THE ANCIENT SECRET

THE ANCIENT SECRET

Fire from the Sun

Flavia Anderson

RESEARCH INTO LOST KNOWLEDGE
ORGANISATION

c/o R.I.L.K.O. Books
B. & J. Hargreaves,
10 Kedleston Drive,
Orpington,
Kent BR5 2DR

Distributed by
THORSONS PUBLISHING GROUP
Wellingborough, Northamptonshire

First published 1953
This Edition 1987

Additional text illustrations by Joyce Hargreaves

British Library Cataloguing in Publication Data

Anderson, Flavia
The Ancient secret : fire from the sun.
— 3rd ed.
1. Grail
I. Title   II. Research into Lost Knowledge
Organization
809' .9337   PN56.G67

ISBN 0-902103-13-X

Printed and bound in Great Britain

Contents

Due acknowledgements to Faber & Faber for permission to quote from 'Four Quartets' by T.S. Eliot.

Acknowledgements

I have already in my first and second editions acknowledged the help of many kind friends, some of whom have now departed this life. I therefore do not think it necessary to restate my gratitude to all who were concerned in the past, but would like to repeat my thanks to Mr T.E. Hope of the Romance Department at Glasgow University and Mr John Rillie of the English Department there. I would, however like to thank those who aided my recent and up-to-date researches: Mrs Philippa Glanville, Assistant Keeper of the Department of Metal Work at the Victoria and Albert Museum for her recommendations on reading matter about reliquaries and monstrances; Mrs George Davson for her researches at Oxford on my behalf into the group of heretics led by Tanchelm of Antwerp and Eón de Étoile; and Mr Cyril Aldred, F.R.S.E.; Egyptologist.

I am specially grateful to Dr Elizabeth Kirby, to whom I was introduced by the relevant department of the British Museum because of the line of research the Museum knew she was pursuing. Her recent discoveries reinforce and substantiate my own findings, and the Epilogue she has kindly contributed puts the seal of authority on my own theories.

I also wish to thank the Council of R.I.L.K.O. and particularly Miss Elizabeth Leader for arranging publication of my own latest discoveries in this almost entirely new composition and compilation of my original theme.

List of Illustrations

Photographic Plates

"Five things were missing in the second
Temple. The ark, the mercy-seat, the
cherubim; the heavenly fire; the Shekinah; the Holy Spirit; and Urim and
Thummim."   Babylonian Talmud. Yomah.

"Father Hesper, Father Hesper, Watch,
    watch night and day
Lest the old wound of the world be healed,
The glory unsealed,
The golden apple stol'n away,
And the ancient secret revealed."
                    Alfred, Lord Tennyson.

A Summary of the Various Legends of The Holy Grail

If you go over the Brendon Hills, and then, leaving the heights of Exmoor, drop down to the coast of the Bristol Channel, you can look north and see the silver line of the Welsh coast. If you then travel eastward along the shore road you will presently come to a wide, green plain, and from many miles away you will see the Tor of Glastonbury, rising above the level of the land like a blue pyramid, very much alone. To the left the Mendip Hills appear to form only a low rampart to this lake of green meadows. Once long ago it was indeed a lake, or rather a marsh: the delta of the Parret, the Brue and the Axe, the three rivers which crept sluggishly by many winding waterways into the estuary of the Severn. The Tor of Glastonbury was then the highest point of one of the many islands in this network of channels, and from the earlies times of which we have any record it was a holy place.

To-day only the fluted Gothic pillars, roofless, at the foot of the Tor show forth the lines of the once great Abbey, to which Christian pilgrims journeyed from far and near. But long before the coming of the Gospel to Britain, tradition has it that the "Druids" – a term employed by the country-folk to describe all pagan priests in this island, regardless of race or date – worshipped the sun from the summit of this very Tor. Indeed, some people see in the flat green ways which wind in zigzag fashion up to the top of the hill, the remains of the processional avenues of these Celtic sun-worshippers, and compare them to the twisting slopes of the Ziggurat temples of Chaldea. Certainly nature could

have provided no better point of observation of the
heavens, for, although it is only five hundred feet high,
nevertheless from the top of the Tor one can see the earth
laid out in a flat circle, which the swell of the Mendip Hills
hardly interrupts.

If the histories written by the monks and the traditions of
the people may be trusted, the Gospel was first brought to
these Druids of Glastonbury within the life-time of the
Apostles, and by no less a person than St. Joseph of
Arimathea. It is not the purpose of this book to go fully into
the evidence of whether or not St. Joseph did in fact come to
Britain. There exists a marginal note in the original of
William of Malmesbury's *Antiquities* by a hand later than
William's to the effect that not only did Joseph come to Britain but was accompanied by his dearest friends, Philip and
James. The marginal note appears to be concerned with
later Arthurian heroes and may be spurious. Nevertheless
Joseph of Arimathea was a rich man, and, when nearly a
thousand years earlier, Solomon joined himself to King
Hiram of Tyre to send ships to Tarshish, i.e. Spain, it is probable that Jewish interests would have been involved with
the known journeys of Phoenicians to Cornwall for tin. The
coast from Spain to Britain was a well used shipping route.
The iron of Gijon now stands in mountains of refined ore
for shipment to British steel plants, and silver has been
mined in Spain since earliest times, in fact Spain is a
treasure house of metals. Of Toledo I shall write later. Sufficient to say here that tradition attributes the origin of the
Jewish colony that once inhabited that city, not from the
Dispersion in 70 A.D. when Titus sacked Jerusalem, but
from the days when refugees fled there rather than be carried off to the Exile in Babylon in the 6th century B.C.
Moreover Jonah was on his way to Tarshish when his ship
was wrecked.

So it is very possible that Joseph of Arimathea's riches
did derive from the Spanish-British shipping route and
profits therefrom; and the early date at which the Church
Councils accorded a high precedence to British Bishops, on
the grounds that the Church in Britain had been founded in

Apostolic times, adds weight to the tale of his coming. The Saxon kings took infinite pains to preserve the measurements of the little church of wattles and thatch which was reported to have been the original church which St. Joseph built. Every history written by these monks of Glastonbury and other sources attest the truth of St. Joseph's mission.

However, be that as it may, the subject of this book is not Joseph of Arimathea but an enquiry into the origins of the various legends of the Holy Grail, which some of the legends suppose was brought by Joseph to Glastonbury.

Some of the legends assume that the Grail was the cup of the Last Supper. But none of the monks or any ecclesiastical history mention it. In fact the Church frowned on this story for fear that such a vessel, if it should be known still to exist, could become a kind of fetish, which might put in doubt the validity of the Blessed Sacrament in the humblest cup in any parish church.

To those unfamiliar with the sources of the legend I should make clear that the poets and troubadours who wrote later than about 1220 A.D. can be discounted as they (including Sir Thomas Malory, famous for his Morte d'Arthur) were merely embroidering a theme, the meaning of which they did not understand, though they were anxious under the influence of the Cistercians to emphasize any Christian association possible.

The authorities on Romance Literature and scholars only attribute importance to the two earliest versions: one, that of Chrestien de Troyes in Romance French, which is believed to have been written between 1188 and 1190; and two, that of Wolfram von Eschenbach in German who died in 1220. Both claimed to have had their different accounts from earlier sources, so that it is hardly possible to say that one source predated the other.

There has lately (1982) appeared a book by Messrs Baignet, Leigh and Lincoln, entitled "The Holy Blood & the Holy Grail" which has startled, indeed scandalised the Christian world by inventing a marriage between Christ and Mary Magdalene, and that families in France derive their lineage from this union, and that the Magdalene herself was the sacred "vessel", bearing within her womb the progeny of such a mating. I find it surprising that these three authors never quote any of the world authorities on the subject, in particular Professor R.S. Loomis, Professor Urban T. Holmes and Professor Leonardo Olschki, all of whose different theories happen to be reconcilable with my own interpretation, which, while acceptable to Christians, is also acceptable to all religions world-wide that identify Light as the symbol of the good as opposed to darkness identified with Evil.

I will here give as briefly as possible an account of Chrestien and his version, entitled *"Le Conte du Graal"*. He claimed to have obtained his subject matter from a little book given him by his patron, Count Philip of Flanders:– The hero, Perceval, leaves his widowed mother in order to seek adventure. At his first encounter he takes from a certain lady a jewelled finger-ring. Without knowledge of feats of arms he then slays the Red Knight who has carried off the Queen's golden cup, and himself assumes the Red Knight's armour. He comes to the aid of a maiden, Blanchefleur, with whom he falls in love, and who will one day be his bride. Although in his beginning he is a simple lad, the Fool of folklore, he has now become a skilled warrior and is attached to the court of King Arthur.

He arrives at the Castle of the Fisher King – "concerning this tower one might seek as far as Beirut without finding one as noble" – note the unnecessarily intrusive comparison with a locality in the Middle East. In a square hall there reclines on a couch a nobleman with grizzled locks and a sable cap as black as mulberry (The Heraldic term for black is sable, so that fur is not necessarily indicated.) There are bronze pillars round the fire. A squire presents Perceval with a sword that could never break save in one peril only. Presently another squire enters carrying a white lance of which the point drips blood. Then come two more squires bearing candelabra of gold. Next comes a damsel holding in two hands a grail which gives forth a brilliant light so that the candles lose their brightness just as the stars do when the sun shines. (Note that a female was never allowed by the

Church to bear the chalice of the eucharist except by very occasional permission to elderly, dedicated abbesses; and that Chrestien never explains what a "grail" is.) After the damsel with the grail comes another damsel carrying a *talleors* of silver (variously translated as platter, bowl, dish, aumoire, tabernacle or casket by various commentators or in other accounts by medieval authors). The grail itself was of refined gold set with precious stones of many kinds. The procession enters another, further chamber. While Perceval is at supper the grail passes again before them, and still Perceval did not ask whom one served with it and for what it was used. The Fisher King, owner of the castle, whom Perceval had met by chance while the king was in a boat fishing the lake, was reclining at supper because he had been wounded through the thighs, a wound that would not heal. Perceval retires for the night, and wakes to find the castle deserted. He rides forth to search for his host and, as soon as he has crossed the draw-bridge, the castle vanishes. He comes upon a maiden holding a strange dead knight in her lap, and lamenting. She tells Perceval that the Fisher King was long ago wounded by a spear-thrust through both thighs, and that the wound would have been healed had Perceval asked concerning the mysteries which he saw. She tells him that the sword he received as a gift may break, but can be mended by dipping it in a certain lake. Perceval eventually returns to King Athur's court, and the next day there arrives a hideous and loathsome damsel, who curses him for having omitted to ask concerning the lance and the Grail; had he done so, the Fisher King would have been healed of his wound and the land restored to prosperity.

Perceval goes forth vowing to learn more of the Grail and the lance. He wanders for five years without thinking of God, yet performing many feats of arms. He is reproached by some pilgrims for riding in full armour on Good Friday, for he has forgotten Christian custom. He confesses his sins to a hermit who tells him that his mother died of grief because of his absence, and declares: "great was your folly when you did not learn whom one served with the Grail. It was my brother, and his sister and mine was your mother.

And believe me that the Rich Fisher is the son of the king who causes himself to be served with the Grail. But do not believe that he takes from it a pike, a lamprey or a salmon. The holy man sustains and refreshes his life with a single mass-wafer. So sacred a thing is the Grail and he himself so spiritual that he needs no more for his sustenance than the mass-wafer which comes in the Grail.''

Chrestien's *Conte du Graal* includes some adventures of another knight of the Round Table, namely Gawain, King Arthur's nephew. In gratitude for her rescue a damsel leads Gawain to a subterranean crypt, where is kept the Sword of the Strange Girdle, which had been the brand of Judas Maccabeus. He is ferried across a stream to a magic castle to rescue more maidens, and there he sees a magnificent bed on which he attempts to lie, but is immediately assailed by invisible arrows and by a lion.

Here Chrestien's version breaks off, and the future deliverance of the Fisher King from his pains is dealt with only by three different poets who continued the poem at a later date, Gautier de Doulens, Manessier and Gerbert, writing within the next fifty years after Chrestien's death, but not necessarily having direct access to Chrestien's source.

Wolfram von Eschenbach, a native of north Bavaria, wrote his poem *Parzival* in German verse. As he died in 1220 he must have brought out his work within about thirty years of Chrestien's death. He frequently refers to Chrestien's version with great contempt. They both admit to drawing from earlier sources, so that it is beside the point as to whose poem predated the other. Wolfram claims to hold the true version from Kyot, the singer, a "Provenzal" who found the tale of Parzival written in Arabic by a Jew in Toledo.

This Semitic account goes as follows:– Parzival's father goes to the Middle East (including Alexandria) and in the East wins the love of a heathen queen, Belakane. She bears him a son named Feirefiz. Parzival's father then returns to Britain, and marries a Welsh queen, mother of Parzival. The story then continues on much the same lines as Chrestien's

Conte du Graal, except for one important difference. The Grail is not a cup brought by Joseph of Arimathea from the Holy Land, but is a *stone* confided by celestial powers to Titurel and his dynasty. It was a stone from which the phoenix periodically arose rejuvenated, and to this talisman there descended every Good Friday a dove, who laid upon the stone a consecrated wafer: the Host or Bread from Heaven. But it is the stone which is identified with the Grail and not the heavenly bread. From time to time the names of the knight destined to achieve the Grail appear miraculously inscribed on the stone. The cause of the Maimed King's (Anfortas') hurt is his having taken up arms in the cause of worldly and unlawful love. More stress is laid upon the episode of the broken sword. Parzival's love is called Condwiramur and the loathly damsel is Kundrie, who reproaches him for not having asked concerning the Grail on his first visit. Eventually Parzival returns to the Grail castle with his half-brother Feirefiz. At the feast to celebrate his return the Fisher King wears his black cap. The Squire appears again with the lance dripping blood, and the maidens appear again bearing candelabra. A table of transparent Jacinth is loaded with food, a veritable cornucopia to satisfy all appetites, and is set before the king. But the Grail itself is carried by a maiden upon a cushion for display (a hardly suitable means of balancing a chalice). But the Grail was *not* a chalice according to Wolfram; it was a stone (presumably white as will be explained later). It had hitherto been guarded by the fallen angels, but is now in the charge of the Templars, who hold it hidden from strangers' eyes. Parzival's name appears upon the stone. Anfortas, now healed, therefore relinquishes the kingdom to Parzival. Parzival's son is the Lohengrin of Wagner's opera, and Feirefiz baptised, weds the bearer of the Grail-stone, the damsel Repanse de Schoie, and becomes the father of the legendary Prester John (believed to have reigned in Ethiopia, if he ever existed).

To follow Wolfram let us take the important points of those who presumed to add to the original versions:–

Diu Crône in German: Here it is Gawain who searches for

the Grail. In the Fisher King's castle the procession of the Grail is much the same: the damsels enter bearing lights, followed by two knights with a spear and two more damsels with a *toblier* (a word of which the translaters are uncertain of the meaning) made of gold and jewels. In the *toblier* are three drops of blood. In a box or casket borne by the fair lady is a piece of bread. Gawain enquires what these wonders mean and the old man replies that what he has seen is the Grail. In another passage of this work the Grail is described as a crystal vase. The Fisher King explains that he is really dead, but only waiting this long while for the suffering of the dead and the living to be relieved before he disappears.

The *Didot Perceval*, written after 1225 in French, asserts that Merlin told King Arthur that the Grail was given by Our Lord to Joseph of Arimathea, who passed it to the Fisher King, now old and sick. A knight of the Round Table must ask what *use* is the Grail, then the Fisher King will be cured. The son of Alein le Gros is Perceval. Alein's father is Brons of Ireland. Perceval rescues a maiden bound to a tree, and receives her ring as a reward. It is set with a magical stone which will protect him. He comes to the Round Table, and sits in the forbidden Perilous Seat, forbidden in memory of Judas, and the stone of that throne cracks and will only be joined together again when the adventures of the Grail are accomplished. For the sake of a damsel Perceval goes hunting the White Stag. He then comes to the Grail castle. All happens much as in Chrestien's account, except that Chrestien never said that the Grail had anything to do with Our Lord or Joseph of Arimathea. But this version includes a lance, a damsel bearing two silver plates, and a squire with a vessel containing Our Lord's blood. After various further adventures Perceval is found on Good Friday fully armed, having forgotten all Christian custom. He eventually returns to the Grail castle and asks the Rich Fisher to what purpose the vessel is put, and forthwith the king is cured. The lance is the one with which the centurion pierced the side of Jesus Christ, and the vessel is that in which Joseph caught the blood as it ran to the ground. He teaches Perceval the secret words, which Our Lord on the cross told to Joseph, but the writer cannot and may not say what these words are.

It can be noted that whereas Chrestien never said what exactly the Grail was, apart from a description of its brightness, and Wolfram asserted that it was a stone, the subsequent versions are becoming more and more concerned with the Passion of Christ.

Gautier de Doulens and Manessier each in turn continued Chrestien's half-finished poem. The former tells of Gawain's failure to ask the vital question; and in one room of the castle is an ominous bier. Departing on his way again, he enters a chapel where the one and only light is quenched by a mysterious Black Hand. The lance is identified with the one that pierced Christ's side, and it bleeds into a silver cup. Perceval also comes to the chapel of the Black Hand, passing first a tree on which burn many lights. A dead knight lies upon the chapel's altar. A damsel explains that these mysteries concern the Grail.

Manessier asserts that the Grail is the vessel in which Joseph of Arimathea collected the blood at the foot of the crucified Christ. Joseph, freed by Vespasian from imprisonment by Christ's enemies travelled via the Saracen kingdom of Ptolemy in Egypt to King Evelac, a sun-worshipper, whom Joseph converted. Perceval defeats the devil in the chapel of the Black Hand, fights his way to the altar, where he find a golden cup covered with a veil. The light upon the altar, which the Black Hand has quenched, relights itself in a miraculous way. In old age Perceval retires to a hermitage, and when he dies, Grail, lance and dish were doubtless carried up to heaven, for since that day no man has ever seen them.

Let us now turn to a purely pagan and Celtic version: the *Mabinogi of Peredur*. It begins with the simple lad and the widowed mother who, amongst other exhortations tells him that if he sees a fair jewel, he is to take it and give it to another. He begins his adventures by acquiring a jewelled finger-ring from a certain damsel. He slays the Red Knight, thus avenging the stealing of the Queen's cup, and arrives at

King Arthur's court. In due course he discovers the castle of
the Lame King. Two youths enter the hall bearing a spear of
giant size from which flows blood. Two maidens follow with
a salver on which a man's head swims in blood. Peredur
fails to ask concerning these mysteries. He goes on his way
and slays a serpent, which is lying upon a gold ring, and he
wins the ring. He comes to the Mound of Mourning, a
cairn, and in the cairn lies a serpent with a *stone* in its tail, the
virtue of which is to give as much gold to the possessor as he
may desire. He slays the serpent together with three hundred knights, and gives the stone to his friend Etlym (which
is what his mother told him to do if he should find a fair
jewel). At Arthur's court he is reproached by the loathly hag
for his silence at the court of the Lame King. He is found
armed on Good Friday. It is to be noted that no mention is
made of the Grail although there is an allusion to a bleeding
lance and an unpleasant appearance of a decapitated
head.

Sir Perceval of Galles is the earliest version in English
(c.1440), and the only point of interest is that after slaying
the Red Knight Perceval does not know how to unbuckle
the Red Armour, until he recalls his mother's injunction,
"out of the iron burn the tree", and so he kindles a fire to
burn the body and free the armour and thus acquire it.

The next version to study is a prose romance in French
called the *Queste del Saint Graal* written by a certain Walter
Map very shortly after Chrestien wrote, for Walter died in
1210. It was translated into Welsh under the name of *Y Seint
Greal* and later still Malory used the French for his account
of the search for the Grail, so I here give a rather longer
account of it than I have accorded to the authors who
followed on from Chrestien and Wolfram.

La Queste Del Saint Graal

On the Perilous Seat at the Round Table is written that on
the 454th year after the Lord's Passion the seat shall find its
master on Whitsunday. According to custom, the Court of
King Arthur awaits an adventure before the knights can sit
down to meat. A youth comes to tell them of a floating stone

which had appeared in the river. It is a block of red marble in which sticks a sword, and upon it is written that none may draw the sword from the stone save the best knight in the world. None of the knights who try can draw it forth. They return to the hall, and an old man leads in a young knight in red armour, whom he claims to be the desired hero, of the seed of David and kin to Joseph of Arimathea, who shall achieve the adventures of the Holy Grail. On the Seat Perilous is now found to be written: "This is Galahad's seat," and the young knight forthwith sits in it. Lancelot recognises him as his son, whom he got upon the daughter of the Fisher King (King Pelles). Galahad easily draws the sword from the floating stone. After Vespers the Court sits down to table; a clap of thunder is heard, followed by the brightest of sunbeams, so that all are as if lighted by the Holy Ghost. None knows whence the light comes, and none has the power to say a word. The Holy Grail enters, covered with white samite, but none may see who carries it; the hall is filled with sweet odours and, as the Grail passes along the tables, all receive such meat as each one longs for. Then the vessel departs, none may say how. The knights make a vow to search for the Grail.

Lancelot comes to an old chapel. He dismounts and enters, but an iron rail hinders his progress. Through it he sees an altar whereon burn (French version) seven candles, or (Welsh version) one wax taper. He lies down to sleep outside the chapel, and sees come a knight on a bier drawn by two horses. The candlestick and the Grail approach this sick knight and give him relief. The Grail disappears, and Lancelot still says never a word, for which after times much mischance was his. The sick knight arises well, and swears never to rest until he knows why the Holy Grail appears in so many places of the kingdom of Logres (Britain), and by whom it was brought to England. Lancelot awakes, wondering whether what he has seen is dream or truth.

The story returns to Perceval. He learns that his mother has died from grief because he left her. He comes to a monastery where an old man lies upon a sick bed to hear mass. The old man is Evelac, the heathen king whom Joseph of

Arimathea converted to Christianity, and he had been struck blind for daring to approach too near the Holy Grail. He is four hundred years old, and is waiting until the good knight shall come, who is to achieve the adventures of the Holy Grail. Perceval continues on his journey and mounts a horse which is in reality, a fiend. They approach a river. The knight makes the sign of the cross, and the horse rushes howling into the water. Perceval is tempted by the love of a woman. Again he makes the sign of the cross, and she disappears in flames. In his contrition, he pierces his thigh with his sword.

The story continues with the adventures of other knights. A hermit explains to Lancelot and Hector the allegorical and Christian significance of their past adventures and dreams, which have been so many experiences or revelations in the progress of the soul. But as to the hand with the taper, which appeared and vanished, and the voice which foretold that they, being of poor belief, could not attain the Holy Grail, the hermit may not and will not explain as evil may come of it.

Perceval's sister conducts Galahad to meet Perceval and Bors. They all sail to a desert island, off which is another ship. On this fair ship is written in Chaldee that those who would enter must be full of faith. They go on board and find a rich bed with a crown at its head, and at its foot a sword six inches out of the scabbard. The pommel of the sword is a stone of all the colours of the world; its handles are made out of the bones of two creatures (from the watery abyss): the serpent Papagast and the fish Orteniaus. It is covered with a cloth whereon is written that only the first of his line would be able to grasp the sword. The hangings of the scabbard are of poor stuff. They can be changed by a king's daughter only, and she must be a virgin. On turning the sword over, the other side is found to be black as pitch, and bears the words that he who should praise it most would blame it most in his greatest need. Perceval's sister explains this as follows: The Maimed King, Pelles, once came to this ship on the shore of the sea over against Ireland, and entering found the sword, drew it, but was straightaway wounded through the thigh by a lance, and may not be healed till Galahad come. They then examine the bed and find that it has on it three spindles, fashioned from the Tree of Life, which tree remained unharmed by the Deluge and lasted until Solomon's time. A voice told Solomon that a woman of his line should bring men more joy than ever her sex had caused sorrow, and that a virgin knight should be the last of Solomon's lineage. Solomon consulted his wife as to how he should let this knight know that he had foreknowledge of his coming, and she advised the building of the ship and the taking of David's sword from the temple to be fitted with a new hilt, the pommel of which should be of one precious stone only and this stone to be of all the colours of the world. It was to be placed in the ship together with Solomon's crown and the bed. Only the maiden who can change the tattered hangings or girdle of the sword can put a name to the weapon. Perceval's sister makes new hangings from her braided hair, and names the brand "The Sword of the Strange Girdle", and the scabbard she names "Memory of Blood."

Galahad girds on the sword, and on the morrow they all set sail for Scotland. They meet a White Stag led by four lions; these beasts come to a chapel beside a hermitage and they there hear mass, whereat the stag becomes a man (Christ) and sits on the altar; the lions become the four beasts of the Evangelists – man, lion, eagle and ox, all winged.

The story returns to Lancelot. He comes to a castle and enters a room wherein are the holy vessel and a priest celebrating mass. Lancelot approaches too near, is struck by a fiery wind, and remains fourteen days dumb without food or drink. He finds that he is in the castle of Corbenic (The grail Castle, called Montsalvat in Wolfram's versions) and a damsel tells him that his quest is ended.

The story returns to Galahad. He heals the wounds of Mordrains – who was known before his conversion to Christianity as Evelac – and Mordrains then dies in his arms. Galahad, Perceval and Bors come to castle Corbenic, and are greeted by King Pelles. The King's son, Eliezer,

brings the broken sword with which Joseph of Arimathea
had been pierced through the thighs. Galahad makes the
sword whole. At Vesper time four damsels bring on a
wooden bed, a man, crowned, in evil plight, who greets
Galahad as his long expected deliverer. Borne by angels
from heaven comes St. Joseph clad as the first Bishop of
Christendom. He places before Galahad the table on which
stands the Holy Grail; he opens the doors of the ark, and
four angels issue from it, two bearing burning lights, the
third a cloth of red samite, the fourth a lance which is bleeding so hard that the drops run into a box which he holds in
his other hand. The candles are placed on the table. The
cloth is placed on the holy vessel, so that the blood falls into
it. The Grail, it is explained, is the *dish* of the Last Supper,
and Galahad shall see it more clearly in the city of Sarras,
whither it is going. Galahad heals the Maimed King with the
Holy Blood, and then follows the Grail to Sarras (i.e.
Saracen territory), where he is made king of the city. There
he fashions a tree of gold and precious stones *over* the Grail
to *cover* (i.e. hide) it, and prays before it every morning. A
hand from Heaven then takes Grail and lance and bears
them heavenward, so that there is no man bold enough to
say that he has seen the Holy Grail. Bors returns from Sarras
to tell of these adventures, which were written down and
kept in the Abbey of Salisbury, and from these writings
Master Walter Map drew to make his book of the Holy
Grail.

The following is a prose version in French entitled *Perceval le Gallois*, and written by an unknown author probably
before A.D. 1225. It is to be found printed in M. Potvin's
edition of Chrestien's *Conte du Graal*. To distinguish it from
the English metrical *Sir Perceval of Galles* and Wolfram's German *Parzival*, I shall refer to it in future as the *Prose
Perceval*.

The story follows closely the account given by Chrestien,
but there are one or two points of interest. Instead of one
loathly damsel three ladies, queens, arrive at the Court of
King Arthur to complain of Perceval not having asked con-

cerning the Grail. One of these queens has her hand attached in a strange fashion to a golden star which hangs from her neck. The position of the hand, it is claimed, concerns the mystery of the Grail. Perceval comes to Arthur in a ship drawn by a swan, and claims the shield which the three queens have left for him. Thereafter he meets his sister, and she goes to a haunted chapel to fetch Christ's grave-clothes which are kept there. Eventually Perceval achieves the Grail and is crowned king of its castle. Gawain's origin, like that of Moses, is wrapped in mystery, for he was found in an ark or vessel abandoned in the water. Lancelot must draw a sword from a roof-tree. He is invited to be king of a city whose fires have burned for a year. Only Lancelot can quench these flames, and for this service he shall receive the crown, but shall die at the end of the year. He enters a haunted chapel and takes from it a sword and Christ's grave clothes.

We now come to a whole new class of legend concerning St. Joseph of Arimathea and his descendants in Britain who were of Jewish stock. There are only two early MSS and they are both in French and by the same author, Sire Robert de Borron, who wrote sometime between 1170 and 1212, that is to say at a date more or less contemporary with Chrestien and Wolfram. By such authorities and great scholars such as Professor Loomis and earlier Jessie Weston, who both favour a Celtic or heathen origin for the legends, it has been suggested that de Borron, under the influence of the Cistercians, was attempting to overlay Celtic legend with inventions in order to augment the importance of Christ's Passion and of the then fashionable veneration of relics in particular. It is true, as Messrs Baignet, Leigh and Lincoln are anxious to point out, that Wolfram in his poem asserts that the guardians of the Grail were Templars, and that St. Bernard, who founded the order of Cistercians, was a great upholder of that order of knighthood, but, as will presently be shown, a Celtic, a Christian and a Jewish origin of the legend are not theories in conflict, but on the contrary reinforce my own theory and reconcile all the various versions to each other; although they have nothing whatever to do

with Mary Magdalene and her supposed union with Our
Lord – supposed that is by the previously named three co-
authors. On the contrary regarding St. Bernard and the
Templars, de Borron's sources are taken almost entirely
from the Apocryphal New Testament, excluded from the
Canon by the Church centuries before the days of St. Bernard as being largely fairy-stories, and de Borron has drawn
on and muddled up such fairy-stories to an astonishing
degree, a truly inventive author.

That Joseph of Arimathea did share with St. John the care
of Our Lady is stated in the *Apocryphal Assumption of the Virgin
by Joseph of Arimathea*, who calls her ever-virgin and the
Lord's temple, and has himself been called *Paranymphos*
(guardian of the lady) a title shared only with St. John. Certainly in the Roman Liturgy she is acclaimed as *Vas Honorabile*, the holy or honourable vessel of the Saviour. But
neither has this anything to do with the Jewish origins of
those knights who achieved or guarded the Grail, and that
their lineage was Jewish deriving from Joseph of Arimathea
is clearly claimed by Sire Robert de Borron.

His longest work entitled *Le Grand Saint Graal*, and the
important points to be learned from it are as follows:– in the
year 717 A.D. a certain monk suffers terrible doubt concerning the doctrine of the Trinity. Christ appears to him
and gives him a little book, the second part of which is
entitled "The Holy Grail". According to this book Joseph
of Arimathea lived in Jerusalem with his wife and his son,
Josephes. After the Crucifixion, Joseph goes to the house of
the Last Supper and carries off the *dish* wherein Christ had
eaten (presumably eaten the Paschal lamb). When Joseph
takes down the body of the Saviour from the Cross and
gives it burial, he collects the blood flowing from the
wounds in the dish. The Jews throw Joseph into a dungeon,
and leave him without food. Christ appears to him in the
dungeon and restores to him the dish which had been left in
Joseph's house. (With the exception of the dish, the story of
Joseph's imprisonment and vision of Christ is taken directly from the *Story of Joseph of Arimathea* in the Apocryphal *Acts
of Pilate*, believed to have been written in the 4th century.)

For forty years Joseph is miraculously sustained by the Grail. The Emperor Vespasian is healed of leprosy by St. Veronica's cloth, and becomes a Christian and rescues Joseph from prison. Joseph and his son make a wooden ark for the Grail and set out to carry the gospel to foreign lands. They come to the city of Sarras and go to the temple of the sun, where the Saracens are assembled in council with their king, Evalach, on whom the Egyptians, under their king Tholomes (i.e. a Ptolemy) are making war. Evalach is baptised and given a new name, Mordrains, as also his brother Nasciens. Josephes is given charge of the ark by his father Joseph, and all the various relics of the Passion, cross, nails, bloody lance, sponge and scourge emerge from the ark. (Here de Borron is embarking on a truly impressive but purely inventive list of relics). Nevertheless there emerges from the ark at last a rich vessel of gold and precious stones identical with the Grail as described by Chrestien, and only later does an angel (the eighth) carry the holy *dish*, while a ninth carries a head, reminiscent of the decapitated head which appeared in the Welsh *Maboinogi of Peredur*. There is a faint possibility that de Borron's "head" might refer to the head of John the Baptist at present venerated in the mosque of Damascus, though de Borron never gives a reason for a head appearing from the chest containing the Grail, and certainly the tale of Peredur is too full of Celtic slaughters to suggest that a decapitated head in a salver at a dinner party is anything but an unpleasant occurrence.

Robert de Borron claims that Josephes was smitten through the thighs by an angel with a lance for his laxity in not working sufficiently hard at his task of converting the heathen. Nasciens is struck blind because he dares to approach too near the Grail. (It gives off a blinding light and is sufficient to eclipse candlelight, as we know from Chrestien.) Both men are eventually healed. Mordrains is protected from the black bread (of sin) by a wonderful bird, the phoenix. Nasciens finds Solomon's ship with the bed whereon lies a sword. It snaps in his hands, but he mends it. Joseph begets a child who is called Galahad. They all cross the sea to Britain. Joseph appoints the youngest son of his

kinsman, Brons, to be guardian of the Grail when he himself shall die. The young man's name is Alein le Gros. He is
told to take the net from the Grail table and to fish with it,
and he is thereafter called the Rich Fisher. Joseph is wounded in the thigh, and must await healing from the man who
shall achieve the adventures of the Holy Grail. Joseph dies,
and Alein takes charge of the Grail, and builds for its keeping the castle of Corbenic.

The Metrical Joseph (also by Sire Robert de Borron)

When the Jews carry off Jesus to be crucified, one of them
takes the very fair vessel wherein Christ made his Sacrament, and gives it to Pilate. Pilate in turn gives it to Joseph of
Arimathea. Joseph and Nicodemus take down the body of
Jesus from the cross and wash it, which makes the blood
from the wounds flow afresh. Joseph puts the blood into
the vessel. After the Resurrection the Jews are incensed
against Joseph, and thrust him into a horrible dark prison.
To him appears Christ with his vessel in a great light, and
instructs Joseph, telling him that for the love which he had
to Him, he shall have the symbol of His death, and shall
bequeath it to whom he will. He teaches Joseph concerning
the Sacrament: the bread and wine are Christ's flesh and
blood; the tomb is the altar; the grave-cloth is the Corporal
(that is to say the linen cloth in its burse, which together with
the veil conceal the chalice before and after celebrating
mass). Joseph is rescued from prison by the Emperor Vespasian, newly (but quite unhistorically) converted to Christianity, and Joseph goes forth to preach the gospel. In all de
Borron's work there is a fearful confusion between Joseph,
son of the Patriarch Jacob, who was thrown into a pit, sold
into Egypt and could interpret dreams, and Joseph of
Arimathea; the only possible bond between the two being:
one a true, and two, a supposed sojourn in Egypt. St. Joseph
is accompanied to Egypt by his brother-in-law Hebron,
shortened to Brons for convenience. Brons catches a *fish*
and places it *on* the Grail table. One seat at their dinner
table, the Perilous Seat, is to be left empty to signify the seat
of Judas, until there comes one pure and perfect enough to

sit there without danger. He shall be a descendant of Brons
by his son Alain. An angel tells Joseph that he is to instruct
Brons concerning the holy words which God spake to
Joseph in prison, which are properly called the secrets of
the Grail. Brons is called the Rich Fisher from the fish he
caught. Brons is to wait for the son of his son (Galahad, the
second of that name), and then give him the vessel. Then
shall the meaning of the doctrine of the Blessed Trinity be
made known.

Let us now see if we can recapitulate the essentials of
these tales: the hero is at first a simple, untutored lad. It is
generally claimed that he is of Jewish descent. He acquires a
jewelled finger-ring. He avenges upon the Red Knight the
stealing of the Queen's cup. He is concerned in the rescue
of a lady, who is either imprisoned in a tower or bound to a
tree. He arrives at a castle where certain sacred talismans are
held. The king of the castle suffers from a wound in the
thigh which will not heal. Because the hero fails to enquire
what these talismans may mean, the king must continue to
suffer and the land remain waste. The hero's mother dies of
grief because he has deserted her. The hero is found to be
without knowledge of Christian customs. He is concerned
in a head-hunt for the head of a stag or man. In one version
an angel issues from the shrine of the Grail carrying a head,
and in another a head is borne in a bloody salver round the
table where the knights are eating. The hero's visit to the
castle of the talismans is in some way connected with an
ordeal in a haunted chapel. In one account it is Christ's
grave-clothes which must be taken from this evil place; in
another a veil from a golden cup must be removed and
dipped in holy water to scatter purification around. Once
the veil has been removed, the knight is imbued with power
to cure a sick man or to exorcise the Black Hand, which has
extinguished a flame. The flame relights itself. The hero
must mend a broken sword before he is allowed to know the
true history of the talismans. One of the talismans is a spear,
from which some effluence flows into a receptacle. There is
a silver dish or bowl, whose import forever remains unex-

plained. If the talismans are indeed of Christian origin, this *talleors* may have been introduced to describe the very small silver paten used at mass for the consecrated bread. If the legends are Celtic, we shall have to explain its purpose. The Grail itself is declared to be either a relic of the Passion or a stone; if a stone it can be connected with the dove and the Sacrament, or alternatively with a serpent or ring. Out of the ten earliest versions of the story, four (*Wolfram, the Mabinogion, the Thornton MS and Diu Crône*) speak either of a talismanic stone or a crystal vase. The other six describe a relic of the Passion, but the various authors are not united as to whether it was a cup in which St. Joseph collected the Holy Blood from the wounds (*Manessier and the Didot Perceval*) or the dish in which Our Lord ate the Paschal lamb (*Queste and Saint Graal*) or the cup in which Christ instituted the Sacrament (*Metrical Joseph*) or even the small box containing the Holy Bread *(Diu Crône)*. In other words the writers are not very clear as to how and in what fashion the divine effluence entered the cup, but that it issued from the spear is strongly illustrated in the Mabinogi of Peredur, where the spear produces the effluence, but there is apparently no cup to receive it, for Peredur's quest was for the serpent-stone, and the Grail is not mentioned in the lay. Whether it is a cup or stone, in either case it is an inexhaustible source of something precious: food, gold, or the heart's desire. In the procession at the Grail castle the holy vessel is carried by a maiden, and several authorities have seen in this an argument for a pre-Christian source, for a woman was never allowed to bear the chalice except in very special circumstances such as an elderly abbess being allowed speccial dispensation in her convent. The castle of talismans can only be approached by crossing water, and its king has something to do with fishing or with a fish.

Although I have tried to be as brief as possible in these summaries, the reader, if he is not specially interested in medieval literature, may be beginning to wonder whether any valuable conclusion can ever be reached from all this wealth of legend, often so conflicting and so full of apparently insignificant details. It is perhaps as well here, therefore, to reassure those in doubt. We shall presently find that all these legends bear witness, not to any imaginative world of dreams wherein spiritual progress is described by means of allegory, but on the contrary to a very precise and particular ritual practised by out most ancient ancestors as well as in later times by the Christian Church.

2 THE CAULDRON OF WISDOM AND INSPIRATION

In the last century Mr Alfred Nutt in *The Legend of the Holy Grail* and Monsieur Potvin in the preface to his first printing of Chrestien's *Conte du Graal* came to the conclusion that all these tales have a Celtic origin and that the talismanic vessel was the old Celtic Cauldron of Inspiration and Wisdom, an inexhaustible source of food, but they do not postulate any theory as to what the ancient cauldron was. Time and again the knight in quest of the Grail is bidden to ask what the vessel is used for, and to what purpose, and by whom. Since the original editions of this my book, one of the great world authorities of Romance Literature, Professor Loomis first postulated that the sword of the Grail hero was a sun-sword, a loose term for a very real phenomenon, which I shall describe in the next chapter. Then, alas, he retracted his first belief, which was so near the truth, in favour of quite a new theory: the Grail he wrote was a cornucopia, a horn of plenty, and the *cor benit* had been confused with the *corps benit* of the Blessed body of Christ*. To my knowledge neither cauldron nor cornucopia have ever inspired men to undertake a spiritual quest, however enticing food and drink may be.

Miss Jessie Weston, who first translated Wolfram's German into English, saw a similarity between legends of the Grail and the cults of the vegetation gods of the Near East: Attis, Adonis, and others of the same type. She understood

---

* The Fisher King's castle is in some versions called Corbenic which could derive from either the body or the horn.

rightly that the whole purpose of achieving the talismans was to restore the land, the widowed earth, to life and the renewed vigour of springtide; and she came therefore to the conclusion that the spear and the Grail represented in Celtic fashion the symbols of the male and female powers of procreation. The craze to see these particular symbols everywhere and in everything appertaining to religion was in fashion at the end of the last century, a fashion probably set by Sir James Frazer's *Golden Bough*. But Miss Weston's theory does not in fact fit the legend of the Grail, for if the spear is held to be the symbol of the male powers, then what does the broken sword signify? And if the reverse is held to be the case, we are still left with two symbols of the male of which one must be superfluous.

Of the various serious commentators I believe the two theories of paramount importance are, first that of Professor Urban T. Holmes, Professor of Romance Philology in the University of North Carolina in his work *A New Interpretation of Chrestien's Conte du Graal*, published in 1948. He propounds a Jewish source associated with the famous Rabbinical school of Rashi at Troyes. According to Holmes, Chrestien was a converted Jew and the Grail castle was a memory or symbol of the temple of Solomon. The Fisher King's robe fringed with purple refers to the purple fringes required by Mosaic law (Num.XV.38). Aaron's rod is likened to Excalibur, which according to Jewish legend could not be pulled from the ground save by Moses who knew the name of God engraved upon it. The failure to ask the requisite question at supper could be the omission of the duty of the youngest member of a family at Passover to ask "Why is this night different from all other nights?" The black cap embroidered with gold thread worn by the Fisher King could, in my view, reinforce Professor Holmes' theory.

Second, and perhaps the most important of all theories, is that of the Italian Professor Leonardo Olschki. I shall be referring to this in detail later on, but here it is sufficient to say that he realized that the one common denominator of all appearances of the Grail was the blinding light; and he postulated an over-emphasis by a secret sect of Gnostics on the lst Chapter of St. John's Gospel with its verses concerning Christ as the light of the world and the words of the Nicene creed: Lumen de Lumine.

I must not anticipate however, for we shall not be able to judge fairly concerning a Celtic origin unless we first attempt to enumerate the very little that has come down to us from ancient manuscripts concerning the Celtic "Cauldron".

When in mythical times the Tuatha De Danann (literally the folk-of-the-god-whose-mother-is-Dana) invaded Ireland, they brought with them four treasures: The Stone of Destiny; a magic spear; the sword of Lugh, the god of light; and the cauldron of the god, Dagda, the All-father. This vessel had the property that it could feed a host of men without ever being emptied.

Another magic cauldron is mentioned in the Welsh account of Bran, King of Britain. (There is a faint possibility that he could be identified with the Brons of Grail legend but it is not very probable.) He gave his sister Branwen in marriage to the King of Ireland.* With her dowry she took a wonderful cauldron which had the property that, if a dead man were cast into it, he would come forth well and sound. Bran seems to have been a solar hero, "as big as a mountain and two lakes were his eyes." In a war with the Irish he was mortally wounded in the foot, and at his death his head was buried in London's Tower Hill, where it remained oracular for some time.

In another Welsh myth from the *Mabinogion*, Llew, the sun-god or solar hero, could either be slain or changed into an eagle by means of a spear.

In a poem by the Welsh bard, Taliesin, there is a description of a cauldron which was part of the spoils of Hades (Annwn or Uffern as it was known in Wales) and which was brought down from the underworld by King Arthur.

---

* The story of Branwen in the *Mabinogion* translated by Lady Charlotte Guest.

The first word from the cauldron, when was it spoken?
By the breath of nine maidens it was gently warmed.
Is it not the cauldron of the chief of Annwn? What
is its fashion?
A rim of pearls is round its edge.
It will not cook the food of a coward or one forsworn.
A sword flashing bright will be raised to him,
And left in the hand of Lleminawg.
And before the door of the gate of Uffern the lamp
was burning
When we went with Arthur – a splendid labour –
Except seven, none returned from Caer Vedwyd.*

Taliesin, the bard, is a more of less historical character,
but his mythical birth is connected with a magic cauldron in
a tale from the Mabinogion hardly relevant to our enquiry,
but of how he was found as an infant will concern us
later. †

For the present it is necessary to review what we can learn
from these myths. The inexhaustible cauldron of the Dagda
is connected with a king's throne, a magic spear, and the
sword of the sun-god; the stag also plays a part in the story
of Llew. In Taliesin's verse he who finds the cauldron of the
underworld will find in his hand a "sword flashing bright"
and a lamp burning.

It is true that in Wolfram's version there is an inexhaustible supply of food in the Fisher King's hall, but the Grail
itself is shown to Parzival lying on a cushion, hardly a suitable place for a cauldron or cup, although I suppose a cornucopia could be so presented. But who has ever heard of a
quest for a particular horn of plenty, attribute of Plutus, god
of wealth, or alternatively of Fortuna? The cornucopia was
used as a decoration in architecture, but never to my
knowledge as a single source of inspiration, except perhaps
to the greedy for food or gold. Moreover Chrestien's Grail

---

* This translation is by T.W. Rolleston in *Myths & Legends of the Celtic Race*.
† The *Mabinogion*.

emits light and is bejewelled and bears one single mass-wafer.

Before we can put a definite name to the vessel and give a satisfactory explanation to the mystery, we shall have to examine first the names of the heroes.

Now Gawain in the Welsh versions of the Arthurian legend goes by the name of GWALCHMEI, the meaning of which is "Hawk of May". The name Gawain itself is a derivation of GWALCH-GWYN, "the White Hawk", and Galahad is derived from the Welsh GWALCH-HAVED, meaning "Summer Hawk". The name of Peredur, whom we have seen to be the Welsh counterpart of Perceval, comes from the Welsh "par", meaning a spear, and is sometimes written PALADR-HIR, in other words "He-of-the-spear"; some etymologists might question my own opinion that Lancelot derives from the lance or spear of Lot, Lud, Lugh or Llew*, the various Celtic spellings of the god of light (Lud in London), but by inference drawn from the other heroes I think my suggested derivation can be deduced rather than searching for a French root.

We can now make a list of the names of the Grail heroes as follows:

Gawain (Gwalchmei) Hawk of May son of the god of light, Lot, or his namesake.

Lancelot, the Spear of Lot, god of light.

Perceval (Peredur), He-of-the-Spear.

Galahad (Gwalch-haved) the Summer Hawk, Son of the Spear of Light.

Miss Weston long ago pointed out in her *Legend of Sir Perceval* that although several knights are mentioned as being concerned in the Quest, in fact they each played similar roles. Every locality had its particular way of naming the hero, and as tribal localities united, each and all of the heroes had to find a place in the story. She came to the conclusion that Gawain, son of King Lot, was the most ancient

---

* For the meanings of these names see *Studies in the Arthurian Legend*, by John Rhys, and *Zeus* by A.B. Cook Vol 1. p. 243.

of names. In time he was superseded by Perceval, and he in his turn had to yield first place to Lancelot and finally to Galahad. By the time Malory came to write, Gawain had degenerated into a coarse buffoon. Nevertheless, if the legends are examined with care, it will be found that in fact each of the knights undergoes almost exactly the same adventures. Indeed it is this very duplication which tends to make the legends long and tedious.

Gawain, Lancelot and Perceval all in turn visit the chapel of the Black Hand, the Chapel Perilous. Perceval and Lancelot both visit a haunted chapel for the purpose of removing a veil from a cup. Perceval receives a sword from the Fisher King which can break and yet be mysteriously mended in water. Gawain receives the sword of Judas Maccabeus. Lancelot draws his sword from a roof-tree, a legend curiously reminiscent of Sigmund's drawing of Wotan's sword in the *Volsunga Saga*. Yet, as I shall presently hope to show all these swords are in fact manufactured in the same way. All three knights and also Galahad behold the Grail and are concerned in the cure of a sick man. Finally, Arthur himself plays the major role: he visits a strange chapel, he possesses the magic sword, Excalibur, also the magic spear, Ron; and he is one of those to behold the Grail.

From all this it might seem that we are on the track of a Celtic origin for our Grail legends, but if we are to succeed in showing that Grail and Cauldron are identical, we must be able to explain the four major points which the legends have in common:

1. The vessel was an inexhaustible source of something precious.
2. Its association with a spear.
3. Its association with a hawk-like hero.
4. And finally its association with a sword.

Is there any myth which can provide a clue to associating these four points? Indeed there is, and moreover some artist, who lived in Egypt more than two thousand years ago, has kindly provided us with an illustration, which is

Fig 1. THE STARS OF THE PLOUGH FIGURED AS THE HAUNCH
OF A BULL, BEING EXTINGUISHED BY THE RAY OF THE HAWK-
HEADED SUN-GOD RÊ.
From the great temple of Denderah; after Professor Maspero's illustration
in "The Dawn of Civilization".

reproduced here (see Fig 1.) It is drawn from the rectangular zodiac carving upon the ceiling of the great temple
at Denderah, and shows the first ray of the risen sun, Rê or
Horus (the sun-god who in Egyptian symbolism is always
portrayed with a man's body but with the head of a hawk)
extinguishing the polar stars of Draconis (known in Egypt
as the Hippo goddess) and of the Plough. What is very
significant is the fact that the spear or sunbeam is pointed
directly at the group of stars which we today call the Plough,
but which the Egyptians called the "Thigh" or sometimes
the "Haunch of the Bull", and may just possibly have
something to do with the wounding of the thigh in Grail
legend, although there are other equally possible and
perhaps more probable explanations. The illustration in
Fig 1. is taken from Professor Maspero's *Dawn of Civilisation*,
and he holds that Rê the sun-god, and Horus the hawk, are
for all purposes indistinguishable as gods of light and sky,
though their life stories differ. It should be noted here that
this ray of the sun depicted here is veritably built into our
English language, where we talk of a shaft, a beam or a dart
of sunlight.

Since the first two editions of this book I have received

even more convincing evidence from Mr Cyril Aldred, F.R.S.E., Egyptologist, who has kindly provided me with the illustration on Plate 1 of a carving in the Louvre Museum. It shows Horus, hawk-headed and *mounted* like a true *preux chevalier* slaying a monster with his spear. It is, says Mr Aldred, of late Roman date, hence the armour of a legionary, but it represents the prototype of St. George of Cappadocia, patron saint of England (who is roughly identical with St. Demetrius of Thessalonica, a saint much venerated in the Greek Church). They are both represented as slaying a monster with a spear. The crocodile and the hippo were the "dragons" of the Nile, and the crocodile particularly was the representative of the powers of evil, called Set or Typhon in Egypt.

The Church claims that both George and Demetrius were Christian martyrs, but there is little historical evidence to support such a claim, though it is not impossible that some one person (George and Demetrius are almost certainly identifiable as one person) was holy enough to be represented iconographically as the personification of the bearer of the spear of light subduing the monster of the evil watery abyss. As a Christian, I do believe that St. Michael is the supreme commander of the angelic "Hosts" of the Lord, but to represent St. Michael clad in the sartorial elegance of the Roman armour of an Imperator is to exaggerate poetic licence. To me, much more convincing is the description of C.S. Lewis of archangels whose streaks and speed of light make everything else in the world appear crooked or aslant. I admit that no artist could portray such a vision, so we usually have to accept a picture of St. Michael in Roman armour, *faute de mieux*.

When we come to St. Margaret of Antioch we shall find that as early as the 12th century Pope Gelasius II tried to strike her from the Calendar of Saints as the heroine of a mere fairy-tale, but local sentiment was too much for him. Lately, St. Catherine of Alexandria and St. Barbara, both connected with the real truth behind the Grail legend, are by order of the present Pope John Paul II no longer allocated special saints' day festivals, while in respect for

English sentiment, St. George has retained his festival for April 23rd.

Whether or not George of Cappacocia did in fact kill a Typhonian monster, symbol of evil, of which hawk-headed Horus had first initiated a picture, what we can accept is that *someone*, a Christian, before any such historical records existed, followed St. Paul's advice (Romans 13.12) and put on "the armour of light" as first worn by Horus.

The important thing for public sentiment is to realise that clarity and reason demand that we differentiate strictly between actual historical facts and the allegories and parables, which may convey important truths, but are non-existent historically; and if we forget that they are allegories, parables or iconographic symbols, we may miss the important message they should convey to us.

A priest lately told me of a young child, a boy, who, looking at a beautifully stained glass window, declared: "Oh, now I understand! The saints let the light come through to us." But the boy was not tempted to worship the mere glass.

A more modern analogy would be to say that it would be absurd to venerate and adore a television set, whereas the voice coming from afar *through* the set may be giving us very important information. So we must differentiate between the medium (the stained glass or the T.V. set) and the light or sound that issues *through* these purely earthly objects. In this way it will be found that St. Margaret of Antioch (the flaming pearl) St. Catherine of Alexandria (with her fiery wheel) and St. Barbara (with her special window) probably had no historical existence, and were not people at all, but *objects*, and if properly understood can be very inspiring, as for instance when St. George (alias Horus) rescues St. Margaret (the flaming pearl) from the embrace of the Typhonian monster.

To return to Egypt and pagan times, the representation of the "dragon" in the adventures of Horus in his life lived on earth, and therefore distinguishable if rather vaguely from Rê, the sun, is carved in a whole series of stone tablets round his temple at Edfu, where he avenges the murder of his earthly father, Osiris, upon the hippopotamus, who represents the same evil powers of the deep dark water (Set or Typhon) as does the crocodile. At Edfu the sculptor portrays the Typhonian monster as a very small little beast, which when finally speared has its "paws" upended in the water beside the boat of Horus in a rather pathetic gesture, like a small dog surrendering to death. When we come to the terrible Celtic water-horse, the *each-uisg*, which attempts to drown various Grail-legend heroes and also knights in other medieval lays, it will appear that we have once again come across the Typhonian monster, the hippo, whose very name, hippopotamus, means the river-horse.

To those who have read Professor W.J. Perry's *Growth of Civilisation* it will be no surprise to find that the culture of Egypt spread to our shores in neolithic times, but much later the Romans came, and the Romans in turn had drawn their learning from the Greeks. It is probable that one of the first confusions between the Grail and the spear from which flowed a mysterious effluence (which gave birth to Christian tales of the Passion) and the original spear of the sun is due to the fact that the Greek for spear is *Longkhe*, and this probably gave birth to the supposition that the centurion who pierced Our Lord's side was named Longinus. Undoubtedly the centurion existed, but there is no scriptural authority or historical evidence whatever for his name, except in Apocryphal writings written three or four centuries after the Crucifixion. And if Longinus does indeed mean the holder of the spear, the *Longkhe*, then his name in Greek is exactly equivalent to that of the Welsh Grail-hero, Peredur, the Spear-holder.

Apart from Egyptian blue faience beads found in neolithic tombs in Britain, Geoffrey of Monmouth claims Trojan ancestry for the first British kings, but such claims are largely discredited today. Pliny, however, can hardly be ignored, and he says that the Britons were so accomplished in the art of magic and their practice of it so similar to that of the Persian Magi, that he suggests a British origin for the Persian cult*. The fact that the Phoenicians came to Cor-

* Pliny, *Natural History* XXX. 4.

nwall for tin is known to all. They probably first arrived in
the 10th century B.C. at a time when Tyre had succeeded to
Crete's place as mistress of the seas and had only recently
freed themselves from Egypt's domination; and when the
Tyrian king, Hiram, was allied to Solomon and they were
sharing the sea-traffic (round about Tarshish or Spain) so
that there were very possibly Jews aboard such tin-ships.
And the Phoenician sailors of that same King Hiram who
had helped build the temple for Solomon, would have been
able in any case to spread tales of the grandeur of Solomon
and Jerusalem. All this points to the fact that Europe and
the Middle East formed a very small world, and were much
closer to each other than some previous centuries have
supposed.

It is interesting to remember that Toledo in Spain was at
first a Punic settlement, and that it was in Toledo that
Wolfram von Eschenbach claimed that the true story of Parzival and the Grail had been found from a writing discovered by a Provencal troubadour, a certain Kiot.

I give the words as translated by Miss Weston:–

Since I did but as Kiot bade me, for he would I should hide
the tale,
And tell none the secret, till the venture so far were
sped
That the hidden should be made open, and the marvel of
men be read.

For Kiot of old, the master whom men spake of in days
of yore,
Far off in Toledo's city, found in Arabic writ the lore
By men cast aside and forgotten, the tale of the
wondrous Grail;
But first must he learn the letters, nor black art might
there avail.
By the grace of baptismal waters, by the light of our
Holy Faith,
He read the tale, else 'twere hidden; for never, the story
saith,

Might heathen skill have shown us the virtue that
hidden lies
In this mighty Grail, or its marvels have opened to Christian
eyes.

'Twas a heathen, Flegetanis, who had won for his wisdom
fame,
And saw many a wondrous vision (from Israel's race he
came,
And the blood of the kings of old-time, of Solomon did
he share).
He wrote in the days long vanished, ere we was as a shield
might bear
The cross of our Holy Baptism 'gainst the craft and the wiles
of Hell.
And he was the first of earth's children the lore of the Grail
to tell.
By his father's side a heathen, a calf he for God did
hold,
How wrought the devil such folly, on a folk so wise, of
old?

And the heathen, Flegetanis, could read in the heavens
high
How the stars roll on their courses, how they circle the silent
sky,
And the time when their wandering endeth – and the life
and the lot of men
He read in the stars, and strange secrets he saw, and he
spake again
Low, with bated breath and fearful, of the thing that is
called the Grail.
In a cluster of stars was it written, the name, nor their lore
shall fail.

From this we learn that a Jew, whose forefathers once
worshipped the golden calf of Egypt (Apis) is here
associated with a knowledge of the Grail. The Jews in
Medieval Spain wrote nearly always in Arabic, and Pro-

fessor Olschki, who asserts that the one common denominator of all accounts of the Grail is the light issuing from it,
guessed that Flegetanis was merely the name of an Arab
tract. But the Department of Islamic Studies I consulted in
Edinburgh was unable to trace any such tract. It seems
likely to me that the name comes from the Arabic *falak*
(Aramaic *pilak*) a word for the pre-Copernican spheres; and
Tanan or *Teni* is the designation for 1st century Jewish
teachers of Rabbinical tradition after the Dispersion in 70
A.D. following the sacking of Jerusalem by Titus. This
could fit exactly with Professor Olschki's ideas if, as I
believe and as Wolfram asserts, Flegetanis was a Jewish
teacher studying astronomy in Toledo, the Mecca of all
learning under Moorish rule, not only of astronomy but
mathematics and Aristotelian theories and general science;
a place to which Frederick Stupor Mundi sent his own tutor
and best scholar from Sicily for extra instruction, namely
the so-called magician Michael Scot, native of our Scottish
borders. That Flegetanis studied the pre-Copernican
spheres once again fits exactly with Professor Olschki's
assertion that the Grail was associated with a sect of Gnostics. For before the discoveries of Copernicus no one could
study the stars without studying the "spheres", thought of
as a series of transparent or glassy parasols, one above the
other, on which the planets revolved; and for the very
reason that sunlight could not, it was supposed, reach earth
without penetrating these glassy parasols, the Gnostics
assumed that the ultimate and supreme God, the En Soph
of the Cabbalah, could not reach mankind except by
gradual descent through these tiers of glassy floors. We
know that there was a particular Jewish and famous
astronomer living in Toledo in the mid 11th century, by
name Ibrahim abu Ishaq Zarkal. But Toledo's Jews did not
suddenly appear in Spain after the Dispersion in 70 A.D. It
is claimed that their original colony there goes back to 500
B.C. when they fled as refugees from the transportation of
their race to Babylon by Nebuchadnezzar. Jonah was on his
way to Tarshish (Spain) when his ship was in danger of foun-
dering, and there is an unauthenticated legend that

Adoniram, Solomon's master of tribute and levy master of the corvée to build the temple (naturally unpopular therefore, as are all tax-men and employers of forced labour) survived being stoned to death (see 1. Kings IV.6 and XII.18) and escaped to Toledo.

It is very possible therefore that Jews of ancient lineage in that city knew more about Solomon's temple from their forefathers than the Rabbis who only arrived in 70 A.D. and were merely recording in the *Mishnah* and *Talmuds* their memories of the Herodian temple, whereas two other temples predated that of Herod, namely the first built by Solomon with the help of King Hiram and Hiram Abiff, and the second largely rebuilt or at least restored by Nehemiah after the Exile, because Nebuchadnezzar had burnt the first (IIChron.V1.19).

To return now to Egypt and its connection with our shores: the Tuatha de Danann, the mythical folk who invaded Ireland and brought with them the Cauldron of the Dagda, are believed by most students of Irish history to be not a people but the gods of the people called the Milesians, who invaded Ireland in remote times. According to the Irish *Book of Conquests*, Miledh, the king of this Milesian folk, brought with him his wife Scota, who was a daughter of the Pharaoh, and from whom the Scots, her descendants, took their name. *The Book of Leinster* and the 11th century *Acts of Saint Cadroe* both mention the legend but give Scota another Milesian husband called Nel or Nellus*.

There were well-known trade routes by which the culture of the Near East could reach Britain. One came from Asia Minor up the valley of the Danube, crossed over to the Elbe and made contact with the shores of the Baltic, where amber could be obtained. Any culture which came to the north by this route was influenced by the civilisations of the Euphrates and Tigris valleys and Troy. The other route was by sea, through the Pillars of Hercules (straits of Gibraltar) and round the coast of Spain, or alternatively by sea as far as

* For accounts of Scota see *Celtic Scotland* by *W.F. Skene.*

the Greek settlement of Marseilles, and then overland to Brittany. By this route came the culture of Egypt, the Aegean and Phoenician cities, and finally of Greece and Rome.

In Greece the spear-bearing Rê becomes Apollo with his dart. In Rome Romulus, whom we shall presently see is a child of the Sun, becomes metamorphosed after death into Quirinus, meaning the "spear-holder" and is worshipped on the hill of the Quirinal*. In Britain a special hill or Tor is dedicated to the spear and its accompanying hawk or eagle, and Geoffrey of Monmouth attempts to put a date to the arrival of this magic eagle by making it contemporary with Solomon's building of the Jewish Temple in the 10th century B.C. I quote from the Welsh version of his history "And this Rvn (a king of Britain) built Kaer Kaint and Kaer Wynt and Kaer Vyydd Y Paladr (the Caer of the Mountain of the Spear) and there the eagle prophesied, foreboding evil to this island. And Salyf (Solomon) son of Dafyd finished Jerusalem."

The legendary King Lot of the Lothians is generally conceded to have been the Celtic god of light, or at least a solar hero. He was married to Anna, and it is possible that she is none other than Anath, the Great Mother of the Phoenicians. At Ephesus in Greece she is known as Di-ana, the goddess Ana. In Ireland she is Dana. In Wales many royal or saintly genealogies are preserved which go back to a certain Avaloc, who was the son of Belli, who in turn was the son of Anna, the first ancestress. We shall presently see who these heroes Belli and Avaloc were, and that the latter is identical with the Evelac of Grail legend.

I hope that I have now given sufficient evidence to show that is is very possible that some contact was at one time made between the civilisations of the Aegean and these islands, whereby the cult of a hawk-headed sun-god with a spear could have become known. But the purpose of our enquiry is to find the real meaning of the Grail. If the spear of the Grail legend was indeed the shaft of the sun-god, into

* Re Romulus see Ovid, *Fasti* 11,475.

what vessel could this seemingly divine ray of light flow? The answer is supplied by many classical references: it is a vessel or any other medium whereby the sun's rays can be focused to a point so as to light a fire. The fire was considered sacred, because it was a manifestation of the sun-god's point of arrival or incarnation upon earth. The following Homeric hymn illustrates why such a fire was held to be holy.

Then from the ship sprang the far-darting Apollo
Like a star in the middle-day, and there flew
Sparks from him in myriads, their brightness ascending to
the heavens.
He entered the shrine, where stand the glorious tripods,
And lit the fire therein, making visible his bolts.

If then we are to learn more about the vessel through which the fire descended, we must turn to the accounts of sacred and so-called perpetual fires. The majority of such accounts are contained in works of the 1st century A.D., a date rather late for the exploring of origins, but ritual practice continues long after its purpose has been forgotten. As an example, the Beltane fires were lit by Christians in Scotland to the very end of the 19th century.

There was a sacred fire at Delphi and another at Athens, and Plutarch in his *Life of Numa* tells us how these were lit from the sun's rays.

"Wherever in Greece a perpetual fire is kept, as at Delphi and Athens, it is committed to the charge, not of virgins, but of widows past the age of marriage. And if by any chance it goes out, as at Athens during the tyranny of Aristion the sacred lamp is said to have been extinguished, and at Delphi when the temple was burned by the Medes, and as during the Mithridatic and the Roman civil wars the altar was demolished and the fire extinguished, then they say it must not be kindled from other fire, but made fresh and new, by lighting a pure and unpolluted flame from the rays of the sun. And this they usually effect by means of metallic mirrors, the concavity of which is made to follow the sides of an isosceles rectangular triangle, and which converge from their circumference to a single point in the centre. When, therefore, these are placed opposite the sun, so that its rays, as they fall upon them from all sides, are collected and concentrated at the centre, the air itself is rarefied there, and very light and dry substances placed there quickly blaze up from its resistance, the sun's rays now acquiring the substance and force of fire."

While it is difficult to follow Plutarch's mathematical explanation of the angles at which light is reflected, my task is made easier in this latest edition of my book by Television, which now gives us all periodic demonstrations of the lighting of the Olympic torch by means of such a large metalllic mirror.

Apuleius in his *Apologia* also refers to the phenomenon, and asks: "Why do concave mirrors, when held at right angles to the rays of the sun, kindle tinder set opposite them?"

Anthemius, a Greek mathematician at the court of the Emperor Justin in Byzantium (contemporary of our King Arthur) was one of the first men to attempt a scientific study of the behaviour of light. Only fragments of his work have come down to us, but in one of his experiments he mentions "a mirror in the shape of an oven". Here, perhaps, is our link with the word "cauldron", for cooking utensils in ancient times were not so carefully differentiated as they are to-day. Any metal receptacle which would hold food or water was put to use by the common folk to boil or to bake, and to serve alternately as cauldron or oven upon a hearth, in much the same way as a Scots wife "bakes" her scones upon an open girdle. Thus a concave bowl of reflective metal (for instance, the now popular Chinese Wok) could as easily be termed an "oven" as a "cauldron". But the Celtic Cauldron of the Dagda or of Annwn was far too precious for culinary purposes, for we are told its rim was set with pearls, so that it is more likely to have been the concave mirror wherein Anthemius attempted to study the behaviour of light.

We come now to another means whereby men could

bring down fire from heaven. The following will be found in *The Orphic Book of Stones**:

"Take in your hands, a crystal – a glittering transparent stone, a ray of clear, divine brightness. In heaven it particularly delights the heart of the immortal gods, and if you go to a shrine carrying one in your hands, none of the gods will refuse your requests. Listen then, that you may learn the powers of this gleaming stone. If you wish to stir up flames without living fire, you order the stone to be laid on top of dry firebrands. Then, when the sun is shining from the opposite direction, it will immediately unfold above the brands a thin ray. As soon as this touches the dry, thick material, it will give rise to smoke, then slight fire, and finally a great flame. This, the ancient goddesses called the Sacred Fire. Therefore I trust that haunches, so pleasing to the immortals, burn with no other flame. In addition I shall tell you as a friend this great miracle: As soon as you lift from the fire that very crystal which is the cause of the flame, it is cold to the touch, and, if placed on the kidneys, will relieve pain."

The crystal described here was probably a sphere, for the following reasons: In the case of a crystal ball the focal point would lie just *within* the surface of the sphere, but the emergent beam would still be strong enough to ignite dry timber in *contact* with the ball's surface. We shall presently see that in the case of a crystal lens or a hollow glass sphere filled with water, the focal point lies *outside* the surface, and would therefore need to be held or fixed above or away from the tinder. I am indebted to the late Sir James French, Chairman of Barr & Stroud's glass and telescopic works in Glasgow for the above information re focal points, a subject he knew well for his firm was manufacturing all our lenses and telescopes for our armaments in the war.

We shall meet in further references the astonishment of the ancients that a stone which could cause fire should itself remain cold and unconsumed. It is also interesting to

---

* See *"De Lapidibus"* – 'An Orphic Poem in both Greek and Latin'. From J.M. Gesner's Edition, annotated by Thos. Tyrrwhitt in 1781.

observe that here the crystal is credited with curative powers. That this was no empty superstition is shown by Pliny, who first records a "sun-treatment" as follows: "I find it stated by a medical man that the very best cautery for the human body is a ball of crystal acted upon by the rays of the sun."* Furthermore, he asserts that rock crystal is a form of ice which has been more or less permanently solidified. "Crystal is only to be found in places where winter snow freezes with the greatest intensity, and it is from the certainty that it is a kind of ice that it has received the name it bears† in Greece.. Rain water and pure snow are absolutely necessary to its formation."

If such mirrors or crystals were kept in the temples ready to light the sacred fire, their existence and whereabouts, at least in early times was wrapped in mystery and as closely veiled to all but initiates as was the Grail itself. Dionysius of Halicarnassus, writing in 7 B.C. about the temple of Vesta's sacred fire in Rome, says: "And Numa enacted in accordance with the ancestral custom of the Latins, that the guarding of the holy things should be committed to virgins. There is some doubt, however, what it is that is kept in the temple and for what reasons the care of it has been assigned to virgins, some affirming that nothing is preserved there but the fire, which is visible to everybody."

He goes on to say: "They regard the fire as consecrated to Vesta because that goddess, being the earth and occupying the central place in the universe, kindles the celestial fires from herself. But there are some who say that besides the fire there are some holy things in the temple of the goddess that may not be revealed in public, of which only the pontiffs and the virgins have knowledge."

Continuing, he explains that a strong confirmation of this story is the fact that when the temple caught fire during the First Punic War, a certain Roman called Metellus dared the flames in order to rescue the holy things. He proceeds: "Some affirm that the objects preserved here are part of

* Pliny, Natural History, XXXVII. 10.
† Ibid.9.

those holy things which were once in Samothrace: that Dar-
danus removed them out of the island into the city which he
himself had built, and that Aeneas, when he fled from the
Troad, brought them along with other holy things into Italy.
But others declare that it is the Palladium that fell from
heaven, the same that was in the possession of the people of
Ilium; for they hold that Aeneas, being well acquainted with
it, brought it into Italy, whereas the Achaeans stole away a
copy." He concludes:

"For my part I find from very many evidences that there
are indeed some holy things, unknown to the public, kept
by the virgins, and not the fire alone."*

It has so far been shown that a concave mirror dedicated
to the use of the sun-god could pass for the pearl-rimmed
Cauldron of Celtic myth. It is to all purposes an inexhaustible vessel, for the sun as a source of energy certainly
appears inexhaustible, and the shining silver vessel can produce fire indefinitely. Is it possible then, that either a mirror
or a crystal could be the Grail? The answer, I think is that
both *sacra* were displayed to the initiates of the Grail cult.
"Li saint talleors d'argent" is the silver bowl-shaped mirror;
and Wolfram, while denying indignantly the truth of Chrestien's version of the story, expressly tells us that the Grail
was a stone. He is referring to the chivalrous company of
the guardians of the talisman and he says:

And this brotherhood so gallant, doest thou know what
to them shall give
Their life and their strength and their valour – then
know by a *stone* they live.
And that stone is both pure and precious – Its name
has thou never ever heard?
Men call it Lapis Exilis – by its magic the wondrous bird
The Phoenix, becometh ashes, and yet doth such virtue
flow

* *Roman Antiquities* Bk II, 66 and 67.

From the stone, that afresh it riseth renewed from the
ashes' glow,
And the plumes that erewhile it moulted spring forth yet
more fair and bright.

Then after a few more verses, Wolfram declares:
  And this stone all men call the Grail.

There will be more to say about the Phoenix in a later
chapter. Here it is sufficient to admit that the bird's powers
of resurrecting itself did in medieval times make it an allow-
able symbol of Christ amongst the very many symbols of
the Saviour, but from more ancient times, as Herodotus
tells us, it is concerned with the resurrection (or relighting)
of fire, and it is this characteristic which Wolfram's poetry
describes, because he mentions it as rising from the ashes,
and is telling us that the Grail-stone was a stone which produced fire. We can leave until later the question of the
meaning of *Lapis Exilis*, which has so far puzzled all commentators, and also the all-important question as to why a
crystal lens should be connected with the idea of bread
from heaven. Meanwhile I can only assure readers that
Chrestien was correct in his assertion that the Grail contained one mass-wafer only, and that Wolfram was equally
right that the wafer was placed upon a stone.
    Let us now go on to Wolfram's description of how once a
year the wound of the Lame King, Anfortas, becomes more
than usually painful, and how the spear (which we have
shown to be the sun's ray) is then plunged into the wound to
give some small measure of relief. If we compare the following passage with Pliny's description of cauterising a
poisoned wound by means of a crystal ball, which was
believed to be ice, there can be little doubt that as far as
Wolfram's version of the legend is concerned, the talisman
was a crystal; and the Jew, Flegetanis, had recorded not only
its ability to inspire men with mystical ideas about God, but
its purely physical powers to effect certain cures by
cauterisation. Here are Wolfram's words:

And deep in the wound empoisoned once more do they
plunge the spear,
One woe shall help the other, the spear cure the frost's
sharp pain.

In the time that erst I have told thee then the king little
rest may gain;
His flesh through the frost it groweth colder than e'en
the snow,
But men know that the spear sharp-pointed doth with
fiery venom glow,
And upon the wound they lay it, and the frost from his
flesh so cold
It draweth and lo! As crystals of glass to the spear doth hold,
And as ice to the iron it clingeth, and none looseth it from
the blade.

So far I have endeavoured to trace the identity of the sacred vessel, but now we must return to our four main points.
It has been shown that a crystal or mirror is an inexhaustible source of fire, and that is is associated with a hawk-
headed sun-god and his spear of light, but we have not yet
identified the magic sword. Miss Weston guessed that it was
a sun-sword, and originally Professor Loomis was of the
same opinion before he openly rejected his earlier writings
about its solar symbolism in favour of his later theory concerning the Cornucopia. But a "sun-sword" is a term which
has in the past been very loosely used to describe what was
thought to be the mythical weapon of a solar hero.

In fact the "sword" of the Grail was as much a material
object and had as useful a purpose as the Grail itself, but in
order to know what it was, it is necessary first to understand
the reason of man's original veneration for the sacred flame
– the fire from heaven – and this will be reserved for the next
chapter.

3 ODIN'S SWORD AND THE BRAND EXCALIBUR

With all our knowledge of modern science, as far as we know there is nothing of a material nature which penetrates daily to our world from outer space except light rays, cosmic rays, the solar wind and a little meteoric dust. The scientific explanation of how light traverses empty space is about as mysterious as the nature of the light itself. It is not surprising, therefore, that all religions, including our own Christian faith, should have seen in light the symbol of that invisible something which we trust and pray reaches out to us from the realms of the spirit.

The sacred fire was the symbol of the visible arrival of this divine spirit, and therefore it was always associated with the Divine or Priest-King of early times, because it explained to the eye how his supposed incarnation from the sun-god was effected. Just as light descended from heaven to kindle a flame, so, it was thought, did the sun-god's spirit descend to enter the body of the king. For this reason the kindling of fire from the sun was very much the king's business, and the torch which he kindled was the symbol of his divinity. From it in turn he lit the fires of his people, and when he died his special torch was extinguished.

In a letter to Pharaoh Akhenaten, a Hittite king addresses him as "My Sun, the great Bil-Fire Torch."[*]

In the story of Meleager, his life-span is determined by the time it will take for a certain brand to burn away. "There

* *The Phoenician Origins of Britons, Scots and Anglo Saxons* by A. Waddell.
† Ovid. *Metamorphosis* Bk VIII.

was a billet of wood", writes Ovid,† which, when the daughter of Thestius lay in childbirth, the three sisters threw into the fire and, spinning the threads of life with firm pressed thumb, they sang: "An equal span of life we give to thee and to this wood, O babe new-born"." In order to preserve her son, the mother snatched the blazing brand from the fire, and quenched it with water, but later, when her son had displeased her, she consigned it once again to the flames, and when it was altogether consumed he died.

Sir James Frazer tells us that in Uganda the fire was put out when the king died, and his death was announced as "The fire has gone out!"* In Sparta the kings had a special officer known as "fire-bearer", whose duty it was to carry the flame into battle like a standard.† Diodorus Siculus records that the sacred fires of Persia were extinguished at the king's death.§ In Greek art, Professor James Clark says that death was sometimes symbolized by a youth with an inverted torch.‡ Monsieur Franz Cumont, in his book *The Mysteries of Mithra* writes as follows:

"They (the monarchs) ruled by the "grace" of the creator of heaven and earth. The Iranians pictured this "grace" as a sort of supernatural fire, as a dazzling aureole, or nimbus of "glory", which belonged especially to the gods, but which also shed its radiance upon princes and consecrated their powers. The *Hvareno*, as the Avesta calls it, illuminated legitimate sovereigns and withdrew its light from usurpers as impious persons."

Then on another page he continues: "The celestial fire which shines among the stars, always victorious over darkness, has as its emblem the inextinguishable fire that burned in the palace of the Caesars, and which was carried before them in official ceremonies. This lamp, constantly lighted, had also served the Persian kings as an image of the perpetuity of their power; and it passed with the mystical

---

* *The Golden Bough*, Sir J. Frazer Vol II, *The Magic Art* p. 261.
† ditto.
§ Diodorus Siculus XVII, 114.
‡ *The Dance of Death* by James Clark M.A. Ph.D.

ideas of which it was the expression to the Diadochi, and from them to the Romans."

In Ireland all fires were extinguished by the Druids on the Eve of Samhain, and the king then lit the new flame at Tara. According to the Brehon Laws, neither gold nor silver might redeem from the death penalty he who dared to light a fire before the king had done so.* For certain offences men were excommunicated, and thereafter no member of the tribe might give the outlaw fire on pain of similar excommunication. † We can see, therefore why the Celtic Cauldron would not cook the food of a coward or a man forsworn. In plain language, it would not provide him with the fire on which to do his cooking. To return to the lighting of the king's fire: when St. Patrick arrived in Ireland, he kept alight the candle upon the altar of his little church on the hill at Slane. It was visible to the Druids at Tara, and when all their fires had been extinguished in preparation for the ritual of the king rekindling the flame, St. Patrick's light continued to burn. Whereat the Druids cried out: "O King, unless the fire which you see be quenched this same night, it will never be quenched; and the kindler of it will overcome us all and seduce all the folk of your realm." The king and the Druids thereupon mounted their chariots and drove to Slane, but St. Patrick and his companions escaped death by being miraculously, but fortunately only temporarily, changed into stags §. While on the subject of St. Patrick, amongst his miracles it is recorded that he brought fire out of an icicle, not an impossible feat if water is frozen in a dish hollowed to shape a lens, and then loosened from it; but ice and crystal were, as we have seen, hardly differentiated by the ancient world.

A special torch was borne by the powerful and princely chiefs of Ireland as late as the 16th century A.D. It was known as a 'richainnell,' or king-candle, and was of enormous size, with a great bushy wick. It burned at night in the

---

* *A Smaller Social History of Ancient Ireland* by P.W. Joyce p. 90.
† *Druidism* by Dudley Wright.
§ Life of St Patrick by Professor J.B. Bury.

royal presence; in the palace it was placed over the chief's head; during war it blazed outside his tent door; on night marches it was borne before him. This custom is mentioned very often in the records, and in *The Four Masters* is described Shane O'Neill's bodyguard in the 16th century. Shane was the mighty chief of Tyrone with whom Queen Elizabeth negotiated, and in front of his tent burned a great fire "and a huge torch, thicker than a man's body was constantly flaring at a short distance from the fire."*

We can scarcely doubt but that the Oriflamme (meaning the golden flame), which was borne by the Frankish kings into battle, was not originally a silken banner with an embroidered flame, but a torch of living fire.

I have left until last the reference to such a custom in the Old Testament, because they are the most interesting to us. In II Sam. XXI 17 we find: "Then the men of David sware unto him, saying, Thou shalt go no more out with us to battle that thou quench not the light of Israel." And I Kings XI.36 gives: "And unto his son will I give one tribe, that David my servant may have a light always before me in Jerusalem." Job XVIII.5 is more explicit: "Yea, the light of the wicked shall be put out, and the spark of his fire shall not shine. The light shall be dark in his tabernacle, and his candle shall be put out with him."† Finally we have the verses of II Chron. XXI.7, "He (the Lord) promised to give a light to him (David) and to his sons forever", and of Psalm CXX-XII.17, "I have ordained a lamp for mine anointed." These verses describe an actual contemporary Hebrew ritualistic practice, which foreshadowed and prophesied the coming of the Messiah, whose Sanctuary lamp lights our Christian churches to-day.

It is not necessary to enter here into long explanations of Sir James Frazer's theories concerning the cult of a dying and reviving god of vegetation and light; briefly the theory is that the god was represented by the king; the virility of the

---

* *A Smaller Social History of Ancient Ireland*, by Professor J.B. Bury.
† Other references to the same practice will be found in II Kings VIII.19 Job XXI, 17 Prov.XIII, 9 and XXIV.20.

king was therefore thought to influence the growing corn and the yearly course of the sun; the King, the Divine Youth, was for that reason sacrificed yearly, or at any rate before his vigour departed. As civilisation advanced, he won free from such a fate, at first by the substitution of a slave, and finally by the substitution of a scapegoat.

In the course of time, the life and term of office of the Divine Youth was prolonged, and therefore a gradual disassociation between the yearly fire-kindling feasts of Beltane, Samhain, or St. John's Eve and the person of the king came about, until at length some sacred fires were thought by the common folk to be never extinguished, and were therefore called perpetual fires. But actually they were not perpetual. Ovid tells us that the Calends of March were really the beginning of the year when "the withered laurel is withdrawn from the Ilian hearth, that Vesta also may make a brave show, dressed in fresh leaves. Besides 'tis said that a new fire is lighted in her secret shrine, and the rekindled flame gains strength."* Solinus attests the same fact about Vesta's fire.† When the life of the king was no longer forfeit, and the offices of king and priests had been divided, it is probable that the priests (perhaps with the help of the king) kindled a sacred fire yearly, while the king's special torch remained unextinguished for the period of his life.§

Remembering that Arthur's sword is always called the *brand* Excalibur, and that any magic sword is generally likened in the French MSS to "un brandon de feu", I must now take a big jump and assert that the magic sword Excalibur, identical with the sword of the Grail, is nothing else but the king's torch, which at Arthur's death was extinguished in the water of the mere by Sir Bedivere. Various attempts have been made to equate the name

---

* Ovid, *Fasti* III.135.
† Solinus. Ch.2.
§ If Vesta's fire went out by accident, the virgins were whipped by the Pontifex Maximus, and were compelled to rub a board of wood with a borer to produce fire by friction, but whipping shows, I think, that this task was a punishment for carelessness. The inference that the annual lighting was effected, as at Delphi and Athens, from the rays of the sun remains good. See Festus s.v. "Ignis" p. 106 ed.C.O. Müller.

Excalibur with variations of Celtic sources such as Calibur-nus, but remembering how easily Horus/Rê and his spear of light could travel to England and become St. George, and to Greece to become St. Demetrius, is it not possible that the name of the sword derives from the Greek – Ex Kylike Pyr – meaning "out of a cup – a fire!" The reader will have the opportunity of judging whether the evidence I shall now give bears this out.

To obtain that evidence we must go as far afield as Iceland and the Norse myths. But this is not really so far from the Near Eastern source of the Grail legends as might at first be supposed. While mirrors and glasses were still venerated as *sacra* in the temples of Delphi and Athens and Rome, nevertheless some centuries before the Christian era an increasing familiarity with the laws of nature and science, particularly in Greece, led mathematicians to regard the behaviour of light from a scientific as well as from a mystical stand point. So that Archimedes in the 3rd century B.C. used reflective mirrors to set the Roman fleet on fire, and even earlier, Aristophanes made casual mention of a burning glass in *The Clouds*. Plutarch's account of how the sacred fire was lit at Delphi, where he was a priest, is illustrative of how both the scientific and mystical approach to light could exist in the same mind at the same time, for he speaks of a flame as being "unpolluted" and yet cannot resist a mathematical explanation of the angles of reflection. No such scientific study of the subject occurred amongst the northern peoples, who continued to regard the phenomenon of fire-from-heaven as the supreme and divine mystery until superseded by the Christian mysteries. The farther away a country is from the source of its culture, the longer are the myths preserved in their original form, and thus Iceland and Britain both acted as sounding-boards, which echoed back the old tales long after the people of the Mediterranean had begun to speak first of mathematics and optics and then of the Gospel story.

The most archaic version of the Norse myths are to be found, therefore, not in Germany or Scandinavia, but in Iceland; and the earliest MS is the *Poetic Edda* of the 13th century, but it was probably first written down in the 9th, that is to say before Iceland became a Christian country. As many of the original Icelandic settlers were drawn from Britain, these lays are recognized to have been influenced by Celtic myth.* In about A.D. 1222 Snörri Sturluson wrote the *Prose Edda*, which was a kind of commentary on the *Poetic Edda* and an instruction to skalds on how to compose such metrical lays. Snörri, a Christian, must have been something of an antiquarian, for his advice to would-be skalds concerns not so much the laws of metre as the rules for preserving the old legends intact. His view was that a poet, although Christian, might compose new songs about the old pagan heroes, but he might not tamper with the canon of ancient tradition, and he must first understand and then continue to employ the traditional synonyms, similes and periphrases, by which certain characters or objects in these myths were recognised by reference to their adventures.

From Snörri we learn that the Norse gods came from Troy by way of the Danube valley, Odin, he says, was descended from Priam, whose daughter had a child called Thor. Thor was fostered in Thrace, and seventeen generations divided him from his descendant Odin. Odin was the All-Father. The earth was his daughter and his wife. On her he begot the first son, which is Asa-Thor. Then he and his people left the east and came to Saxland. Snörri seems to ascribe a human origin to Odin and yet to assign to him the powers of the All-Father, but if we try to separate history from myth, we arrive at the probable truth that the traders of the Danubian route brought with them their Trojan gods.

Now Snörri shows us very clearly that in his day the skalds still enjoyed a sort of Freemasonry, whereby words served as masonic signals between one brother-poet and another. It was, no doubt, a delightful game, comparable to our cross-word puzzles, and it must have lent them some self-importance. It is certain that, without Snörri's explanations, a large part of the *Elder* or *Poetic Edda* would

---

* Foreword to Olive Bray's translation of the *Poetic Edda*.

have been incomprehensible to the modern reader. Every skald, he tells us, must use the art of periphrasis, and use it, moreover, in the traditional way. Thus (to choose my own analogy) we must not call a spade a spade, but rather "that which first caused Adam's brow to sweat". If the reader happened to be unacquainted with the story of the Fall in Genesis, he would be entirely at a loss. Snörri gives us a list of the traditional modes of periphrasis, together with the legendary adventures which explained them. For instance: Thjazi was a mighty man, and his father possessed much gold. When he died, the giant and his two brothers inherited the hoard and, in order to guard it, carried it about in their mouths. "And", writes Snörri, "we have it as a metaphor among us now, to call gold the mouth-tale of the giants; but we conceal it in secret terms."* To quote one more example from Snörri, "Aegir asked, "What manner of metaphor is used for skaldic writing?" "Three are the types of skaldic metaphor", answered Bragi. "Thus (first) calling everything by its name; the second type is that which is called substitution; the third type of metaphor is that which is called periphrasis."

Amongst Snörri's list of traditional substitutions, he tells us that "swords are called Odin's fires", and he explains the origin of the substitution as follows: "And at evening, when it was time for drinking, Odin had swords brought into the hall, so bright that light radiated from them: and other illumination was not used while they sat drinking." Snörri was a Christian writing a late (13th century) commentary on pagan myths. It is not therefore surprising that in this instance he got his "substitution" the wrong way round, for by the inference of further evidence he should have said that fires were called Odin's swords, but at least he links them together. Did he make the same mistake when explaining the substitution for gold? "Wherefore he asks, "is gold called Aegir's fire?" and he answers: "Aegir (who gave a banquet to his fellow gods) had bright gold brought

* All quotations from the *Prose Edda* of Snörri are taken from the translation of A.G. Brodeur, Ph.D.

in on to the floor of the hall, and the gold gave forth light and illuminated the hall like fire: and it was used there for lights at his banquet, even as in Valhall swords were used in place of fire." We shall meet often with this last substitution of gold for fire, and it will be remembered that in the *Mabinogion*, Peredur's serpent-stone had the property of producing as much gold as was desired. But now let us return to Odin's sword.

In the hall of Volsung grew a big oak-tree, and "the limbs of the tree blossomed fair out of the roof of the hall, while below stood the trunk within, and the said trunk did men call Branstock".* It was in this tree that Odin had thrust his sword ready for the hero who could draw it out. In modern language we should say that the property of fire was hidden deep within the wood, and that man had not yet learnt to draw out the fire. The Branstock derives from the same Teutonic root which gives the words brand, burn, etc., and the name simply means the "fire-tree".

The most primitive way of making fire is to rub two sticks together and this was generally effected by a bore of hardwood twirled in a cup-shaped matrix of soft wood, and these two parts of the fire-drill were for obvious reasons conceived to be of different sexes: male and female. In archaic ritual, therefore, it was thought fitting that a woman should hold and steady the matrix, while the man employed the bore, and this is the practice amongst certain primitive tribes to-day. † To digress: swords and fires may have been associated as far back as the Book of Genesis, because the knapping of flints produces sparks and could give birth to the idea of a fiery sword. Sunlight flickering on steel could not be the origin of antediluvian ideas because neither iron nor steel had been discovered.

But to return to the fire-drill: the earliest myths will tell us of how the magic sword was drawn forth from a tree, and generally by a man and a woman. Odin's sword was drawn forth from the Branstock by Volsung's son, Sigmund, and

---

* *The Volsunga Saga,* translated from the Icelandic by Eirikur Magnusson & William Morris.
† *The Golden Bough* by Sir James Frazer Vol: II Magic Art p.208

his sister-wife Signy. The story of how they drew forth not only the brand but also the wrath of the gods upon their heads, just as did Prometheus when he stole fire from Olympus, is well known to those who are familiar with Wagner's opera cycle of *The Ring*. Sigmund's sword is broken, that is to say extinguished, by the power of the All-Father, who takes upon himself the characteristics of Thor, god of thunder and lightning: the rain and storm and the spear of lightning quench the poor little brand of primitive man.

To explain how the brand was next "mended" or renewed, we must return to how Arthur first got the sword Excalibur, and to Malory's account of how there was found "a great stone four square, like to a marble stone, and in the midst thereof lyke an anvylde of steele, a foot of height, and therein stooke a faire sword." This stone – though Malory was almost certainly unaware of the meaning of the legends he was transcribing – is really a description of a flint, *a stone used as an anvil*, on which iron striking will produce a spark. And Arthur "handled the sword by the handles, and lightly and fiersly he pulled it out of the stone". Whereat he was proclaimed the only rightful king of Britain, or more accurately *because* he was the rightful king he kindled a king's torch. As we shall presently see, this was not the only fashion in which the sword could be "mended" for Malory gives us another account of the finding of Arthur's magic sword when it was drawn from the Lady of the Lake. It is difficult in cold and rainy Britain to light a torch from the sun's rays for the sun is seldom hot enough, though broken glass bottles in Forestry plantations seem to ignite unwelcome fires in very hot weather. But although Arthur used iron and flint on the first occasion he may have been very well acquainted with the concave mirrors of the Middle East and also with the mysterious powers of water, for Chrestien's Grail sword given to Perceval could only be mended in water.

So far we have dealt only with the more primitive ways of making fire by friction or percussion, and both these methods necessitate the action and intervention of man, and were thought to be effected by the conjunction of a male and female element in the materials used; for in the Iranian scriptures of Zoroaster it is laid down that the stone of mother-earth is female and that metal, on the contrary is male.* Since communication obviously existed between Northern Europe and the Near East from the earliest times, the belief that stone and iron had these sexual qualities was probably common to most peoples. It is often maintained that the earliest iron to be worked was meteoric iron. The Egyptians called it always ba-n-pet, "the metal of heaven", even when eventually imported and well known.† The point of contact of iron on stone was therefore not only the union of male and female but of celestial and terrestrial qualities, and the spark which resulted from the blow of a primitive iron axe upon stone may perhaps explain its adoption as a sacred emblem in Crete, for the Labyrinth probably takes its name from "the place of the axe".

Nevertheless, fire produced from percussion necessitated a good deal of activity on the part of man, whereas the more man could eliminate any human action in the production of fire, the more would he feel that this divine brightness came directly and miraculously to him from the gods and their dwelling in the sky. Far more desirable, therefore, than fire-drills or iron and flint was a talisman which merely by holding it to the sun would draw down fire from heaven. Any "vessel" which could thus receive the sun's rays and beget the fire-child without the intervention of an earthly male element was thought of as a "virgin" vessel.

We have seen that this receptacle of light could be either a metal mirror or a crystal. But there is a third kind of virgin-vessel, and the Grail legend bears this out. Arthur goes to the Grail castle and there sees the 'sacra' of its mysteries, and "the history testifies that there was not at that time in the whole of great Britain either (sic) a chalice. The Grail then appeared at the consecration of the Mass in three ways. The

* *The Bible of the World* edited by Robert O. Ballou.
† See *Zeus* by A.B. Cook Vol. III p. 922 note 9.

king was well pleased to see what he saw and he took into his memory the name of the chalice and the form... and he commanded to make the like in every place in his dominion for serving God the more honourably."* What was this third type of chalice? Was it Christian or was it a means of focusing sunlight – or was it both? I think it was the means whereby Arthur drew his magic sword out of water, for there is no more powerful way of focusing sunlight than by a hollow glass sphere filled with water, as many scientists have found to their cost when a large retort filled with water has been left in the sun, and a laboratory has consequently gone up in flames.

That this phenomenon was known to the ancients is proved by references in Lactantius[c] and by Pliny, who says first that "vessels in glass have been brought to a marvellous degree of resemblance to crystal,[†] and secondly that, "we find that globular glass vessels, filled with water, when brought in contact with the rays of the sun, become heated to such a degree as to cause articles of clothing to ignite."[§]

That in drawing his magic sword (let us always call it Excalibur) from the Lady of the Lake, Arthur was drawing fire out of water, is supported by the following references. Pliny says that, "at Dodona the spring of Zeus is cold, and puts out torches that are plunged in it, but kindles such as are put out and brought near to it".[‡] Wolfram tells us that Parzival's sword "which Anfortas gave him, as ye once in this tale did hear, sprang asunder one while, yet 'twas welded afresh in the mystic spring."[¶] In the poem known as the *Chair of Taliesin* by the Welsh Bard, a boat of glass (and we shall see later that such a boat is globular or coracle-shaped) is, in the hands of a stranger, a sign whereby he is known as an initiate and admitted to the mysteries: "With priests of

---

* *Y Seint Greal*, the Welsh version of the *Queste* translated into English by the Rev. Robert Williams pp.673 & 685.

[c] See the article by H.C. Beck in the Antiquaries Journal Vol VIII.327.

† Pliny. Natural History Bk XXXVII Ch. 10.

§ Ibid Bk XXXVI Ch. 67.

‡ Ibid Bk II. CVI. 228.

¶ Jessie Weston, *Parzival* p. 252.

intelligence, to officiate on behalf of the moon, and the con-
course of associated men, under the open breeze of the sky,
with the maceration and sprinkling, and the boat of glass in
the hand of the stranger, and the stout youth with pitch.''[c]
The pitch, of course, refers to the torch ready to be
lighted.

It will be necessary to go more deeply into the science
and dates of glass-blowing in a later chapter, but it is time
now to postulate what was the actual ritual practised in
pagan and particularly in Celtic pre-Christian times; and,
more important, what was the spiritual meaning or yearning which underlay it.

The virgin-vessel was a symbol of earth, of Kore the
Maiden. At the close of summer it was solemly entombed in
a cave (a mouth of the nearest and most impressive entrance
to Hades) if possible beyond a subterranean stream, the
mythical river Styx. When springtime came, the Divine
Youth had to ford the subterranean stream at considerable
peril, and brave the truly awful depths of such an underworld. Having suffered this ordeal, he then won the symbol
of the Maiden, and carried it in a priestly procession to the
top of a Tor or a hill, where the rays of the morning sun
passed through it to light his torch and symbolize his incarnation and consecration as a son of the Sun.

Before going on to give further evidence of this ritual, let
us consider its significance. Some readers may feel that such
a practice might very well explain the Celtic Cauldron.
Others may feel a certain disappointment and even
repugnance in supposing that the Grail, which has always
been associated with Our Lord and which has called forth
from so many poets the highest expression of their art and
faith, is no more than the *sacrum* of a fire-cult. I would like
therefore to assure such readers from the outset that any
loss they may feel now will be made good again in due time,
and a glance at Plate XII will perhaps reassure them that they
are following a line of detection, labyrinthine but reward-
ing, if they will remember that light was a fore-ordained

[c] *Mythology and Rites of the British Druids.* Translated by Edward Davies p. 277.

symbol whereby we might have some idea of the relation of God to Christ, the Light of the World. For the sake of brevity, I shall in future use the phrase "fore-ordained symbolism" or "picture-writing" when I want the reader to understand that the rhythm of the sun's course and the behaviour of light and its refraction were not what gave birth to Sir James Frazer's idea of the dying and reviving god, but that on the contrary, the Creator set lights in the firmament "for signs" for the purpose of preparing man for the advent of His Son. He could have created quite a different pattern, rhythm and behaviour in the sky, had He so chosen.

If I am right, there was never a time when some man did not raise his head and, beholding the beauty of descending light, long to be endowed with it, stretching up his hands in anticipation of the descent of the Holy Spirit. An early Chaldean prayer to Gibil, the god of fire, went thus: "Cause then the limbs of man, the son of his god, to shine, – make him to be bright like the sky, – may he shine like the earth, – may he be bright like the interior of the heavens."*

At the heart of all the old religions which spread from the Near East was the apprehension that there was only the One God, the Creator, and though he might delegate some of his powers to attendant Archangels or punitive demons, who were unfortunately numbered as gods – a veritable Civil Service of innumerable departments, each of which had to be placated – yet the Creator remained supreme. In Egypt Rê was addressed as "O thou Only One, O thou Perfect One, O thou who art eternal", and as "Divine Youth, who art self-created. I cannot comprehend thee. Thou art the lord of heaven and earth, and didst create beings celestial and beings terrestrial."†

In the Indian epic the *Mahabharata*, the hero Yudhishthira prays: "O sun, thou art the eye of the universe, the soul of all things that are; thou art the creator; thou art Indra, thou art Vishnu, thou art Brahma, thou art Prajapati,

---

* *The Dawn of Civilisation* by Professor Maspero p. 636.
† See *The Book of the Dead*, pamphlet by the British Museum.

lord of creatures, father of gods and men, thou art fire, thou art Mind; thou art lord of all, the eternal Brahma."*

For those who regard Christ as the Light of the World, the secrets of Camelot will, I think be welcome, for Arthur's Camelot and the ancient British town of Camulodunum both take their names from the Celtic "camu" – (bent) and "Lot" – (light), and it is the secret of how to bring together (angle) the rays, not of light but of the Spirit to a focal point in our hearts for which we are all seeking.

* See *Indian Myth and Legend* by Donald A. Mackenzie.

4 THE TREE, THE APPLE, AND THE SERPENT

Henceforward it will not be difficult to recognise a pearl-rimmed cauldron or bowl for what it was. It is less easy to recognise in the many legends which will presently be examined the references to a crystal or glass sphere, and to do so one must be able to pick out the allusions to the metal setting in which the jewel or glass was framed. If a crystal ball is cut in half it forms a lens, and a fire is more easily lit by this means than by a complete sphere, because the focal point being then outside the surface, greater heat is obtained than when only the emergent beam is available. Lenses of rock crystal have been found in Crete dating from 1500 B.C.,* and a similar find has been made in Assyria. † In the case of a lens, however, it is necessary to hold the crystal above or away from the tinder, and it is essential to hold the hand steady. While a crystal ball required no metal setting, for it must be laid directly on the tinder, it was necessary to set a lentil-shaped crystal or a hollow glass sphere in some form of ring attached to a handle or pedestal in roughly the same way as we set a magnifying glass to-day. If this is not done, there is a risk that the slippery crystal will fall to the ground and receive a crack or flaw. Alternatively, if the gem is held securely, the hand obscures half the light.

It must also be realized that the symbol of the virgin earth-goddess is never alluded to as "it" but always as

---

* *Antiquaries Journal* Vol VIII p. 327.
† *Ninevah and Babylon*, by Austen H. Layard P. 197.

"she"; and "she" is always the heroine of the story. Thus, for example, Danae, locked in her tower of brass, conceived by means of a golden shower of light, which transpierced her, and she gave birth to Perseus. Perseus is a dual character. His "birth" is the rebirth of an initiate: his consecration as son of the Sun. He is the mortal and immortal brother, or, as the Egyptians would have expressed it, the Pharaoh and his double; and it is the fire, symbol of his divinity, to which Danae gave birth.

From this brief illustration let us presuppose certain standard types of golden settings which the ancient employed, and then we shall see if the myths and legends prove the supposition correct. In the story of Danae the framework is called a tower. We shall presently see that it is sometimes called a "bed", and this is very understandable, for we still speak to-day of a jewel being "embedded" in its setting or matrix. But we need to know the detailed design of this tower or bed.

In Egyptian, Chaldean and Norse mythology the earth was conceived to be the shape of a lentil. (This plant was first cultivated in Egypt, and our word lens derives from it. The offering of first-fruits to Horus was always lentils.*) Whether the Pythagorean taboo against eating beans originated in the connection between the lentil's shape, the earth, and the mysteries of optics is pure speculation, and the reason for the taboo has never been explained to anyone's satisfaction. Pythagoras himself, however, seems to have thought that the earth was a sphere, and later some of the Romans believed likewise. But, as has been said, the early peoples of the Nile, Chaldea, and the North believed it to be lentil-shaped, the round surface uppermost, and that it was entirely surrounded by a sea – the wide Atlantic and Indian oceans – and this circular moat around the lentil was thought to be, or at any rate was symbolized as, a great serpent. When the Sun rose above the Indian ocean he was said to have escaped from the coils of this monstrous reptile, which the Egyptians called Apapi, and when he sank

---

* Plutarch, *On Isis and Osiris* LXV.3.

into the Atlantic he had once again to pass through the underworld realms which the serpent guarded. In the Norse myths this all-surrounding sea was known as the Midgard serpent or Lind-worm, and was believed to hold his tail in his mouth so as to form an endless ring. "He lies," writes Snörri in the *Prose Edda*, "in the midst of the ocean encompassing all the land and bites upon his own tail." In the mythology of the Near East the ring of the endless serpent often symbolizes eternity, partly because it has no beginning and no end, and partly because a snake, which casts its skin, suggests an endless sequence of rebirth. Broadly speaking, all the peoples in the world have associated the serpent with the watery element.

It will not be surprising, therefore, if the gold ring surrounding the crystal or glass symbol of earth took the form of a serpent biting its own tail, for there he would seem to challenge his old enemy, the Sun, for possession of the Maiden, and his powers over water and ice would appear to defy the passing of the solar rays, all to the greater glory of the conquering light.

For easier handling, and for displaying the talisman in a shrine, such a ring would need to be set firmly upon a flat base, and, since man first drew fire from the wood of a tree, the tree would naturally jump to his imagination as a fitting symbol for the purpose. Compare with my supposition the account of such a tree by Nonnus in his *Dionysiaca*. The Baal of the Phoenicians, the sun-god whom the Greeks identified with Heracles, told Dionysus that the city of Tyre owed its firm foundation to his having inspired men to find the tree of the goddess (Nonnus, being a Greek, called her Athena), which grew on the Ambrosial Rocks. On the top of this tree perched an eagle and a well-wrought bowl. From the flaming tree fire, self-made, spat out wonderful sparks, and the glow devoured the tree all around, but consumed it not. A snake writhed round the tree. The fire kept to the middle of the tree and sent out a friendly glow, hurting neither serpent nor eagle. Only by the sacrifice of this bird to Zeus could Tyre be firmly founded.*

* Nonnus. *Dion.* XL lines *469 et seq.*

Fig 2. BABYLONIAN SEAL, SHOWING SOLAR-HERO IN CONFLICT WITH EAGLE-HEADED MONSTER BESIDE GRAIL-TREE.
From Professor Langdon's "Semitic Mythology".

Now let us look at the illustration of a Babylonian seal in Professor S.H. Langdon's *Semitic Mythology* (Fig 2.)

The stylized form of the tree should be noted, and particularly the suggestion of a jewelled centre; also the three whorl-shaped knops on the stem. Beside the tree a solar hero is in combat with strange unearthly powers, in much the same way as in Fig.1 Rê/Horus is defying the stars of the night. The conjunction by the artist of a solar hero or solar-god, and a Grail-stone or Grail-tree, is eminently suitable. Some Assyriologists might argue that the Babylonian seal represented the date palm; and the "flaming palmettes" of the Persian rugs in the Burrell Collection could either be dates or flowers but as far as the definitions in the Burrell Collection are concerned they are designated as "flaming". However the date palm and vine have been from ancient times proposed as possible origins of the Tree of Knowledge in Paradise, so our interest need not be deflected from the great jewelled circle above the branches.

Apuleius, who was an initiate of the mysteries of Isis and Osiris, gives us in the last pages of his *Golden Ass* a description of a procession of the priests and priestesses of Isis. The women wore polished mirrors tied to the back of their heads, in imitation of the goddess whose head was crowned with a mirror supported by vipers. The High Priest held a golden, boat-shaped lamp with a tall tongue of flame mounting from a hole in the centre. Behind him came a priest who carried a *miniature palm tree with gold leaves*." And amongst several other priests came one "with a box containing the secret implements of her cult."

Remembering that Snörri tells us that the old name for Asgard was Troy, among his traditional lists of periphrases we find the following: "Why is gold called the Needles, or Leaves of Glasir? In Asgard, before the doors of Valhall, there stands a grove which is called Glasir, and its leafage is all red gold, even as is sung here:

> Glasir stands
> With golden leafage
> Before the High God's halls.

Far and wide this tree is fairest known among gods and men.

Virgil recounts that Aeneas escaped from Troy to Italy, and that there the Sibyl told him that his only means of entering and returning safely from the underworld was to grasp and bear with him into Hades the fruitage of a golden bough. The actual words of Virgil are important, for Sir James Frazer jumped to the conclusion, and I think incorrectly, that it was the mistletoe which had to be cut from the sacred oak, and he built up a large part of his theories on this assumption. The Druids have likewise been credited by many writers with a great veneration for the mistletoe, because of one very brief account by Pliny that they cut it at certain times of the year with much ceremony. That they culled many other plants with ceremonies just as magical and august is ignored. Frazer came to the conclusion that the mistletoe on the oak-tree was believed by primitive man to have been sown there by lightning, and that therefore it symbolized the arrival or incarnation of the son of the sky-god. That the golden bough was connected with the arrival of light is, I think correct, but I see no real grounds for supposing it to have been the mistletoe. Virgil

certainly compares it to the mistletoe, as any poet is entitled
to use an analogy, and the berries are not unlike small
spherical crystals. But he states very definitely that "the foil
tinkled in the light breeze", a most significant phrase,
which would be most descriptive of the delicate gold foil-
work of the Mycenean and Etruscan wreaths for the head,
which can be seen in the British Museum. Furthermore,
Aeneas is told not to cut the bough but the Sibyl instructs
him to pluck the fruit:

> Sed non ante datur telluris subire,
> Auricomos quam qui decerpserit arbore fetus.

The words *auricomos* and *fetus* have been translated as
"golden-tressed fruitage". It is no doubt difficult to give an
exact translation of what Virgil meant – and Virgil himself
may have only half-understood the legend about which he
was writing. But certainly *fetus* concerns fruit or the bringing
forth thereof. And this is a most important point, for, as will
presently be shown, the crystal was referred to as the "fruit"
of the golden tree.* Sometimes indeed the crystal was described as an apple, and in fact the attribute of Diana of
Nemi was an apple branch.† It seems more likely,
therefore, that the apple branch rather than the mistletoe
was the golden bough in question.

The Romans believed this golden bough to be situated at
Nemi beside the lake known as "Diana's mirror". Also to
Nemi came the image of Tauric Diana, brought it was said
by Orestes, who took it from the Tauric king, whom he had
slain, and brought it to Italy in a bundle of faggots. Frazer
states that the title of Vesta was borne by Diana at Nemi,
where she had a perpetual fire. § The image of this Tauric
Vesta hidden in a bundle of faggots bears a strange and
haunting resemblance to the crystal which the *Orphic Book of
Stones* described as laid on top of fire-brands.

---

* *Aeneid* Bk VI 124 et seq.
† *Zeus* by A.B. Cook Vol I p. 274.
§ *The Golden Bough* Bk I Ch. 1 pp 1-17.

It will be remembered that the Golden Fleece which Jason sought to steal was kept in the midst of a tree round which a guardian serpent coiled itself. Whether or not the Golden Fleece was a periphrasis for the Golden Apple of the Hesperides (of which more on a later page) is speculation but seems very likely, for the Greek word *melon* has the alternative meaning of sheep or apple. Such a possibility is intriguing because in 1429, at a period when French and German poets had already made the Grail legend widely known, Philip, Duke of Burgundy, founded his famous Order of the Golden Fleece, a company of knights who on terra firma closely resembled in their chivalry and devotion to the Christian faith the ideal Templar knights who in Wolfram's version guarded the Grail in the Castle of Montsalvat. The famous collar of the Order portrays alternate flint-stones, steels and flames between the horns of a ram, and the motto on the embroidered velvet hood is that of the House of Burgundy: "Ante ferit quam micat", which is generally translated as "First strike and then the flame will shine", perhaps one of the oldest ways of expressing: "Knock and it shall be opened unto you. Seek, and ye shall find." Whether or not the Duke of Burgundy had esoteric knowledge, that the Fleece and the Golden Apple of the Hesperides were one and the same, is the intriguing question. If the Fleece was indeed yet another legend concerning the Golden Apple, then such a tale is almost identical with the adventure of Hercules in the Hesperides, of Jason in Colchis and of Siegfried in the far north of Europe, for all three found a serpent-dragon coiled round a tree guarding a golden hoard. Both Jason and Siegfried were guided to the dwelling of the monster by the kindly offices of a bird: Jason by the wry-neck* (whose habit is to hide its egg in the hollow of a tree) and Siegfried by the "Wood-Bird". The hoard of gold would have been unlimited if that gold was the sun's light issuing from the sacred crystal in the "hole" of the metallic "tree".

Thus the miniature tree of Isis, of Glasir, of the Golden

* *Zeus* by A.B. Cook. Vol I. pp253 and 257.

Bough, and very probably of the Golden Fleece, all point towards the existence of a small golden tree. Coming now to the Grail legends, it will be remembered that in the Thornton MS Perceval comes to a damsel who is attached or bound to a tree, and that in the *Queste*, when Galahad disembarks at Sarras (which was the city of the Saracens, pagan or infidel) he makes a tree of gold and precious stones round or over the Grail: "Quant Galahad fu venus a terre tenir, si fist par desus la table un arbre d'or et de pierres precieuses qui couuri le saint graal".* If the Grail had been a chalice, such a covering does not make sense, though there does exist a wooden cup, a relic called the Cup of Antioch, which is decorated on the exterior with metal filigree work. Little is known of it historically, and there was such a plethora of relics genuine and false that no one can any longer distinguish what is truth and what fantasy. But if Galahad's "Grail" were a crystal lens or glass sphere we can very well understand how it was set amidst the branches of such a tree as is pictured on the Babylonian seal.

Compare now the illustration (Fig.3) with the early Babylonian design. This illustration is to be found in a very curious little book published in 1825, of which Glasgow University has a copy, entitled *The Astrologer of the Nineteenth Century*, by a certain Raphael. Raphael claims that he copied it from an ancient German manuscript, obviously a treatise on Alchemy, on which subject more will be found later on in this book, for he describes the conjunction of the several necessary metals to make the tree-like "stand" for the crystal. Raphael (from his *nom de plume* probably a Jew) claims for what he describes, the names of Urim and Thummim. It should be noted that although very stylized, the leaves of the old tree are still present; so are the three spinning-whorls or knops on the stem; and the lettering intimates a tradition that Hebrew characters were inscribed on the metal setting. The oval shape of the lens would be quite as efficacious for lighting a fire as a circular lens.

---

* *La Queste del Saint Graal* of Walter Map, edited by F.J. Furnival printed for the Roxburghe Club. p. 245.

Fig 3. THE THUMMIM OR URIM, A CRYSTAL SET IN PRECIOUS METALS.
As illustrated by Raphael in "The Astrologer of the 19th Century".

We know very little about the sacred objects known as Urim and Thummim, of which Aaron and his descendants had charge from the days of Moses until the exile. The meaning of the words in Hebrew are Thummin (perfect), and Urim (light), so that together they might be said to mean "Perfect Light". The Thummim was the metal stand, the tree-like stand, according to Raphael, the Alchemist. The Urim (probably not the Thummim if I am right) could be slipped or clipped into the jewelled breastplate of the High Priest (Exod.XXVIII.30) and Urim and Thummim were *par excellence* the symbol of his office.* How could a fairly large crystal be clipped or hung from an already

---

* Deut. XXXIII.8.

jewelled breastplate? The important answer in bridging the gap in Christian era dates between a small unostentatious box shaped pyx as described in *Diu Crône* for reserving the Host (and historically used for the sick until about the 10th century) and the more complicated varieties used later, is the existence of the Amulet of Charlemagne, a relic incapsulated between two crystal lenses hung from his neck, as we shall see later on, but meanwhile the reader might like to view Charlemagne's Talisman on Plate IX.

The Urim (but apparently not the Thummim) was oracular in so much as a king could ask counsel of God, and the Lord might answer by Urim (light).* The Jews, returning from the Exile, were unable to find these sacred objects, which were no doubt with the Ark which Jeremiah had hidden for safe-keeping but which was never discovered.† From the above information it is quite possible that the Urim was a crystal, for crystal-gazing has been a practice of mystics since ancient times. The Egyptian seers were accustomes to look into a bowl of water for the same purpose, and a hypnotic trance can be more easily induced, so the medical profession tells us, by the patient gazing at a bright point of light. Indeed, the notes to the comparatively new Jerusalem Bible in the translation of the Old Testament, suggest that the Patriarch Joseph's silver cup hidden in the sack of his brother, Bemjamin, was likely to have been Joseph's "seer's" cup. Is it mere coincidence that both Grail-stone and *talleor* (the silver dish of the Grail legend) could both be used to induce trance? Some Biblical scholars have suggested that the Urim, admittedly an oracle, was merely a bunch of yarrow stalks for casting down and interpreting their positions as employed in the *I Ching* by the Chinese, or arrow shafts as used at Delphi, considered even by the pagan Greeks as a very second-rate means of divination. Although the Jews did cast lots, it is much more likely that an object taken into the Holy of Holies on the heart of the High Priest was an object

* Num.XXVII.21 & Sam.XXVIII.6.
† Ezra ii 63 and II Macc ii.

superior to a pouch of sticks – in fact an object that produced meditative states in which prophecy is possible.

The Cabbalah differentiates between two states of grace or power. The faculty for extraordinary prophetic knowledge as vouchsafed to Moses is called the Luminous Mirror or Specularia, while the knowledge of ordinary individuals is termed the non-luminous mirror, and they are respectively represented in the earthly Paradise by the Tree of Life and the Tree of Knowledge. The soul could not bear the brilliance of the Luminous Mirror which proceeds from the Lord of Light without a veil or mantle between them.

The similarity between Charlemagne's amulet in which a fragment of the true cross was held between two slightly lenticular crystals while the whole is held together by metal work, is strikingly like the top half of Raphael's drawing of the Urim, if the crystal is detached from its pedestal (as we shall presently see this done with other relics). The Carolingians of the 8th and 9th centuries were lavish in their use of crystals which is presently going to solve the problem of dates. Whether or not the Jewish High Priest did in *fact* possess a crystal as his oracle will be discussed in full in a special chapter concerning Jewish ritual, but that his pagan neighbours credited him with having such a talisman seems fairly cetain from the tales issuing from the Palestinian coast and from the Grail legends to which we must now return.

It will be remembered that the setting of a jewel can be referred to as its "bed". It can also be described as the "hilt" of the sword, for the brand proceeds out of it. The Grail legend gives us two different references to beds. In Chrestien's *Conte du Graal* Gawain has to achieve the adventure of the Perilous Bed, which was magically connected with a lion, and, as we shall presently see, the Mithraic symbol for fire was a lion. In the midst of a great hall was a bed of gold covered with white samite. It had four posts containing carbuncles mounted on wheels. (Compare Raphael's illustration of the Urim where four spokes adorned with jewels radiate from a central crystal.) Bells were attached to the lower part of the bed. Compare now this description

with the illustration of the four-posted Catholic Mon-
stránce on Plate II which is in the Victoria and Albert
Museum; and do not for the moment worry about dates
and the Monstrance being of the 16th century. The use of
bells in Jewish ritual is commanded in Exodus XXVIII.33-
35. Gawain finds it difficult to reach the Perilous Bed
because the "shining floor as glass lay smooth beneath
him" and the bed was on rollers. These two descriptions
appear to come straight from Jewish legend where the
polished marble of Solomon's palace floor frightens the
Queen of Sheba because she thinks it is water, and the
throne of God is supposed to roll about the heavens.

In contact with the "bed" Gawain was assailed by arrows,
shot from he knew not where. He nevertheless gains mas-
tery of the lion. In *Artus de la Petite Bretagne* and the *Vulgate
Lancelot* the same Perilous Bed is attacked by a magic lance,
the point of which is ablaze.

The most important and revealing reference to a "bed",
however, is that of Solomon, which the Grail characters find
in Solomon's ship, and if I am right, we have here a detailed
description of the very vessel which has been sought for so
many ages. The bed of Solomon referred to in the Song of
Solomon 111.7. was according to Cabbalist tradition a code
word or traditional periphrasis for the radiance of God,
which the Jews called the *Shekinah*.* Allow me to be more
accurate: let us say the "bed" was the means whereby the
fire, deemed holy, because it issued from the sky, visited
mankind. But the Shekinah was on the contrary the Jewish
word for the *true* presence of God. The accounts of
Solomon's bed are to be found in four different MSS: The
Grand Saint Graal † of de Borron, and Henry Lonelich's
fairly close translation of it; § The *Queste* of Walter Map and
the Welsh version of the *Queste* known as *Y Saint Greal*.‡ The
gist of the story will be remembered from the summaries j of
these works in Chapter I of this book: Solomon dreams that
his descendant shall be the "good knight". He prepares for him

---

* *Zohar*, translated by H. Sperling and M. Simon Vol III pp. 13 and 45.
† § all printed for the Roxburghe Club edited by F.J. Furnival.
‡ Translated by Robert Williams. pp. 514-516.

a sword, places it upon a bed, and a ship carries both bed and sword to Britain; where first Nasciens, a contemporary of St. Joseph of Arimathea, and then Galahad, a contemporary of Arthur, find it.

I shall substitute the word "setting" for "bed", so that the reader may see how quickly the details then fall into place to make a picture of the sacred vessel.

De Borron and Lonelich state that the knight who came to the magic ship found the "setting" covered with a veil, just as Gawain found the Perilous Bed covered with White Samite. Apuleius recounts that the *sacra* of the mysteries were accustomed to be wrapped in linen.* The knight removed the veil and was astonished at the beauty of the "setting".

Upon the length (that is to say the stem of the pedestal) of the "setting" was a threefold spindle. "As long they were as lengthe & brede of the bed everywhere". (Lonelich.) These spindles had been made by Solomon's wife out of wood from the Tree of Life which grew in Paradise, and we can recognise the most ancient type of spinning-whorl in the knops on the stem of the Babylonian and German illustrations. (We can feel reasonably sure that these spindles were indeed a decoration of the stem of the sacred vessel and that the "bed" and sacred vessel are identical not only because spindles as long and broad as a real couch are an impossible conception, but because in the *Vulgate Lancelot* these same spindles are expressly described as appearing with the Grail in the manifestation of the sacred vessel to Bohort at Corbenic.)† On or amidst the "setting" is the "hilt" of the sword: its handle decorated by two scaly creatures; one was a serpent called "Papagast", a name not unlike that of the Egyptian Apapi, and it was intertwined with a water creature from the Euphrates, perhaps another rendering of the Set/Typhon fishy monsters of the deep which Horus and also St. George and St. Demetrius are at

* *Apologia* of Apuleius p. 56 "Flax, the purest of all growths . . . is used by the holy priests of Egypt, not only for clothing and raiment but as a veil for sacred things."
† *Vulgate Lancelot*, edition of Oskar Sommer Vol V. p. 300.

pains to overcome. The "handle" could be the metal ring (in the form of the endless serpent, the Lindworm) by which the lens-shaped jewel could be safely grasped. But the important feature is the pommel of the so-called "sword" because it was of one stone only. Great stress is laid on this by all four versions. Solomon's wife had bidden him decorate the hilt with many precious stones. This he did, but for the pommel he disregarded her advice and chose a stone "in which were all the colours of the world" (*Y Seint Greal*).

but Onliche to the pomel An hy
he putte but on ston sekerly,
Whiche of Alle Manere Colowrs it was
That Ony Man Cowde thenken in Ony plas.
(Lonelich).

That is to say that, like a crystal, it could be prismatic.

On the "hilt" was written that one man only should be able to stretch his fist around it. "I am wonderful to be looked upon and more wonderful to be known; for there never was a man that could shut his fist about me, however great might be his hand; and there never will be but one". (*Y Seint Greal*). This is a most beautiful tradition, and points to the truth of the assertion that Solomon desired it to be known that he had fore-knowledge of the coming of the "good knight", for the crystal lens represented the wide earth, and only the Creator, or God-made-man, could take it in his hand. The inscription also supports the tradition, shown in Raphael's illustration, that there was lettering upon the Grail's setting, if Grail and Urim be identical: in fact if the illustration be correct, it was the very name of the Creator, Elohim and Tetragrammaton being the Jewish substitutions for the unpronounceable name of Jehovah.

At the head of the bed (or above the setting) was a crown. I must digress for a moment here in order to show that there is a foundation for this idea in other sources of Christian legend. Mr Harold Bayley, who worked for years in and studied the history of paper manufacture, made it his special task to record the earliest water-marks, and published his findings in a book entitled *A New Light on the Remaissance*. The conclusions he reached are that paper-making first flourished among the heretical Provencals and Lombards of the early Middle Ages and that their water-marks, which are nearly all symbols of a religious character, were a secret language bringing messages of hope and encouragement from one colony of an esoteric cult to another. One of their favourite marks was that of the mystic vessel or Grail, and it was very frequently surmounted by a crown, as will be seen in the illustration from Mr Bayley's book (Fig 4). In Cab-

Fig 4. 15TH CENTURY WATERMARKS, SHOWING HOLY VESSEL SURMOUNTED BY CROWN.
From "A New Light on the Renaissance", by Harold Bayley.

balistic tradition as given in the *Zohar*, crowns signified in technical terms the various proper names of the Deity formed by combinations of letters. Kether was the crown of the En Soph, the one and only God from which all other emanations descended. A "crown" surmounting the Grail would therefore help to confirm the tradition that the Tetragrammaton was inscribed on the gold setting. Perhaps it is because of this identification of a "crown" and the Sacred Name that in Jewish ritual a crown is hung above the scrolls of the Law: a point which shall have great importance in a later chapter, but the reader might like to glance now at Plate III showing the crown which hangs above the Torah and of the breastplate showing a crown above the two tables of stone.

To return now to the "bed" or setting of the mysterious something on Solomon's ship. Across the foot of the "bed" slanted the blade of the sword. That is to say that the sun caused a beam of light to slant through the crystal. The torch itself is referred to as the "scabbard", and it was made of the red wood of the Tree of Life: "del fuerre qui fu fais del arbre de uie" (*Queste*). The identification of scabbard and Tree of Life is easily understandable when we remember how Sigmund drew the sword from *out* of the Branstock. From the "scabbared" issued a thousand branches, and he who bore the brand and was girt with the branches would always be safe:

> For what man Abowtes him bereth Me,
>
> he ne schal neuere ben schamed In non degre
>
> as longe as with these brawnches he is gert.

(Lonelich).

Here we are forced to move away from Jewish tradition to Celtic legend, a very natural process for civilised and barbarian cults become fused and integrated by conquest and trading between one and the other. The individual clad in the thousand branches of a tree is the Divine Youth or "Green Man" who will live just so long as he is crowned with the yearly leaves of the oak and no longer. This "Green Man", peering from his oak leaves, and so like the vegetation gods of the Near East, is a favourite subject of the medieval sculptors on the bosses of cathedral roofs, of which the illustration (Fig 5.) is typical. But, alas! when the knight turns the scabbard round (when the torch is

Fig 5. FOLIATE HEAD FROM NORWICH CLOISTERS.
After illustration in "Roof Bosses in Medieval Churches", by C.J.P. Cave.

extinguished and inverted) its other side is not bright red but coal black, and on it is written that he who praises it most will blame it most in his greatest need (de Borron and Lonelich).

Only a virgin – and she must be the daughter of a king and queen – can put a name to the sword:

In the manere as here Is seide,
Wheche scholde ben be A wommannes hond,
bothe kynges dowhter & qweene, I understonde.
this womman be the riht name schal clepen this swerd,
and Me by my Name Openly & Apert;
For neuere to-foren In-to that day
Non Creature be oure riht name Clepen ne may.
(Lonelich).

And if she should have lost her chastity, she shall die the most shameful death: "Et s'il auient qu'ele enfrainge sa uirginite, asseur en soit qu'ele morra de la plus vilaine mort que nule feme peust mourir" (*Queste*). This is strangely reminiscent of the Vestals, who were immured alive in the walls of Rome if they broke their vows of chastity. Perceval's sister, being of royal descent and a virgin, puts a name to the sword. She dubs it "The Sword with the Strange Girdle" (*Y Seint Greal*) – "l'espee a estranges renges" (*Queste*).The reason why she so called it may perhaps be sought in Ireland, where in olden times flint and steel with tinder were commonly used for striking fire. The whole kindling gear – flint, steel, and tinder – were carried in a girdle pocket, so as to be ready to hand. And accordingly fire struck in this way was called *teine-creasa*, fire of the *crios* or girdle.* In the same way the Scottish sporran takes its name from the Gaelic for flint, *spor*, and means the "flint bag". The Fir-bolgs, who lived in Ireland before the coming of the Milesians with the Cauldron of the Goddess Dana, were probably called after their fire-bags, from *bolg* a bag, and *pur*, the Greek which had a common origin with our word

* *A Smaller Social History of Ireland* by P.W. Joyce p. 90.

fire. In other words, they were the more primitive men who drew fire from flints in contrast to the Milesians who possessed the Cauldron. In Brittany the fairies known as Korrigans, whose speciality was to haunt the megalithic stones, were believed to carry red pouches slung over their shoulders in which they kept their treasure. According to legend, a mortal who found one of these pouches discovered in it only dead leaves, hairs, sand and a pair of scissors; but when holy water had been sprinkled on this rubbish, the leaves turned to gold, the hair to pearls, and the sand to diamonds. What happened to the scissors is not recounted, but on the tomb stones of Iona they are used to designate the burial place of a female, and might therefore have served in Breton legend as an emblem of the goddess. Of the other treasure one can only say that the golden leaves of Glasir, and the sand which makes glass are ingeniously represented; and as for the pearls (remembering the pearl-rimmed cauldron of Annwn) it may be this very vessel from which the Korrigans took their name, for the Gaelic for kettle or Cauldron is *coire*.*

The French medieval writers, however, declared that the girdle, which dated from King David's day, was torn and tattered and in shreds, and that therefore Perceval's sister cut off her hair, wove with it a new girdle, and gave the sword its name as a memorial of her sacrifice. I think this is an interpolation to explain the name which puzzled the medieval transcriber, but the sacrifice of hair no doubt represented to the medieval mind the taking of monastic vows of chastity, and therefore only emphasizes that Perceval's sister was a dedicated virgin. If the legend should prove to be of Jewish origin, then the torn girdle may have another significance, but again connected with fire, as will be explained in the chapter on Jewish ritual.

To complete the study of the sword upon the bed: rightly or wrongly, tradition credits Solomon with having introduced the ritual to Britain. Moreover the ritual was not of

* For the legends of the Korrigans see *Le Foyer Breton* by Emile Souvestre Vol. II pp. 132 et seq.

his own institution, but was the brand of his father, David, and was kept in the Temple. "Je vous dirai", says Solomon's wife, "quele arme li serroit souffissans. El tample que vous aues fait en l'onneur de ihesu crist l'epee le roy dauid uotre pere" (de Borron). The other versions say the same. And the king follows her advice:

> Owt of that temple the swerd they browhte
> the wheche kyng davy his fadyr owhte
> and that they helden as riche and as worthy
> Ad Ony thing at In e temple was sekerly. (Lonelich).

If the Urim was indeed a crystal, it is plain that Solomon did not rob the temple of such a precious gem. It was only the blade or brand which was sent to Britain – as the Olympic torch is sent about the world to-day. But perhaps he did send a new stone for the pommel, a crystal similar to that kept in the Temple. The distinction between so-called sword and pommel is shown in the following passage, wherein Nasciens, having broken the sword (extinguished the fire-brand) Mordrains welds it together (lights it again).

> Thanne took the kyng this swerd on hond,
> And *stille* there-with he gan to stonde
> In the ton hond the swerd, the tother the pomel,
> And hem departed Every del.
> And A wondir Aventure behappede tho, –
> that Azen to Gederis Anon gonnen they go;
> And so faste to-gederis weren they Ioynt,
> that Nevere sethenes In on poynt
> Neuere departed Asonder they were
> For non Man that lyf beere. (Lonelich).

There is a similarity between this passage and the account of Peredur's snake-stone, for "whoever should hold it in one hand in the other will have as much gold as he may desire". It should be noted that in order to renew the brand it is necessary to stand very still, and this is no more than the truth, for otherwise the focal point will move and the heat be dissipated.

If the pommel and the gold-producing snake-stone of Peredur were both crystals, Miss Jessie Weston was right when she suggested that the search for the Philosopher's Stone originated in the search for the Grail-stone, though she presumed that the "gold" was a mystical light, whereas we know it to be a traditional substitute for fire. That Alchemy did have a mystical approach is true, but for the moment let us confine ourselves to fire. In Alchemical treatises fire was denoted by such terms as sword or scissors, says Professor J. Read in *Prelude to Chemistry*. The Hermetic Vase, in which the alchemists sought to produce the fabulous Stone, was a spherical glass flask with a neck which was "hermetically" sealed. In diagrams it was often decorated with a serpent. It was sometimes depicted surmounted by a crown, and in the frontispiece to Professor Read's book an illustration from the Harley MS shows it between two pillars reminiscent of Jachin and Boaz. Within the glass is portrayed a peacock to symbolise "all the colours of the world". Raphael's illustration of Urim and Thummim, the one surrounding the other, would certainly have been taken from some old Alchemical MS, for he describes the stylized tree, the "setting", of the gem as made of the seven metals. A tree of the seven metals is a fairly common alchemical symbol. It seems the alchemists inherited some esoteric knowledge. They probably misunderstood some ancient directions for collecting the light of the sun in a moon-like glass flask designed to light the torch of the Caduceus of Mercury with "golden" fire. So they spent their lives studying how to mix gold, silver and quicksilver in an attempt to transmute metals. Yet amongst such alchemists there may have been some who *did* understand. An old tradition connects a magical sword-pommel with one of the most famous alchemists ever to search for the Philosopher's Stone. Hudibras writes concerning this same Paracelsus, known as Bombastus:–

Bombastus kept a devil's bird

Shut in the pommel of his sword.

One can hardly doubt that it was the hawk of Horus – the
power of sunlight – which was thus hidden in the pommel
and that Paracelsus knew something about the behaviour of
light seen through transparent stones.

The word pommel derives from the Latin *pomum*, meaning fruit; and we have seen that the golden bough of Æneas
had some fruit-bearing quality. If the reader will look again
at the illustration of the Babylonian tree, he will understand
how the jewelled rosette would easily suggest itself as the
fruit of such a tree. There is strong evidence for supposing
that it was called an apple, and we hear of it at Troy or
Asgard, where, according to Snörri, the goddess Idunn had
charge of the fruit which was the food of immortality
necessary to the gods. The giant Thjazi, taking the form of
an eagle, snatched up Loki, the fire-god, and flew off with
him. In response to Loki's prayers for mercy, the eagle promised him freedom in return for possession of the beautiful
Idunn and her apples, which she kept in a special chest.
Loki lured the young goddess into the eagle's home, but the
gods of Troy grew old and grey-haired, for they no longer
had the food of immortality. Under threat of torture they
made Loki promise to restore the goddess. The fire-god
then borrowed the plumage of a hawk, flew to the eagle's
castle, transformed Idunn into the shape of a nut, and flew
back with her in his beak to Troy. The eagle then pursued
him in wrath, but the gods, seeing Loki's plight, went out
below the walls of Troy and prepared piles of plane-
shavings. *As soon as the hawk alighted they struck fire to the bonfires*,
and the feathers of the eagle caught fire. Snörri goes on to
quote some ancient verses:*

---

* *Prose Edda* by Snörri Sturluson, translated by A.G. Brodeur.

This heard I, that the Staunch Friend
Of Hoenir – oft thereafter
With wiles he tricked the Aesir –
Flew, in hawk-wings hidden;
And the vile Sire of Giants,
Vigorous Wing-Plume-Wielder,
Hurtled on eagle-pinion
After the hawk-shaped Loki.

Swiftly the gods have kindled
A fire; and the sovereign rulers
Sustained the flames with shavings:
Scorched was the flying giant, –
He plunged down in mid-soaring:
'Tis pictured on the giant's
Sole-bridge, the shield which, painted
With stories, Thorleifr gave me.

This fire-producing apple could beget heroes, for in the
Volsunga Saga, Odin hears the prayers of King Rerir and his
barren wife for an heir. The goddess Freyja gives an apple
into the hand of the casket-bearing maiden. The maid
"took the apple, and did on the gear of a crow, and went flying till she came where the king sat on a mound, and there
she let the apple fall into the lap of the king".* The queen
eats the fruit, and thereupon conceives and bears Volsung.
Evidently in this story the king had climbed the Tor and was
all ready to receive the apple from a Vestal.

The *Echtra Condla*, an Irish tale, tells how Connla, the son
of a king in the 2nd century A.D. is invited by a beautiful
and immortal woman to the land of heart's desire. At the
command of his father the king, the Druids do all in their
power to prevent the prince from following the woman,
who is invisible to all but Connla. She tells him that she is of
the people who dwell in the mounds of the *Sidhe* (i.e. the
burial mounds of an earlier people), and gives him an

---

* *The Volsunga Saga* translated from the Icelandic by Eirikur Magnusson and
William Morris.

apple. This he eats; it never grows less, nor does he require other food. After a month she returns to fetch Connla in her boat of glass. He goes with her to another world, but whether to an Elysian Isle or to the underground *Sidhe* is not made clear. It is interesting to note the connection between the apple and the boat of glass.*

There is the famous Apple of Discord, which Paris had to allot to one of the three goddesses, † and this is echoed in Malory's account of how Sir Lancelot falls asleep under an apple-tree; Sir Ector thereupon finds a *bowl* in the hole of the tree; whereupon four queens, amongst them Morgan le Fay, desire Lancelot to judge which of them he will have for his love.

Finally, we come to the Apple of the Hesperides. What was this fruit of which both Hercules and Perseus, son of Danae of the Brazen tower, went in quest? It is significant that only Prometheus, the first fire-maker, could put Hercules upon his way to find it. The alchemists often called the Philosopher's Stone "the Golden Apple of the Hesperides" or the "golden bough". § Mr Lewis Spence tells us that the common apple-tree reached Greece from the *North*. It was adopted by the Greek sun-god as specially sacred to him, and from the Celtic *abal*, an apple, the god derived his name Apollo. ‡ Avallach and Avalooc are Celtic variants of the same word.¶ We have already found that because the Greek word melon means both apple and sheep, the apple is probably identical with the Golden Fleece.

We can now begin to recognise the King Evalach to whose sun-temple Joseph of Arimathea is supposed to have gone to exhort the heathen. Curiously enough, St. David, who was according to the Welsh Books, one of the three hereditary guardians of the Grail, is one of the many princely Welshmen whose genealogy begins with Anna, whose son was Beli, whose son was Avallach. It has already been

* Celtic and Scandinavian Religions by the Rev. J.A. MacCulloch p. 91.
† *Morte d'Arthur*, Vol I. Ch. C et seq. Edited by Thomas Wright 1866.
§ *Prelude to Chemistry* by Professor J. Read pp. 169, 171, 221, 239, 259.
‡ *The Minor Traditions of British Mythology* by Lewis Spence. p. 107.
¶ *Studies in Arthurian Legend*, by John Rhys.

suggested that Anna, wife of Lot, was the Great Mother Anath of the Phoenicians. Lot or Apollo Belinus is both son and husband of the earth-mother. And they beget Evalach, the solar-hero who is a son of the Sun, and whose city of Sarras was not, perhaps, in the land of Goshen bordering Egypt (the usual confusion of St. Joseph of Arimathea with Joseph, the Patriarch's son) but right here in this island of Britain, possibly even at Glastonbury, if indeed St. Joseph did come there, a place of heathen sun-worshippers where St. Joseph converted Evalach to Christianity. (de Borron's *Grand Saint Graal*).

If further evidence is needed that the apple of the sun-god was the crystal, it is demonstrated beyond doubt by the ancient names of Glastonbury itself, which was first known as the Isle of Avalon.* Later, however it went by the name of Inis Vitrin; and Caradoc, a monk who wrote in about A.D. 1150, says in his *Vita Gildas*: "Glastonia was of old called Ynisgutrin and is still so called by the British inhabitants. This in the British language is insula in Latin and gutrin is vitrea. But after the coming of the English and the expulsion of the Britons, that is, the Welsh, it received a fresh name Glastigberi, according to the formation of the first name, that is English *glass*, Latin *vitrum* and *beria* a city; then Glastiberia, that is the City of Glass." It would be nearer the truth, I think, to translate it as the City of *the* Glass. Both of the ancient names, Avalon and Inis Vitrin are perfectly familiar to the local inhabitants of the present day. †

There is reason to believe that Glastonbury may have been the very Garden of the Hesperides, for Hesiod, who wrote the earliest Greek theogony, says that it was beyond the famous sea, that the golden fruit was guarded by a terrible serpent, and that the Garden was situated at a place where Atlas upheld broad heaven, standing on earth's verge. § As Atlas fulfilled the task of one of the four mythical

* William of Malmesbury's *Antiquities of Glastonbury* Ch. V.
† Attempts have been made to discredit Caradoc's derivation because William of Malmesbury suggests that Glastonbury took its name from the little-known family of the Glasteings. I prefer the assertion of the Celtic monk who spoke Welsh to the suggestion of an English monk who paid a passing visit to the Abbey.
§ Hesiod's *Theogony* in Bohn's Classical Library pp 13, 19, and 28.

pillars at the corners of the earth supporting the sky, it is
probable that he would have stood at the furthest point of
the known world in the west – Britain, though the com-
monest tradition is that he stood on the Atlas mountains in
Africa opposite Spain, and was merely a landmark for the
sea-traffic to Britain through the straits of Gibraltar,
thought of as the pillars of Hercules.

I shall come presently to discuss the triple goddess, who
is the earth in her three aspects of spring, summer and winter. It is sufficient to say here that the three nymphs of the
Hesperides are the earth-mother in her threefold aspect,
and are represented on Solomon's "bed" – that is to say on
the little golden tree – by the three spinning-whorls,
emblematic of the female. Indeed the tradition takes great
care that the Mother's emblems shall not be forgotten.

Some verses in the biography of Lord Tennyson by his
son, written in the poet's youth and entitled *The Hesperides*,
seem to be an example of the intuitive powers of a poet.

Kingdoms lapse, and climates change, and races die;
Honour comes with mystery;
Hoarded wisdom brings delight.
Number, tell them over, and number
How many the mystic fruit-tree holds,
Lest the red-comb'd dragon slumber
Roll'd together in purple folds.
Look to him, father, lest he wink, and the golden
apple be stol'n away,
For his ancient heart is drunk with overwatchings night
and day
Round about the hallow'd fruit-tree curl'd –
Sing away, sing aloud evermore in the wind without
stop,
Lest his scaled eyelid drop,
For he is older than the world.
If he waken, we waken,
Rapidly levelling eager eyes.
If he sleep, we sleep,
Dropping the eyelid over our eyes.

If the golden apple be taken
The world will be overwise.
Five links, a golden chain are we,
Hesper, the Dragon, and Sisters three
Round about the golden tree.

Father Hesper, Father Hesper, Watch, watch, night
and day,
Lest the old wound of the world be healed,
the glory unsealed,
The golden apple stolen away,
And the ancient secret revealed.

    To anticipate the chapter devoted to Jewish ritual: it is fitting here to add that a legend existed to the effect that Solomon placed in the Temple golden trees, which bore fruit while the Temple stood. When the first Temple was destroyed, the fruit disappeared. But the trees will put forth blossoms again when the Temple is rebuilt in the days of the Messiah.* The Arabs also have a legend about the jewelled trees in Solomon's temple.

---

* See *Legends of the Jews*, by Louis Ginzberg Vol. IV p.154 and for sources Vol VI. *Solomon* note 558.

5 The Phoenix and the Floating Stone

It is probable that the golden tree with its crystal apple was the most ancient setting for the Grail-stone; but there was, I think, another traditional framework for the jewel. The sun, as it rolled across the sky, was likened in nearly all mythologies to a wheel, and that this idea was used in the construction of a material symbol is shown in the illustration of a plaque in the British Museum (Plate IV), which records the restoration of the temple of the sun-god by a Babylonian king in 900 B.C. The wheel is evidently one of the sacred objects kept in the temple and is placed in a position of importance immediately before the shrine, while the serpent, in the form of a canopy, guards the exit and entrance of the sun-god's home. It is probable that this wheel was made of the bright gold, which reflects the sun's rays so brilliantly and was therefore thought to have an affinity with the god. A very obvious place for the crystal would be at the hub of the wheel, and if many myths and legends support such an idea, we could make a fair guess that such was the case. It does seem to me evident from the stone carving of the wheel in Plate IV that there is an indent in the centre of the wheel as though made purposely to contain some form of boss.

Servius says that Prometheus stole fire from the sun's wheel – *ad rotam solis ignem* – but this, of course, might mean no more than that he obtained fire from the solar orb through some form of magnification of rays.* That the two

* Ecl. VI. 42.

civilizations of the Euphrates valley and the valley of the Indus were in touch with one another is not to be denied, and the following ancient legend from India is more helpful to our enquiry.

Once upon a time the ambrosia of immortality was stolen from the gods by Garuda, who was half-giant half-eagle and the enemy of serpents. This "Lord of Birds" was hatched from an enormous egg five hundred years after it had been laid by Diti, mother of giants; his father was Kaśyapa, a Brahmin identified with the Pole Star, who had sacrificed with desire for offspring. It happened that Diti, having lost a wager, was put under bondage by the demons, and could not be released until she caused the ambrosia, known as *amrita*, to be taken from a celestial mountain where it was surrounded by terrible flames, moved by violent winds, which leapt up to the sky. Assuming a golden body, bright as the sun, Garuda drank up many rivers and extinguished the fire. A fiercely revolving wheel, sharp edged and brilliant, protected the *amrita*, but Garuda diminished his body and entered between the spokes. Two fire-spitting snakes had next to be overcome. Garuda blinded them with dust and cut them to pieces. Then, having burst the revolving wheel asunder, he flew forth with the *Amrita*, which was contained in the "moon goblet".*

The "moon goblet" is a beautiful description of a glass or crystal, and the account of how the eagle-headed god flew *through* the spokes indicates that the wheel was not the solar orb but a symbol constructed to represent it, as in Plate IV of the sun-god Shamash.

In Christian legend the story of St. Catherine of Alexandria is connected with a wheel. Although she was supposed to have lived shortly after the time of Constantine the Great, her history was never recorded until the 9th century A.D. and in the 15th century attempts were already being made to banish her from the calendar on the grounds that the lady had never existed, that her story was apocryphal, and had been drawn from pagan sources. Because of her pop-

---

* *Indian Myth and Legend* by Donald A. Mackenzie.

ularity she survived as a saint until recently when she was no longer allotted a place in the calendar of Saints' days. No firm grounds have ever been found for her having really existed. According to legend, she was the daughter of Pharaoh, and was well versed in philosophy, particularly the works of Plato. She was converted to Christianity, and dedicated her virginity to God, taking Christ as her spouse, and receiving from Him the mystical ring of this marriage. The tyrant Maximin then began one of the periodic persecutions of the Church. Pagan philosophers and rhetoricians were sent by him to the young princess to persuade her to abjure her faith, but she defeated them all in argument, and Maximin therefore ordered her to undergo a most cruel death. She was bound upon a wheel which had sharp spokes projecting from it, so that her flesh might be torn to pieces. But at the last minute fire came down from heaven, sent by the destroying angel of God, who broke the wheel assunder. Maximin had therefore to resort to the more merciful sentence of beheading the saint with a sword. As it was the custom amongst medieval artists to represent a martyr with the instrument of torture which had caused death, and as St. Catherine is always pictured with her wheel, it is not generally realized to-day that in fact the wheel is the symbol of the fire from heaven which rescued her from the more cruel death. It seems very probable from this legend that Pharaoh's daughter (an anachronism in Constantine's day) was in fact the crystal symbol of Isis, the "moon goblet" fixed to the hub of a golden wheel.

It is necessary here to say a word concerning the triple character of the earth-goddess. Apuleius, addressing Isis in the visionary passage of his *Golden Ass*, prays that, whether she be pleased to be known as Ceres, the harvest mother of Eleusis, or as Venus of Paphos, or as Artemis of Ephesus, or as dread Proserpine, she will by whatever name have mercy upon him. In fact, there was only the one goddess, though her names were multiple. Yet this one goddess was of triple character. Hecate's face is turned in three directions, says Ovid.* When King Arthur is mortally wounded he is

* Ovid, *Fasti* I, 141.

fetched by three queens.* Though their names are not specified we can supply them from Grail legend. The first, Blanchefleur, is the earth in spring-time, washed clean of the hot dust and filth by the flood waters (perhaps originally those from the Nile), but as yet unsown. Therefore she is represented as a virgin, and amongst some of her various names Kore, Pallas Athene and Artemis are familiar to us. Her character in summer becomes that of the Great Mother. She bears in her arms either a male child, the son of the Sun, or else the fruits of the earth, and according to the temperament of the race who worshipped her, she may have the nature of a voluptuous queen of love. We know her as Ceres and Aphrodite and Guenevere. Finally, she becomes the earth in its winter habit, hideous, old, barren, revengeful; demanding to be propitiated with sacrifice, seeking the life of the slayer of her child – her child who was both sacred flame and springing corn. Her names are Hecate, Proserpine, the revengeful Juno, and in Grail legend she is both the "loathly damsel" and Morgan le Fay.

In combination the one goddess is known as the Three Fates, the Three Eumenides, the Three Nymphs of the Hesperides, the Three Norns of Scandinavian myth. The spindles made from the Tree of Life for Solomon's "bed" represented by their colours these three aspects of the earth-goddess.† The first was white, in token says the medieval poet, of Eve's virginity; the second was green, in token of Eve's bearing of Cain and Abel; the third was red, in token of the blood of Abel spilt by his brother.§

While I would not for a minute suggest that the monks of Glastonbury lent themselves intentionally to perpetuating a pagan cult, traditions die hard, and I do suggest that some surviving folk-tale or memory may be responsible for the choice of the three female patron saints, which are depicted

---

* *Morte d'Arthur* Vol III Ch. CLXVIII.

† The Three Fates, as also the Three Norns, had spindles with which they spun the thread of life. See *'The White Goddess'* and *'The Greek Myths'* by Robert Graves.

§ *La Queste del Saint Graal*, by Walter Map.

on the Abbey seal used by Abbot Chinnock until the Dissolution, for the three together are intimately connected with the mysteries of the Grail. I would ask the reader to turn now to the illustration of the seal on Plate V. In the centre stands Our Lady, bearing the Holy Child, and in her other hand are the lilies always associated with her. Beside her is the sad St. Margaret with her cross, symbol of mourning, and she stands upon the serpent-dragon over which she was triumphant. I shall come presently to explain the significance of the Madonna lilies and the story of St. Margaret. But for the moment we need study only the figure of St. Catherine, who stands on the Virgin's other side, holding her wheel in her hand.

It will be remembered that in the *Prose Perceval* the position of the hand of one of the three queens who visit Arthur's court to reproach Perceval, is said to have some connection with the mystery of the Grail. The Arthurian queen's hand was pointing to her necklace, of which more anon, but here also the hand of one of the three saints is the clue to the mystery, for she carries the wheel which brought fire from heaven. And what is the inscription or legend round the seal? – *Testis Adest Isti Scripta Matrix Pia XPI Glastonia*: "There is at Glaston, as witness to this writing, the Holy Matrix of God". There have always been legends that either the Cup of the Last Supper or Our Lady herself was buried at Glastonbury. Now *Matrix* is a very curious word to use to describe the Mother of God. *Mater* or *Genetrix* are the words commonly employed. Matrix signifies a mould, cavity, or cup: a something out of which another thing is produced. In this sense it can be used for a mould in which metals are smelted, or for the ore in which jewels are embedded, or for the womb of a woman, but *not* for the woman herself. The words on the seal are, I am convinced, a reference to *a* Grail (there were many crystals taken over by the Church as is shown in Plates II, XI and XII) and that a particular one was treasured at Glastonbury and used to decorate a particular processional cross is no empty boast, as I shall presently make clear. My correspondence with the British Museum re the wording on the seal is given in the

Appendix to the first edition of this book and need not be repeated here.

To turn now to the question of the necklace: articles of jewellery provide an obvious setting for talismanic stones.* Pliny says that the first use of finger-rings was suggested by the rocks of the Caucasus (one of the richest sources of rock-crystal), where Prometheus enclosed a fragment of an unspecified stone in iron for this purpose. Robert Graves in his *Greek Myths*, Vol II.p.49, tells us that "mankind now began to wear rings in Prometheus's honour" and gives several more classical references to the fact. That the institution of ring-wearing should be attributed by tradition to the first fire-bearer is significant, because as many of the myths in this book will lead us to suppose, a magic ring (i.e. a ring set with crystal) together with the fiery brand was the regalia of the Divine Youth, bringing with it the curse in early pagan times of an untimely death; and we have seen how the adventures of Perceval always start with the acquisition of a ring, and end with the need for absolution.

According to the Brehon Laws of Ireland, only a person of royal blood might have his brooch decorated with crystal, but there are references to the Arch Druid's tiara and belt clasp being adorned with the snake-stones.† And from the Druids the privilege passed to the princes and bishops of the Church, whose copes are fastened with such brooches. The association of the privilege with kings and priests indicates the holy qualities attributed to the stone, but it is doubtful whether the size of any stone set in a finger-ring or brooch would be sufficient for the practical purpose of lighting a fire.

The necklace of the Norse goddess Freyja, however, may have contained a much larger jewel. It was called the *Brisinga-men* or "the mighty necklace of Brisings", and plays a most important part in Norse mythology, as we shall presently see, for it was the symbol *par excellence* of the earth-goddess in spring-time. Indeed, on one ludicrous occasion

---

* Pliny. *Natural History* Bk XXXVII Ch. 1.
† *Druidism* by Dudley Wright.

the mighty and masculine god Thor was able to deceive the
giants of the underworld into accepting him as the very person of the gentle and beautiful goddess whom they sought
to possess, because he wore her necklace.* The *Brisinga-men*
may have been made to hang about the neck of some image
of Freyja, for Ovid tells us that a gold necklace decorated the
marble image of Vesta at Rome. At Denderah in Egypt there
is a carving of Pharaoh presenting a wonderful necklace to
the goddess Hathor on the face of the temple "chapel",
known as the "Birth Chamber" (where it was probable that
the rebirth of the sun was celebrated yearly). The mysterious Arthurian queen in the *Prose Perceval* whose hand
points to her necklace and its pendant "star", which it is
claimed concerns the mystery of the Grail, could therefore
be pointing to a crystal talisman such as that of Charlemagne. Equally, the mention of a "star" could contain a
hint as to a Jewish origin of the legend, but the Shield or Star
of David is a subject for a further chapter.

One other article of jewellery can be mentioned here.
That the culture of Egypt and the Near East spread in some
unknown fashion to Mexico and Peru has long been a supposition, and Professor Perry is one amongst many who
believed that ships from the Mediterranean must have
found their way cross the ocean.† The Spaniards recorded
on their arrival in Peru that the heathen priests were accustomed to light their sacred fires from the sun's rays by
means of a concave cup set in a metal bracelet.

It has been shown that the tree, the wheel, the ring and
perhaps the necklace were traditional settings for a crystal
gem. We turn now from the actual setting to the hidden
language for describing the crystal or glass – the substitution or periphrasis of which the Eddas are so fond – and we
shall find it described as an egg, a vessel, and a window.

The followers of Orpheus believed that the god was born
from the Orphic egg.§ Castor and Pollux, the mortal and
immortal twins, were born from the egg of a swan and their

* *The Lay of Thrym* in *Poetic Edda* translated by Olive Bray.
† *The Growth of Civilisation* by W.J. Perry Ch. IV p. 71.
§ *Prolegomena to the Study of Greek Religion*, by Jane Harrison, p. 464.

Fig 6. COIN OF TYRE.
From "Zeus", by A.B. Cook.

sister Helen was worshipped in Rhodes as Helen Dendritis, the goddess bound to a tree, and was probably none other than the crystal within the golden leaves of Glasir, the prototype of all the maidens of Grail legend who are found bound to trees. Fig.6 shows a coin of Tyre, which depicts such a mystic egg, surrounded by the coils of a serpent with a tree behind it. The Hermetic Vase of the alchemists, decorated with a similar serpent, was known as the Philosopher's Egg. It is illustrated on Plates 17 and 32 of Professor Read's *Prelude to Chemistry*.

The serpent's egg was known to be a famous talisman of the Druids. Pliny tells us about this Druidic talisman, but he falls into the error of supposing that the *ovum anguinum* was the production of real reptiles. Furthermore, he goes on to confuse it with a sea-shell, which was held to have magical life-giving properties: a common belief among primitive peoples who compare the shapes of certain types of Mollusca to the female genital parts. But despite this confusion, he gives us a very vivid picture of how the talisman was produced. The snakes meet together on a certain day of the moon. They twist themselves into many convolutions and hiss, and their saliva forms a bubble like a ring above the head of one of them, which the rest blow on till it comes off at the tail.* (This is nothing else but a periphrastic description of blowing glass through the long pipes of the Sidonian glass-blowers, and in Cornwall they used to tell the story and assert that the egg hardened into glass.†) Pliny goes on to say that the egg will float, even though set in gold. And so it will, if it be a glass sphere, empty of all but air. He who could obtain one of these eggs would prosper in all his undertakings, but to steal it from the serpents was not without peril. As it came from the tail of the serpent, it must be caught in mid-air into a cloak, and then he who had seized it must gallop off on horse back and jump across a stream of water in order to avoid pursuit.

It is known in Wales as the *Glain Naidr* (the gem of the serpent), and is erroneously identified with the little glass rings which the Druids wore as amulets, probably slung on a thong round their necks. These amulets have been found, particularly near Aberfraw in Anglesey. They are usually of green glass, but some are blue, and some striped with blue, red and white.§ William Camden, the antiquary who lived in the 16th century says that in many parts of Wales and throughout Scotland and Cornwall, it is the opinion of the people that the snakes meet on Midsummer Eve to form these glass rings.¶ If we discount Pliny's statement that the finished product was a cartilaginous sea-shell, but accept his statement that set in gold it would float, and combine this again with the local folk-lore of its being made of glass, and the actual discovery of glass amulets, we shall arrive at the truth: that the Druids were able to blow glass, but that the egg was a glass sphere, while the amulets were ring-shaped. Pliny derides the possibility of snakes producing eggs only at certain phases of the moon, but when it is realised that the "egg" was the "moon goblet" it is very probable that the glass *was* blown by moonlight at certain festivals with magical rites in honour of the goddess, and particularly on Midsummer Eve, always the greatest fire-festival.

* Pliny. *Natural History* Bk XXIX Ch. 12.
† *The Golden Bough*, Part VII *Balder the Beautiful* Vol I. pp 15 and 16.
§ *Mythology & Rites of the British Druids*. By Edward Davies pp 210 et seq.
¶ *Druidism* by Dudley Wright. p. 100.

It will be remembered that Peredur stole the stone from the serpent's tail. This serpent lived in a cairn surrounded by three hundred knights, who were waiting for him to die in order to seize it themselves. Mr Dudley Wright says that the Druids were themselves called *Nadredd* or snakes by the Welsh Bards. As guardians of the glass egg this would be a fitting nomenclature. We have in the *Mabinogion*, therefore, a picture of Peredur succeeding to the office and regalia of an Arch Druid amongst a congregation of Druids, and that he slew his predecessor is not unlikely if we compare the following account in Caesar of how the Arch Druids were elected.

"Over all these Druids one presides, who possesses supreme authority amongst them. Upon his death, if any individual among the rest is pre-eminent in dignity he succeeds; but, if there are many equal, the election is made by the suffrages of the Druids; sometimes they even contend for the presidency with arms. These assemble at a fixed period of the year in a consecrated placed in the territories of the Carnutes, which is reckoned the central region of the whole of Gaul. Hither all, who have disputes, assemble from every part, and submit to their decrees and determinations. This institution is supposed to have been devised in Britain, and to have been brought over from it into Gaul; and now those who desire to gain a more accurate knowledge of that system generally proceed thither for the purpose of studying it."*

We come now to the "bird" which was born from this egg of the golden serpent or Lind-worm. Herodotus is the first to describe the Phoenix.† He says that it was sacred and that it was very rare even in Egypt, for it came to Heliopolis (*On*, the city of the sun) only once in five hundred years. The five hundred years allotted to the Phoenix and the Indian eagle, Garuda, had an important significance, for the Egyptians who invented the calendar had not perfected their calculations of the solar year. Therefore, the rising of the

---

* *Gallic War*, Bk VI Ch.XIV.
† Herodotus Bk II. Chapter 73.

dog-star Sothis or Sirius, which heralded the annual flood-
ing of the Nile, did not coincide with the month originally
dedicated to it. Therefore approximately every five hundred years the calendar was readjusted so as to remain in
tune with the Great or Sothic year, and was celebrated with
high festival. The Phoenix, who returned periodically to the
sun-temple, or Garuda whose egg took five hundred years
to hatch, is, therefore, the eagle or hawk-headed sun-god
returning to his allotted point in the calendar. Herodotus
says that the bird was reputed to be partly red, partly
golden, and shaped exactly like an eagle; he also added that
it was supposed to come all the way from Arabia. It is
important to remember this claim of Herodotus that the
Phoenix came from Arabia, (i.e. the East or land of the Two
Rivers, the Tigris and Euphrates) for curiously enough, the
eagle-like bird he describes does not seem to be an Egyptian
concept. The Phoenix, as depicted in the Nile valley, is the
grey heron who breaks the silence of the primeval night by
uttering the first call to life, and could possibly be nearer to
symbolising the Logos or First Word of the Supreme Deity,
issuing above "the face of the waters" after arriving from
"the isle of fire". Nevertheless there existed the famous
Benben stone, a conical monument, probably tipped with
gold as were some of the pyramids and obelisks in order to
reflect the first light of dawn. The "fire-bird" represented as
an eagle is however, according to travellers, well known in
the archaeology of the lands lying round the Tigris and
Euphrates. Herodotus says that the Phoenix coming from
this direction brought the dead parent bird with it. To do
this, it first formed a ball of myrrh, and then hollowed out
the ball and put the parent inside. Then it flew with the ball
to the temple at Heliopolis. He makes no mention of the
Phoenix being born again from this ball, probably because
he took it for granted that this was common knowledge. But
both Lactantius and the anonymous Saxon poet who wrote
about the Phoenix in the *Book of Exeter*, recount that the
famous bird was born again from its own egg, placed in the
fire, which became in turn first a worm (i.e. the Lind-worm)
and then the Phoenix: "Yet after the appointed time, new

life again returneth into it, when the ashes once again begin, after the flames force, to combine together, shrunk up into a ball." And the Saxon poet goes on: "Then, after that conflagration, an apple's likeness will be found once more amid the ashes."

From the *Gesta Romanorum* we learn of a similar legend, for Diocletian was supposed to have found an ostrich's egg coated with glass. When the egg "hatched" a worm was found in it. Despite the confusion of eagle and heron between the Middle East and Egypt, one is tempted to return to the latter via Israel, for Solomon had to build his temple without iron tools because of a Mosaic prohibition (Ex.X-X.25). According to legend, Asmodeus, the mischievous fallen but not unkindly angel who helped him, gave the king the mysterious magical worm, the *Shamir*, a puzzle to all Jewish commentators, for it cut the necessary stones for the entire temple by magic. If anyone has ever seen the half-finished obelisk at Aswan and listened to the guide's lecture on how to cut an obelisk as large as Cleopatra's needle, it is likely that such a tourist will recognise the work of the *Shamir*. Wooden plugs half a yard apart are hammered into the naked rock along a line. Then water was poured into the holes. The wood swelled, and the action of the sun no doubt contributed to the heat. The stone (granite) then split in a line, a crack, which ran like a worm along twenty-five or more feet. As it cracked, it must have appeared very like an advancing black worm on the sunny rock. So much for an association between a worm and the fiery Phoenix, and the fact that Moses was learned in all the wisdom of the Egyptians. (Act VII.22)

The Saxon poet's description of the ball or apple found amid the ashes of the Phoenix is reminiscent of the crystal in the *Orphic Book of Stones*, but even more so of the "stone balls" found in the ashes of the perpetual fire at bath in Brittain. Here was kept a perpetual fire to the goddess, whom the Romans called Minerva, but who was known to the British and Irish as Brigit, daughter of the Dagda, who had two sisters also called Brigit. Solinus, who wrote a kind of *Baedeker's Guide* of the known world in the 3rd century, states: "The whole circuit of Britain is four-thousand eight hundred and seventy five miles, in which space are great and many rivers and hot baths, finely kept to the use of men, the sovereign of which baths is that of the goddess Minerva, in whose chapel the fire burneth continually, and the coals do never turn into ashes, but as soon as the embers are dead, it is turned into balls of stone" (*sed ubi ignis tabuit vertis in globos saxeos*).

It must be remembered that Wolfram in his *Parzival* expressly states that the Grail is a stone from which the Phoenix rises. Both de Borron and Lonelich describe this Phoenix in an adventure wherein Evalach (Mordrains) is left alone, hungry and thirsty, upon a desert island. The king is tempted to eat a loaf of black bread, provided by

Fig 7. THE CHRISTIAN PHOENIX.
The use of the phoenix as a Christian symbol of the Resurrection is portrayed on a floor mosaic in a villa at Daphne near Antioch dating from the sixth century. The bird, a wader as is the Egyptian heron, stands on the Primeval Mound of Egyptian mythology (a type of step pyramid) against a background of rosebuds, a possible play on the Latin word *ros*. The bird's head is encircled by the aureole of the sun. From the *Atlas of the Early Christian World* by F. Van der Meer & Christine Mohrmann. Nelson. 1958.

demonic powers, but a marvellous bird swoops down and knocks it from his hand. The history of the bird is then given and closely agrees with the account in the *Book of Exeter*. Because of its powers of regeneration, Evalach is informed that he may accept it as a type or symbol of Christ.

The Phoenix, Evalach is told, is born from a stone found in the vale of Hebron near Jerusalem:

A precious ston of Merveillous kynde,
Wheche in the vale of Ebron is at alle dayes.

And de Borron states that the female or mother "est apielee 'serpolions'. Et la pierre de quoi ele s'art, est apielee 'piratiste'" that is to say, the "Fire-stone" or Pyrites. The connection of this fire-stone or pyrites with the vale of Hebron should be noted, for this tallies with the assertion that the ritual of the fiery sword was spread by Solomon. It is a fact that the story of the renewal of the eagle's life spread from Heliopolis in Egypt to all countries in Europe. We find that the Welsh sun-god Llew is changed, while he has one foot in the magic cauldron, into an eagle, who after a year has lost most of his plumage and sits dejectedly in a tree, until at last he is restored to his old shape. Similarly Psalm CIII – "Thy youth is renewed like the eagle's" shows that the myth was known amongst the Jews.

Opinions are divided as to whether the words Phoenix and the people of the Phoenix, known as the Phoenicians, are derived from the word for "palm tree" or for "red". Were the men of Tyre and Sidon, it is asked, known as the red-skins from their complexions or from the palm-trees which grew on their coast? In my view both derivations are probably correct and both reasons wrong. The word "red" was used by ancient man to denote the mysterious thing which we know as fire. It was the "red thing", and the Phoenicians were a people devoted to the cult of this "red thing", and it is furthermore possible that the palm-tree was their Branstock, as the oak was in Europe. There is a very touching description in Lonelich's version of the *Grand Saint Graal* of how Nasciens takes the scabbard (the brand) in his hand, and cannot understand of what it is made. The *Queste* tells us that it was made from the Tree of Life, but this refers to the wood, whereas Nasciens is puzzled by the actual flames.

but wel he wiste it was Al so Red
And as Ony Red Rose In that sted;

But, alas he never discovers what it is made of, nor did any man until the days of Lavoisier.

In all the legends in this book, therefore, the word "fire" should be substituted for "red". As evidence of this Plate VI shows a charm-stone, which has been in the possession of Major Stewart of Ardvorlich's family since the 14th century, and probably much longer. It is reputed to have great healing powers, and was used to cure the diseases of cattle until comparatively recent times. It is of pure white rock-crystal set in silver, but has nevertheless been known throughout its history as the *Clach Dearg*: The Red Stone. One wonders whether, when in his *Jungle Book* Kipling wrote that the animals referred to fire as the Red Flower, he was drawing entirely on his imagination, or from some Indian village's folk-lore vocabulary. The flint-bags of the Breton Korrigans were "red" bags. The Red Knight, whom Perceval slays, is the Divine Youth who carries fire, and whose place and office (his red armour) Perceval takes. Galahad is similarly clothed in red armour. Mithras also is traditionally cloaked in red. Of the Egyptian god Osiris Plutarch says that "they dress his statue in a flame-coloured robe, since they consider the sun as body of the power of the Good, as it were a visible sign of an essence that mind only can conceive."*

The author of *Y Seint Greal* says all this in so many words: "For as the Lord came to his disciples in the form of fire, so the knight (Galahad) came to you in red arms, which may be likened to the fire. And as Jesus Christ came to his disciples, the doors being shut upon them, so the knight came to you also, to the hall that was shut, without anyone knowing what

* Plutarch, *On Isis and Osiris* L1.4 et seq.

way he came in."* The analogy of the Welsh writer remains
good, for we still do not know how light traverses empty
space to arrive into our atmosphere, any more than we are
able to understand how Christ was able to transcend time
and space after the Resurrection.

To return now to the *Clach Dearg*: It is easily understood
that this fire-stone which was called the "red" stone, was
later confused in legend with rubies, carbuncles, and the
like. Pliny, describing precious stones, groups nearly all
red-coloured gems, whether rubies, garnets, red amethysts
or spinella rubies under the one heading of carbuncle. It is
not surprising therefore that a legend exists to the effect that
the Sangreal was made from one great ruby. While the earth
was still void, Satan led the rebel angels against the throne
of God. In his crest was a shining ruby, the rallying point of
all his soldiers. This ruby St. Michael smote out with his
flaming sword. It fell to earth, and the sea-folk (perhaps the
Cretans or Phoenicians) fashioned of it a wondrous cup,
which Solomon caused to be brought to him. When
Solomon died, no one knew of its fate, until his greater Son
used that cup in which to institute his Sacrament.† It is
interesting to note that once again Solomon is associated
with the Holy Vessel.

Gawain, when he went to Montesclaire to fetch the sword
of Judas Maccabeus, entered a richly adorned grotto, which
was lighted by one great carbuncle, fixed in a central
pillar.§ From this pillar hung the sword. In the stories
which will be given presently, the reader will be able to
recognise such a carbuncle in the hilt of a sword or in the
jewellery of a fairy queen for the fire-stone or crystal: the
Clach Dearg.

Since so many legends, when covertly referring to a crystal, derive from the Near East, it is fitting here to relate that
Madam MacDougall of MacDougall, Chief of Clan Mac-
Dougall owned until it was recently stolen, a spherical crystal about the size of a small apple, which was used in a

* *Y Seint Greal* p. 469.
† See *Glastonbury or the English Jerusalem* by Rev. C.L. Marson, M.A.
§ *The Legend of Sir Perceval* by Jessie Weston. p. 224.

similar fashion to the *Clach Dearg* to cure sick cattle as late as the 18th century. It was known always as "The Crusader Crystal", and was possibly brought back from the Holy Land by some medieval ancestor.

Returning now to a hollow glass sphere being compared to a ship: in several languages a "vessel" can have the double interpretation of a sea-going bark or a receptacle for liquids. Perhaps the reason for this lies in the fact that the earliest boats to navigate the Euphrates, as we know from engravings of them, were very like hollow gourds or the modern gold-fish bowl. The Arabs still use these *kufas* to-day on the Euphrates, and the ancient type (Fig 8.) can be

Fig 8. ANCIENT KUFA.
From Professor Maspero's "Dawn of Civilization".

compared to the Celtic coracle. If such a *kufa* or coracle were to be made of glass it could lead eventually to the construction of a "vessel" not unlike a laboratory retort through which sun-rays can be focused.

In Egypt the sun was supposed to sail in a ship across the sky. The sun itself was the eye of Rê or Horus, and he had but the one, for he had lost the other in a battle with the powers of evil (Typhon). This is worth noting, for later we shall find that Odin, like Rê, was one-eyed, having sacrificed the other as the price of obtaining wisdom. The solar eye in its Egyptian ship is found depicted in many parts of northern Europe, see Fig 9.

A replica of this solar-bark, which through time became more and more like a chest, was carried by the Egyptians on

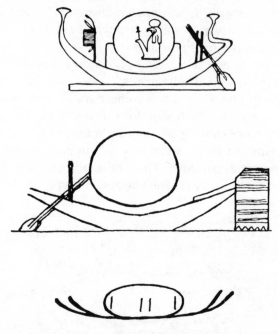

Fig 9. THE EGYPTIAN SOLAR BARK DEPICTED IN NORTHERN
EUROPE.
From "Myths and Legends of the Celtic Races".
Top. Egyptian Bark, with figure of Ra holding an Ankh enclosed in a Solar
Disk. XIX Dynasty, British Museum.
Middle. Egyptian Solar-bark, XXII Dynasty, British Museum.
Bottom. Ship Carving (with Solar Emblem?) from Scania, Sweden (after
Du Chaillu.)

their shoulders in procession, in much the same way as the
Israelites carried the Ark of the Covenant. It was the ashen
chest in which the Trojan Idunn kept her apple. And in the
North the prow of such a ship had a figure-head represent-
ing a swan-like bird. In the *Grand Saint Graal* Nasciens sees
Solomon's ship approaching in the distance:

A lytel thing him thowhte he say Comen there,
No more than a swan As thowh it were. (Lonelich).

In the *Prose Perceval* the ship is guided by an old bald-headed
man. Perceval is asleep therein, and at his feet is a candles-

tick. In the *Conte* of Chrestien the ship is drawn by a swan, and within it is a "blade" which must be drawn out within a year from the body of a prince, who is the son of a fairy.* The swan-ship is, therefore, the processional chest in which the *sacra* of the mysteries are kept, and must be distinguished from the Holy Vessel (crystal or Urim) which is kept inside the chest.

It is time now that we turned to the writing of a certain Greek, Athenaeus, who wrote a monograph all about various types of cups and drinking vessels. First he tells of how the sun descends into its golden cup, and was borne to the land of the Hesperides; then of how Heracles carried off this cup, and sailed across Oceanus. Whether or not this is the solar-bark itself or the glass sphere, through which it was incarnated on earth in the form of holy fire, is uncertain. Heracles was taking the cup westward, but this could apply equally to sun or cup.

A hollow glass sphere must, of course, be filled with water before it will focus the sun's rays. Athenaeus tells us of a "maiden" who had been cast into the sea. A man dives from a ship to rescue her, and emerges with a cup made of gold, so marvellous that the gold he already had, when compared with it, was no better than copper – an apt way of differentiating between metal and the glory of sunlight on glass.

This author writes also of the cup of Bathycles, but here Plutarch is more explicit. † It was drawn up by a fisherman in a net from the sea, as Danae was drawn up by Dyctis, and the Pythian oracle declared that it should be the prize of the wisest man in Greece. After some dispute it was finally kept at Delphi, and was later confused with the tripod, which was another sacred relic kept in the same temple. It is interesting to note here that his offering of a golden tripod or table to the temple of Apollo at Delphi, was taken in the Middle

---

* See M. Potvin's printing of the *Prose Perceval* and Chrestien's *Conte* p. 142 and Bk III pp 24-7 and 56.

† Plutarch's *Life of Solon* trans, by A.H. Clough, p. 171 and A.B. Cook's *Zeus*, writing on the Delphic tripod. Vol II who suggests that its central stem was originally the sacred tree round which a serpent was coiled. p. 193 et seq.

Ages to be a type of the presentation of the pure Virgin in the temple of God. When the glaziers made the windows for King's College Chapel, Cambridge, in the early 16th century, it was stipulated that the subjects should represent "the story of the olde lawe and of the new lawe": the former in a row of windows above to be typical of those of the New Testament below the cross bar. Nothing from Old Testament history would equate with the presentation of the Virgin Mary, so the scene of the offering to Delphi was introduced: the only scene from pagan history in the long series of biblical scenes. The glaziers depicted the offering as a golden table, but Plutarch says that although it was commonly held to be the tripod seen at Delphi, some versions of the tale held that it was a bowl or beaker.*

Athenaeus also in his *Deipnosophistae* refers to a type of vessel named a *kantheros* (a lamp-maker), so called, he presumes, from the lamp-maker who first made one. He says that it was like a ship, and was sometimes called a swan, and on it was figured a distaff and a serpent. He asserts that the *Cylix*, another cup, took its name from the wheel – not, I think the potter's wheel, but rather St. Catherine's, for it was a cup which came to a point (phoxos) and he says it took its name from the place where it was kept. He tells us that the cup-bone of the hip, which we know as the acetabulum and into which the ball of the femur fits, was also called the *cylix* from its shape being that of a shallow cup. This provides only one of the many possibilities of explaining the wound in the thigh of the Fisher King, and of the birth of Dionysus from the thigh of Zeus (of whom, more later) if the cylix-cup or concave mirror was struck by the spear of light.

Let us go back to the ship of glass in Celtic myth. The Welsh Bards describe a ceremony wherein a ship is carried in procession. It is the ship of a god called Hu, who was in Christian times thought to be a Celtic synonym for the Atlantean Noah, because he escaped the great flood in his

---

* See Plutarch, *On Isis and Osiris*, XXXIV.

ship. But in truth Hu was only a Welsh variant of the name of the sun-god in his special character of what we Christians might call the Third Person of the Trinity, and the Jews designate the *Shekinah* or "radiance", being neither the sun nor the incarnate flame, but the light which proceeds from both. I have heard it suggested that the name derives from the Sanskrit "to pour out" and that Hu is "He-who-is-poured-out". Hu-Siris was one of the names by which the Greeks knew the Egyptian man-god Osiris,* to whom, presumably, a measure of the Holy Spirit was vouchsafed. The idea of the pouring out of the Holy Spirit is familiar to the Hebrew prophets from Isaiah to Joel, who prophesies that at the last God will pour out his spirit, not upon the few initiates only, but upon all flesh.

The Welsh Bard Rhys Brydydd wrote of the god Hu thus: "The smallest of the small is Hu the mighty, in the world's judgement; yet he is the greatest, and Lord over us, we sincerely believe, and our God of mystery. Light is his course, and swift: a particle of lucid sunshine is his car." † Mr Dudley Wright gives an account of the procession of Hu's ark, § in which the hierophant represented the Creator, the second carried a torch, and the third represented the moon – that is to say, he probably carried the "moon goblet", for, as will presently be shown, the moon's powers of reflection were understood, and she was venerated, not for her own properties, but as the giant reflecting-cauldron of the sun in the heavens. In this procession of Hu's sacra, the ark is probably the chest visible to all, while the Holy Vessel or "moon goblet" would have been veiled.

Merlin, who was quite possibly a real character at Arthur's Court, took his name at least, if not his identity, from the much more ancient Merddin, another title for the sun-god, whose goddess wife, Elen, built a glass castle to imprison her lord. ‡ Merlin, it is also recorded, constructed a house of glass in which he went to sea, sailing to Bardsey,

† *Mythology & Rites of the British Druids* by Mr Edward Davies p. 110.
§ *Druidism* by Dudley Wright.
‡ *Minor Traditions of British Mythology*, by Lewis Spence.

and taking with him the thirteen wonderful treasures of Britain.* The Hermetic vase of the Alchemists, when "hermetically sealed", that is to say when the neck of the spherical glass was melted and closed on its contents, was known as the House of Glass or Prison of the King, the "King" being a periphrasis amongst the Alchemists for the Philosopher's Stone.† Originally "the King" must have signified sunlight caught in glass.

The following is from Spenser's *Faerie Queene*, and the connection of the glass globe which Merlin made, and the Egyptian Ptolemy or Tholomes (as in Grail legend) is to be noted; also the fact that it was a "looking glass" for the seer who peered into it, seeking visions. This Ptolemy has, of course, nothing to do with the Ptolomaic Pharaohs, but refers to Claudius Ptolemaeus of Alexandria, the great student of astronomy who lived between 127 and 151 A.D.

In Deheubarth that now South Wales is hight,
What time king Ryence raign'd, and dealed might,
A looking glasse, right wonderously aguiz'd,
Whose vertues through the wyde world soone were
solemniz'd.
It vertue had, to show in perfect sight,
What euer thing was in the world contaynd,
Betwixt the lowest earth and heauens hight,
So that it to the looker appertaynd;
Whateuer foe had wrought, or frend had faynd,
Therein discovered was, ne ought mote pas,
Ne ought in secret from the same remaynd;
For thy it round and hollow shaped was,
Like to the world itselfe, and seemed a world of glas.
Who wonders not, that reades so wondrous worke?
But who does wonder, that has red the Towre,
Wherein the'Aegyptian Phao long did luke
From all men vew out of her bowre?
Great Ptolomaee it for his lemans sake

* Lady Charlotte Guest's *Mabinogion* Vol I. p. 115 see note.
† *Prelude to Chemistry* by Professor J. Read p. 150.

ybuilded all of glasse, by Magicke powre,
And also it impregnable did make;
Yet when his love was false, he with a peaze it brake.
Such was the glassie globe that Merlin made.
And gave unto king Ryence for his gard.

The Rev. W. Gunn, in his preface to his translation of
Nennius's *History of Britain*, discusses the question of the
sacred glass ark, the possession of which distinguished the
initiate from the uninitiate, and mentions the legend of
Alexander the Great having once been let down into the sea
in a glass vessel, and then drawn up again. This brings us to
the very important question of what is the true significance
of the story of a man's being drawn out of water in an
ark.

The divine double of Pharaoh (the immortal twin) is the
fire passing through the water in the form of light, and
drawn out from the glass ark to ignite the fiery brand, even
as Arthur drew Excalibur from the Lady of the Lake.
Therefore to say that a man has been drawn from an ark and
water, is to say that he has received genius; undergone
spiritual rebirth; become an illuminatus; been consecrated
as a son of the Sun. Amongst many legends of children
being found in an ark floating on water, I give the following
examples, and it will not be surprising if the ark is described
to the uninitiate as being made of wicker-work, reeds or
bulrushes, like the *kufa* illustrated in Fig 8. Mr Cyril Aldred,
the Egyptologist, is of the opinion that the story of the infant
Moses found in the bulrushes predates all the possible
dates of the historical Moses and was a current Egyptian
folk-tale long before the real Moses could have existed. In
India Karna* is begotten of the sun-god and brought forth
by the Princess Pritha, who, to hide her shame, consigns
him to the water in an ark of wicker-work. Here it is
specifically mentioned that the father is the sun-god. The
infant Sargon, afterwards a famous king of Babylon who
lived about 2500 B.C. is put by his mother into such an ark

---

* A hero of the *Mahabharata*.

and is drawn from the Euphrates by Akki, the gardener.*
The infant Perseus and his mother Danae are set adrift in a
chest and drawn up by Dyctis, the fisher king. Romulus and
Remus (the immortal and mortal twins) born of the Vestal
virgin, Silvia, are drawn out of a similar vessel. Gawain, the
hawk-like hero of Grail legend, was likewise placed by Anna
in an ark as an infant and was rescued by a shepherd.†
Horus, the infant sun-god of Egypt, is frequently figured as
a child with finger to lip (to signify infancy by the babyish
habit of thumb-sucking or possibly to enjoin secrecy). He
rises from the cup or calix of the lotus: the lily-cup or ark of
bulrushes, like a drop of dew holding the light of the sun in
the pure white flower, as did Brahma in the mythology of
the Hindus. "The Jewel is in the heart of the lotus" is the
translation of the Brahmanic saying *Om Mani Padme Hum*.
There will be more to write about the dew in a later chapter,
but here it is enough to say that all the world seems to be in
love with light. I will reserve the story of the birth of Taliesin,
the Welsh poet, and of Lancelot for another chapter but
their stories are very similar to the examples already
given.

Remembering Pliny's description of how the serpent's
egg would float, even though set in gold, we come now to
the legend of the floating stones. The glassy globe which
Merlin gave to King Ryence will of course float if it is full of
air and sealed, and this will be made doubly clear when we
come to the birth of Taliesin. In Brittany the people will
recount to-day how the greater number of their local saints
arrived from Britain, miraculously navigating a floating
stone. At first the picture conjured up is of a venerable old
man paddling a monstrous megalith across the channel.
But, like all traditions, there is truth in the words if they are
properly interpreted. In the *Queste* and in *Y Seint Greal*
Arthur's knights discovered a floating stone of "red" marble. Here Walter Map evidently used his imagination too
freely in translating *Clach Dearg*. "Lord," says the squire

---

* *The Ancient World* by J.A. Brendon p. 42.
† *The Prose Perceval* p. 253 of M. Potvin's translation.

who first saw it, "I have seen a wonderful thing, a stone floating in the stream above the water." And the tale goes on: "And in the stone there was, as they thought, an honourable sword. Its pommel was of precious stone" – "et estoit li poins d'une pierre precieuse." There was lettering on the hilt, which again bears out the tradition that some engraving of characters was figured on the gold setting of the Grailstone. The only knight who could draw the sword from this floating stone was the hawk-like Galahad, son of Elaine, who is none other than the goddess Elen, the virgin glass sphere which imprisoned the sunbeam of Merddin. The Druids, and perhaps even the early Christian saints, probably took such "floating stones" with them, when they went to spread their teaching in Brittany.

6 Glass

All these legends of a floating ark or a floating stone assume the ability of the ancients to make glass, for a solid crystal ball or lens will not float. We have seen that as early as the days of Pliny the phenomenon of focusing sun-rays through a globular glass vessel was known. How early can we presume such a knowledge to have been held, and what references to glass are found in the poetry of the Welsh Bards?

Some of the finest sand for optical glass comes from the coast below Mount Carmel (where Elijah brought down fire-from-heaven), and Pliny tells us that glass-making was first discovered here by some sailors, whose ship was carrying lumps of nitre. They anchored in the harbour and, coming ashore and finding no stones with which to make a hearth for cooking supper, used the lumps of nitre for this purpose, and discovered that the sand and nitre fused to form glass.* Whether or not this story is true, it is certain that for many centuries the coastal strip below Mount Carmel was the only spot which afforded the sand for glass-making, and the sand was transported to other countries for this purpose. † It is also certain that the Sidonians of that coast were the most famous glass-makers of the ancient world from the 9th century B.C. until the Romans began to equal their skill in Pliny's time. But far earlier than the manufacture by the Sidonians was that of the Egyptians, who are known to have

---

* Pliny *Nat. History* XXXVI, 65.
† See *A Dictionary of Assyrian Chemistry and Geology* by Dr R. Campbell Thompson. p. 36.

made glass in 1500 B.C. and probably as early as the 12th Dynasty, that is to say they used glaze. They often used it on the eyes of statues to give a life-like stare. The natural location of these Egyptian glaziers was in the Delta and Fayum, where, in the land of Goshen, there are natron deposits and fuel. It is interesting to note that the two earliest places for glass-manufacture, Carmel, which provided the sand, and Goshen which gave the natron, were both easily accessible to the Jews.

The process of moulding was as follows: on the end of a tapered metal rod, a core of sand was modelled to the desired shape. This was dipped into molten glass, and subsequently the core was removed, and the surface ironed in such a way that its smoothness was as though it had been turned and polished. The account in Herodotus of how the egg of the Phoenix was first plastered with a glutinous substance, and then hollowed out, may relate to this process. In the *Gesta Romanorum* the legend of Diocletian finding an ostrich's egg covered with glaze tells us almost exactly the same story.

Shortly before the Christian era the much easier process of blowing glass became common knowledge amongst the glass-traders of the Mediterranean, as we know from their wares in museums.* Furthermore, Pliny assures us that in his day certain types of glass were entirely colourless and transparent, as nearly as possible resembling crystal. † But we have much earlier evidence than this, for the glass-texts of Ashurbanipal's library show that crystal-like glass was made in the 7th century B.C. in Assyria, and the recipes are given in cuneiform on clay tablets. § The dullness or rainbow lustres (which our museum specimens show of, say, Roman glass) are the result only of age and chemical reaction. My own opinion is that glass-blowing, as distinct from moulding, was a secret known to the priests of Egypt, Sidon, and Babylon long before it was disclosed to traders, just as the knowledge of the temperatures at which different

* *Glass* by E. Harrington Haynes.
† Pliny. *Nat. History* XXXVI.
§ *Dictionary of Assyrian Chemistry and Geology* by Dr R.C. Thompson. p. XXIII.

metals must be treated was closely guarded by the priest-kings of olden times.* Be that as it may, a carefully moulded globular glass vessel would be efficient enough to focus sun-rays in a hot climate if filled with water.

Various attempts, none of them very satisfactory, have been made to find the derivation of the mysterious word "grail" from the Latin *crater* or *gradalis*, meaning a cup or dish, and from *Sang Royal*, the Holy Blood, which is supposed to give "San Greal". The plain truth, however, seems to me to be shown in any dictionary where "grail" is used for certain types of sand or very fine gravel. In Scandinavia today, some types of high quality glass table-ware are advertised as "grail glass". Exactly why this word, grail, should be used by Wolfram von Eschenbach who borrowed it from the Provencal, Kiot, will become evident when we come to the assertion that the stone on which the dove laid the consecrated Host was called *Lapis Exilis*, the literal translation of this Latin being " the slender stone", which makes little sense and has puzzled all commentators. We shall find that it is a French pun.

It would be an interesting study to compare the known sources of sand suitable for optical glass with the famous sanctuaries of the Druids. Not all types of sand can be used, as only a very low iron content, less than 5 per cent, will produce transparent white glass. Fontainebleau, the Western Isles of Scotland and the shores of the English Wash are some of the few sources of such sand in Europe, and these districts are all within easy reach respectively of the great Druid centres of Chartres, Iona, and Branodunum, the latter being connected to Glastonbury by all the most ancient roads – the "green ways" – of England.

The Holy Vessel, says one of the manuscripts "was not of wood, nor of stone, nor of horn, neither of metal.† This

---

* Ibid. on p. XII Dr Thompson, discussing the ancient custom of concealing craft knowledge from the lay world in a fog of jargon, remarks: "Such a palisade of concealment is not confined to antiquity, but has persisted to the present day, particularly among the glass-makers, who preserve not only the tradition of their ancestors' skills, but also their secretiveness.

† See *The Legend of Sir Perceval* by J.L. Weston, and *The Vulgate Lancelot* edition Oskar Sommer Vol IV. p. 343.

leaves us with glass: the crystal-like vase out of which, according to the account in *Diu Crône*, the Fisher-King drinks with a golden reed.

The references to glass in Celtic legend are numerous. The story of how Connla was fetched by the immortal daughter of the *sidhe* in her glass boat has already been given. In one of the many adventures of Maeldun on his famous voyage amongst the fairy islands of the West, he comes to an island whereon is a fortress with a brazen door (Danae's tower) and a bridge of glass leading to it. A woman comes out of the fortress with a vessel in her hand, and, lifting from the bridge a slab of glass, she lets down her vessel into the water beneath, and returns to the fortress. Maeldun, after much patient waiting, is at last admitted to the brazen tower, and is fed from her vessel which is inexhaustible.* Granted that Pliny and his contemporaries confused ice and crystal, one cannot always be sure that such tales really refer to glass and not to icebergs etc., but that Maeldun won his way to an inexhaustible vessel gives a strong suggestion that he is yet another princeling involved in the quest for the Grail.

Mr Wirt Sikes, who was a well known student of folk-lore in the latter half of the last century, writing about the *Glain Naidr* or glass snake-stones found in Wales, says; "They are supposed to have been used by the ancient Druids as charms. There is a Welsh saying, respecting people who lay their heads together in conversation, that the talkers are "blowing the gem". This bears out my supposition that glass-blowing was a priestly secret. Mr Sikes goes on to say: "one of the customs of Easter, at a comparatively recent period in Wales, was getting the children up early in the morning to see the sun dance. This exercise the sun was said to perform at rising on Easter Day, in honour of the rising of Our Lord. The sun was sometimes aided in this performance by a bowl of clear water, into which the young people must look to see the orb dance, as it would be dangerous to look directly on the sun while thus engaged".† I suggest

---

* See *Myths and Legends of the Celtic Race* by T.W. Rolleston p. 319.
† *British Goblins* by Wirt Sikes pp. 273 and 278.

that the original bowl would have been a glass one in order to increase the sparkle and reflection.

Andrew Lang was also a great student of folk-lore, and in his version of *The Princess on the Glass Hill* we have a picture of the king, as son of the Sun, ascending the Tor. As in the case of the name of Glastonbury, the omission of the words *the* and *of* has robbed the legend of sense, for it should be the city or hill *of the* glass. The hero of the tale is called Cinderlad – significant name. Like Cinderella, he is of no account and despised. On St. John's Eve (the night of the midsummer fires) he acquires a magic horse and armour. The king, (god) of the country would give his daughter in marriage only to the knight who could ascend the glass hill. Cinderlad, on his magic horse and clad in armour so bright that it dazzles the spectators, climbs the slippery ice-like pinnacle to the throne, where the princess sits. She gives him an apple as proof of his having achieved the adventure.

In the works of the Welsh Bards are frequent allusions to glass. In *The Spoils of the Deep* by Taliesin, it is written: "Beyond the enclosure of glass (Caer Wydr) they beheld not the prowess of Arthur." I think the "enclosure" probably refers here to the innermost circle of megaliths being reserved for initiates of the mystery, of whom Arthur as king was presumed to be one.

The vessel itself is referred to as "O Wydrin Ban", and the *Gododdin* of Aneurin is full of references to the ritual. The poem describes a mighty battle in a druid sanctuary. Attempts have been made to equate this with some actual battle fought between Saxons and Britons in the 5th century. I must rely on the translations given by Mr Edward Davies,* but to me it suggests the struggle between light and darkness on the dawn horizon, which is frequently described in mythology as a battle between opposing forces. Be that as it may, the sanctuary was a place "where Morien preserved the merited fire". It was "the chief place of distribution of the source of energy" (a periphrasis, I think, for the distribution of fire-from-heaven). "The assembled train

* *Mythology and Rites of the British Druids*, by Edward Davies.

were dancing after the manner, and singing in cadence, with garlands on their brows: loud was the clattering of shields round the ancient cauldron, in frantic mirth; and lively was the countenance of him, who in his prowess, had snatched over the ford that involved ball, which casts its rays to a distance, the splendid product of the adder, shot forth by serpents." Here is Pliny's *ovum anguinum* again, and be it noted that it gives out rays. The hero is described thus: A spear of quartered ash did he extend from his hand over the stone cell of the sacred fire." And the king poured an effusion *as it were* of wine out of crystal vessels. He who extorted silver for his mead paid gold in return. This is almost certainly periphrastic, for the Druids were accustomed to make the people extinguish all fire at Samhain, before giving them back fire lit from the King-candle, for which they extorted payment.*

As for the "crystal vessel", it is significant that only about a century later St. Columba, Abbot of Iona, journeyed, according to his biographer, to meet and try to convert the Arch Druid of the Picts, Broichan, in the vicinity of Inverness. He failed, but while returning he learned that the Arch Druid had broken his glass cup, and this accident had left him gasping for breath and half dead. From that moment the power of the Arch Druid diminished, and Columba was able to establish better relations with the Pictish king, Brude. One cannot but wonder why a small accident to a drinking vessel should have caused such a diminishing of Broichan's power and eventually his death. Did he, perhaps, break his all-imporant "fire-maker" and become unable to light the new Beltane fire from the sun – just speculation!

Of course it is possible and indeed likely that the *Gododdin* does record a real battle between Saxons and Britons, but equally it is possible that the troops were encouraged by the old Celtic rituals, just as medieval armies were exhorted to bravery by Christian celebrations of Mass or displays of relics. Nevertheless the dancing and the garlands seem to

* *The Celtic Druids* by Godfrey Higgins.

suggest a more festive atmosphere than that which would precede bloody warfare.

It is not impossible that the king or Arch Druid did actually drink from the hole in the glass sphere by which it was filled with water, for, in the case of the *Clach Dearg* and similar Scottish charm stones, they were employed to cure the diseases of cattle in the following way. They were immersed in water, and the water was then given to the cattle to drink, in the belief that the magical properties of the stone would have passed into the water. It is quite likely, therefore, that in his passionate desire for the descent of the Holy Spirit, man may have used the glass to bring down light from heaven, and then afterwards have drunk from it, in the hope that he was taking that light into himself. There are references in the Welsh poetry to the "draining of the sacred bowl". This supposition is borne out by two passages in II Esdras XIV. The angel promises that if the prophet will return on the following day, "I shall light a candle of understanding in thine heart". Esdras obeys, and to fulfil his promise the angel bids the prophet drink. "Then", says Esdras, "opened I my mouth, and, behold, he reached me a full cup, which was full as it were with water, but the colour of it was like fire. And I took it and drank: and when I had drunk of it my heart uttered understanding, and wisdom grew in my breast." It is plain that these two passages are intended to describe cause and effect. A candle can be lit by sunlight through a glass cup filled with water, therefore the prophet drinks in order to light the candle of understanding in his soul.

I shall explain later that the followers of Tanchelm of Antwerp (whom Professor Olschki claims to be one of the leaders of a certain heretical sect of Gnostics which he associates with the Grail legend) drank his bath-water because these same Gnostics thought him so holy. More probably they drank the water from the Alchemical vase called the Bain Marie. Well, Catholics have holy water, and bottles of it are brought yearly from Lourdes or from the Jordan, so who dare scoff at our ancestors?

Glain is generally used in the Welsh in contrast to *wydr* (glass) to describe a gem, and would therefore be an appropriate description of a rock crystal. Bardsey was called "the holy island of the Glain to which pertains a splendid representation of re-exaltation", and the Bard Meilyr calls it "the holy island of the Glain in which there is a fair representation of the resurrection." It will be remembered that it was to Bardsey that Merlin sailed in his house of glass, taking the thirteen wonderful treasures of Britain. For Merlin read Merddin, the sun-god after whom Merlin was named. There is no doubt that Bardsey contained an important Druid sanctuary. One Welsh reference describes a bard as being one "who animates the fire."

Taliesin writes: "A holy sanctuary there is – it is rendered complete by the rehearsal, the hymn, and the birds of the mountain. Smooth are its lays, in its periodical festival: and my lord duly observant of the splendid mover, before he entered his earthly cell in the border of the circle, gave me mead and wine out of the deep crystal cup."*

The food of immortality, which the Greeks called ambrosia, probably gave its name to many transparent or life-giving stones in the early days, but one of these, amber, has kept its name. This the tribes of the Baltic, whose language Tacitus says greatly resembled the British tongue, called *glaesum* – i.e. glass. † But when Roman culture made real glass familiar to the common folk of Britain, as distinct from the initiates, it was known not as *glain* or *glaesum* but as wydr or wydrin, which comes from the same Aryan root as the Latin *vitrea* or the French *vitrine*. It is easily understandable, therefore, that, when the uninitiated Latin and French scholars came to tell the stories of saints and Grail heroes, they should confuse the glass (or crystal) through which fire came with the window or vitrine of a temple or church. We shall find the Grail referred to as a "window", "vitrine", or "fenestre", and, according to a book on Freemasonry which I bought and read, the masons who base their ritual on a knowledge of Solomon's temple speak of a window – a

---

* *Mythology and Rites of the British Druids* by E. Davies.
† Tacitus, *Germania*.

"dormer" – through which the light or fire of the Holy Spirit proceeds. The following legends give evidence of how the Grail was called a "window".

St. Brendan (alternative spelling Brandon), sailed like Maeldun from Ireland to find the fairy islands of the West. His fantastic voyage (who knows but that he did not reach America as small boats do today for competitive records?) may very well contain a true account of his having put in his boat to Somerset and visited Glastonbury. For he came to an Abbey and was welcomed by the Abbot to the church. "And there were seven lights there, which had been added since the beginning; and three were hanging down above the High Altar, and the other four were divided into two lots. And he saw that the *altar was of clear crystal.*" The Abbot and St. Brendan remained alone together all night in the sacred building because the Abbot "wanted to show him how God lighted the lamps in the church." Presumably at dawn, "and while they were talking softly together, there came a breath of fire, towards them through the *window*, and it went lighting all the candles which were in front of the altar." The Saint was puzzled and asked, "How can a thing which is spirit burn in a material way?" And the Abbot replied: Have you not read in the Bible of that bush of which the thorns seemed aflame, when God came to Moses on Mount Sinai, which is Armenia, in order that he might talk to him?"*

The legend of St. Brendan confuses the crystal *upon* the altar (where it was almost certainly kept in Christian times as a memento) with the altar itself, and then refers to the flame proceeding from the window, but the inference is obvious. And it should be particularly noted that this phenomenon is associated with the Burning Bush. The abbot's distinction between the spiritual and material types of fire is so important that I must leave the resolution of the problem to the final chapter of this book.

The legend of St. Barbara was introduced from the East

---

* Quotations from *La Navigatio Sancti Brandani of Francesco Novati* and also to be found in the Acta Sanctorum.

about the same time as that of St. Catherine of Alexandria. Mrs Jameson asserts that she is apocryphal.* According to the legend she was the daughter of a nobleman of Heliopolis (the Egyptian *On*, City-of-the-Sun, whence came the daughter of its High Priest to marry Joseph at the behest of Pharaoh once Joseph had become Pharaoh's chief vizier); Barbara was so beautiful that her father was fearful that she should be demanded in marriage and taken from him. So he shut her up in a tower and kept her secluded from the eyes of men. She was converted to Christianity by no less a person than Origen, who lived in Alexandria. Her father, who was violently opposed to the Christian faith, was at this time absent; but before his departure he had given instructions to the masons to build a bath chamber in her tower (glass needs to be filled with water and crystal to be cleansed) and he ordered them to make two windows to the chamber. St. Barbara, in his absence, gave additional commands to the builders to construct a third window in honour of the Blessed Trinity. On the father's return, she confessed to him her reason for having the third window, and he wrathfully consigned her to a dungeon. After much persecution, which failed to shake her faith, the father then (presumably by magic) transformed her into a stone, and took her in this shape up a mountain-top, meaning to behead her. But he then decided to bring her down again, whereupon fire fell from heaven and consumed him utterly. In works of art St. Barbara is always represented carrying a miniature tower with three windows, and sometimes she bears the sacramental cup. She is the patroness of fire-work makers and of anything to do with gunpowder, and thus patroness of warriors with her effigy sometimes stamped on their armour or guns.

Now the earliest form of all the subsequent forms of the Catholic pyx was not for display but for carrying the sacrament quickly to the sick and dying. It was generally a simple box set with jewels similar to that borne by the Grail maiden in *DiuCrône* which contained the holy bread. When the

* *Sacred & Legendary Art* by Mrs Jameson. Vol II. p. 492.

people began to yearn to see the visible sign of Our Lord's presence, the bread was next displayed on the altar in a simple cylinder of glass or crystal, more likely the latter as being more precious; but later came various and more complicated containers known to Catholics as Monstrances (in Italian, *Ostensarios,* and in Spanish *Custodias.* One of the earliest of these types is illustrated in Fig 10, a drawing from

Fig 10. ST. BARBARA'S TOWER.
Reliquary as depicted in J. Braun's work on Reliquaries.

a photograph in *Die Reliqiare des Christlichen Kultes*, by a German, J. Braun. It shows the crystal cylinder set up for display in a stand exactly like a tower, with a roof, a steeple, supported by three metal stays, thus forming St. Barbara's three windows. There is little doubt that Barbara was never a person but was the sacred crystal of pagan religion, and the Church has always been ready and wise enough to adapt an old custom and "baptize" and cleanse the out-dated thing and use whatever it may be to the honour of the true

God. Barbara is none other than Danae, locked in her brazen tower. The third window is the Grail itself, taken from an underground dungeon, (all mystery religions have to have caves, crypts or blindfolding as a prelude to initiation and illumination) to the top of the Tor, or possibly the crystal-bearing rocks of the Caucasus mountains, to bring down fire-from-heaven.

In Rome, Servius Tullius was reputed to have been born of a woman who had conceived by the generative power of the fire. He built a temple to the goddess Fortune, who loved him "and she was wont", says Ovid, "to enter his house by a small window (fenestra) hence the gate bears the name Fenestella (the Little Window)."*

In the *Metrical Joseph* the leprous Vespasian is fed from such a "little window", and as he was *not* in fact a leper, it may perhaps refer to the ambrosia of light being transmitted to him through the Grail, for if held to the hand the focal point of a sun-lit crystal forms a bright white circle on, say, your palm, and a white spot on the skin is one of the first symptoms of real leprosy. †

In Peter Lasko's *Ars Sacra* is described the shrine (escrain) of Charlemagne, alas destroyed in the French revolution, but of which contemporary drawings remain, and the *gyp-*

---

* Ovid, *Fasti*, VI 574 and 672.

† An additional reason for believing the story of St Joseph of Arimathea's coming to Britain is not a mere invention is provided by the following facts: apocryphal literature and the Grail legend both connect the name of St Joseph with Vespasian and Titus. De Borron incorrectly makes Titus the father of Vespasian, i.e. older than Vespasian. It has been supposed that the connection of these Emperors with St Joseph originated in the account of the *historian*, Josephus, of his own meeting with the two Roman generals and his subsequent liberation from prison in Palestine shortly before Titus sacked Jerusalem. De Borron's fantastic claim that Vespasian became a convert to Christianity might lend weight to the supposition that the whole story is based on error. But in fact, however, the claim is not so fantastic as it at first appears. Vespasian was a comparatively humble Roman officer commanding the Second Augusta Legion in Britain at just about the time when St Joseph of Arimathea would have arrived in this island, so it is just possible that a meeting did take place. Vespasian's *elder brother*, Titus Flavius Sabinus was serving under him in Britain (Dio Bk LX, 19) and even Dio on one occasion confused Vespasian's elder brother Titus with his famous son the Emperor Titus. There is reason to believe that Titus F. Sabinus *did* become a Christian. Certainly his son Flavius Clemens died a Christian martyr. The conversion of this branch of the family is discussed in *The Early Church in the Light of the Monuments* by A.S. Barnes. It is not impossible, therefore, that the legend of a connection between St. Joseph of Arimathea and a Christian "Titus" may be founded on truth.

sum fenestra super altare was of semi-transparent stone, probably alabaster cut sufficiently thinly to admit some light,
but not of course sufficient to cause the igniting of anything
upon the altar. Such unpremeditated ignition would have
been not only sacrilegious but high dangerous.

Fig 11. 14TH-CENTURY WATER-MARK OF THE WHITE STAG.
From "A New Light on the Renaissance", by Harold Bayley.

In the following story from the *Queste* and *Y Seint Greal* it
should be noted that the stag was the old stag-headed god of
the Celts, Cernunnos, of whom we shall hear more later.
The story is an allegory of how the pagan god is replaced by
Christ. Galahad, Perceval, Bors and Perceval's sister visit a
chapel, on the altar of which sits a great stag surrounded by
four lions. But even as the knights witness this vision,
behold! the stag becomes a man (Jesus) and the lions are
metamorphosed into the four attributes of the Evangelists –
man, eagle, lion and ox. Christ and his attendants then
withdraw through a glass window and disappear, "without
injuring or breaking any of the window notwithstanding.
And when they were gone away, they heard a voice saying:
"In the manner they went out, without harm or injury to
the glass window, so God descended into the womb of the
Lady Mary without detriment to her chastity and her
virginity." (*Y Seint Greal*) – "en tel maniers descendi li fieus
dieu en la benoite viergene marie, que onques sa virginitei
n'ene pierdi". (*Queste*)

We are about to discover the original source of confusion
between the Grail-stone and the cup of the Last Supper.
Compare the above story with an account in the *Grand Saint
Graal* of de Borron. St. Joseph of Arimathea goes to the tem-

ple of the sun to convert King Evalach, but the king cannot accept the possibility of Christ having been born of a virgin. Joseph convinces him by the following explanation, which I translate from the French for easier reading. "In this vessel (Mary) cleansed by the visitation of the Holy Spirit, the son of God took up his abode. So serene and untroubled was his birth that the virginity of his sublime mother at no time suffered harm – even as the sun's beam, shining through clear water, is traced by the eye into the very depths, but cleaves not the waves, nor yet them divides." Both in the story of the stag and in this last passage, the conception of Christ in the womb of the Virgin Mary is likened to sunlight passing through the glass or water of the Grail – the virgin-vessel of the old religion. In The *Revelations* of Saint Birgitta of Sweden Christ speaks to her in these words, which I take from the edition of Wm. Patterson Cumming, but I have converted the old English into modern spelling for easier understanding: "I am He that spake to prophets and patriarchs, and whom they abode; for whose desire and after mine own behest I took a body without sin or lust, entering the maiden's womb as the sun shining through a clear stone. For as the sun, entering the glass, hurteth it not, so the maidenhead of the virgin abode incorrupt and unsoiled in taking of my manhood."*

Compare now the much later writing of Malory, wherein he says that the sin of the world was one of the causes "that our Lord took flesh and blood of a cleane maiden". And in another passage he writes of "the deadly flesh which he had taken in the womb of the Blessed Virgin Mary". † It is very easy to see how Mary, the vessel from whom Christ took upon Himself flesh, became in legend the vessel from which he took the sacrament of his flesh and blood to give to the Apostles at the Last Supper. The spear of the sun-god, from which the divine effluence of light flowed, would then

---

* I am indebted to Mr John Rillie, Lecturer in English at Glasgow University for this quotation and also a similar one from the *Harley Lyrics* dated circa 1314. I am also indebted to Mr E.G. Morgan of Glasgow University for pointing out a picture of the Virgin portraying her "seemly side" as transparent and ready to receive the rays of light, painted by Grunewald for the altar at Isenheim.

† *Morte d'Arthur*, Vol III, Ch. XL p. 71 and Ch.XC, p. 161.

have to be explained as yet another relic of the Passion. It will be remembered how in the first chapter of this book an examination showed that the poets were not at all at their ease in explaining how blood from the spear of the centurion, Longinus, entered the cup of the Last Supper.

There is no doubt that the Virgin Mary and the Grail have been closely identified, and that the symbol of the god-bearer was transferred to her. In the Litany of the virgin she is addressed as *"Vas Honorabile"*. In the Apocryphal narrative of St. Joseph of Arimathea – *The Assumption of the Virgin* – Joseph says: I am that Joseph who laid the body of the Lord in my tomb and saw him rise again, and always watched over his most holy temple, even the Blessed Mary, ever virgin, before the ascension of the Lord and after it". The two ideas of the Virgin as a temple or vessel are really in one line of thought: she is the God-bearer. What concerns us in this quotation from the Apocryphal New Testament is that St. Joseph had care of the Virgin Mary. The Rev. Lionel Lewis stated in his booklet about Glastonbury that St. Joseph was the only other to share with St. John the title of *Paranymphos* or Guardian-of-the-Lady. Mr Lewis quoted the *Magna Tabula* of Glastonbury as his authority. If the Apocryphal *Acts of Pilate*, chapter XV, be compared with de Borron's *Metrical Joseph* and *Grand Saint Graal* it will be found that a tradition existed that St. Joseph visited the Holy Sepulchre after the Resurrection, and there beheld the risen Christ; that Christ then confided the Holy Vessel to his care, and bade him go to Arimathea and there remain for forty days before returning to Jerusalem. The poets change this into forty-two years in prison (a confusion with the Joseph son of Jacob again), and presume the vessel to have been the Grail. But it is far more likely that the "Holy Vessel" was Christ's mother, and the forty days signify that both St. Joseph of Arimathea and Mary were commanded to return to Jerusalem in time for Pentecost, on which day we know the Virgin to have been present with the disciples. It is extremely likely that the rich man of Arimathea would have given protection and shelter to Mary at such a time and until St. John, who was to act as her son, had made practical arrangements and safe conduct for her reception into his own house. St. Joseph's title of *Paranymphos* is easily confused with that of "Companion or Guardian of the Grail or Basin", which M. Potvin claims was held by Perceval. The title also throws light on the queer and quite unauthenticated tale that the Virgin Mary is buried at Glastonbury. An important crystal Grail almost certainly *is* buried there, and this only shows how carefully traditions are kept, if not always interpreted correctly.

Glastonbury, as the chief centre of Britain's veneration for the Grail (crystal), naturally becomes *the* sanctuary of all others wherein the aid of the Virgin Mary may be sought. St. David, who rebuilt the Abbey, and wished to re-dedicate the old thatched church of St. Joseph, was informed by Our Lord in a vision that the church was already and for ever dedicated to His Blessed Mother, to be a place where at all times men might seek her intercession. Her Immaculate Conception, which the Roman Church hold as part of the faith (the belief that the Virgin was herself from the moment of her conception and birth preserved from the stain of original sin), is borne out if we accept the symbolism of the fire-and-light-cult as a fore-ordained symbolism given us by God. In *Y Seint Greal* Gawain visits the Grail castle and "he saw the figure an angel, which with its finger was showing the chapel, in which was the Holy Greal. And on the front of the chapel was a very precious stone, which said that the Lord of the court was as clean from all sin as the stone itself was from all bespeckling". In the *Wisdom of*

Fig 12. ISIS-HATHOR AS A MERMAID.
From "Dawn of Astronomy" by J. Norman Lockyer.

Solomon the Jewish writer refers to wisdom (Sophia) as "a reflection of eternal light, and a spotless mirror of the working of God".* In other words a crystal, glass or mirror was fashioned of earthly elements common to all matter, but had to be pure and transparent if it was to transmit light.

The study of glass and "windows" has led us to anticipate Christian times. It is necessary now to return to all the wealth of pagan legend which remains unexplored. It was with a mirror that the Titans charmed Dionysus into their power, who was reborn from the "thigh" of Zeus, and the sacra of his mysteries included, says Miss Jane Harrison, a ball and a mirror. † Fig 12 shows an illustration of the goddess Isis as a mermaid with the mirror of the moon above her head. The earth-mother was often pictured thus, because the peak of rock sacred to her, and known as the baetyl stone, rose (or appeared to rise) when the Nile and Euphrates floods abated, while the base of the rock still remained in the water. As Atargatis and Derceto she is portrayed therefore with a fish's tail. § As Aphrodite she rises from the foam. This is the origin of why a mermaid is supposed to sit upon a rock, holding her mirror and combing her hair. In the 18th century Gregor Wilcox, the Scottish warlock of Strathavon, possessed a "mermaid's stone" or clear crystal, handed down by his maternal grandfather, to whom the mermaid had yielded it in return for her liberation. It resembled the knob or bottom of a crystal bottle. ‡

The meaning of Morgan in Welsh is "sea-born", and Morgan le Fay is none other than the mermaid goddess with her mirror and cauldron. That rays shone from the Celtic cauldron of Inspiration is shown in the following verse of the Welsh Bard Llyarch ab Llwelyn: "God, the Ruler, gives me a *ray* of melodious song, as if it were from the Cauldron of Ceridwen." Taliesin also sees in the light of the cauldron the prophecy of the greater revelation of the descent of the

---

* *Wisdom of Solomon.* VII.26.
† *Prolegomena to the Study of Greek Religion* by J. Harris.
§ *De Dea Syria* Lucian.
‡ *Primitive Beliefs in the North East of Scotland* by J.M. McPherson

Word or Logos which inspires men to song: "Manifest is truth when it shines; more manifest when it speaks; and loud it spoke when it came forth from the cauldron of Awen, the ardent goddess."*

In the *Conte du Graal* of Chrestien an episode describes how in Brittany Carados Bris Bras is lured by his wicked (earth) mother to fetch her mirror from a coffer whence two serpents issue to fling their coils round his arms, and from which at long last a magic charm delivered his tightly bound limbs.

When Eochy, High King of Ireland, woos Etaine the daughter of the immortals, the description of her is a description of Ireland itself in much the same poetic vein as Hebrew poets and prophets described Israel as the daughter of Zion; purple mantle for the hills, green silk for the dress, the Emerald Isle in person, but she has a basin of silver set with bright gems of "red" stones (Clach Deargs) around the rim, similar to the Cauldron of Hades in Welsh myth. † In the *Vita Merlini*, Geoffrey of Monmouth says that nine maidens held rule at Avalon (Glastonbury) of whom Morgan was the chief; and there were nine witches of Gloucester who figure in Welsh mythology. Dare one guess that Celtic ritual required nine Vestals to attend the sacred fire, three more than at Rome? A bronze statuette of the Diana of Nemi, who also bore the title of Vesta, shows her holding a torch, just as did Ceres at Eleusis. § Vesta's fire at Rome was known as the Ilian hearth because Aeneas was supposed to have brought the flame from Troy with the Palladium.‡ Of this Palladium, most sacred "Luck of Troy", all that we know is that when Ulysses bore it triumphantly into the Greek camp, it gave out fire, which does not accord with the modern theories that it was a meteorite.

Sir James Frazer has shown that Artemis is not always a virgin, neither was Pallas childless if we examine the story of

---

* *Mythology & Rites of the British Druids* by E. Davies.
† *Myths and Legends of the Celtic Race* by T.W. Rolleston.
§ *The Golden Bough*, Bk I Ch. I pp 10 et seq.
‡ Ovid. *Fasti* III, 418.

Erichthonius. He was supposedly the son of earth (Ge) and fire (Hephaestus) and was handed over by Pallas to three maidens in a chest (ark) which they were forbidden to open. Two of the maidens disobeyed (as did Pandora, the first woman, created by the gods specially to be the wife of Prometheus, the fire-maker who also opened a forbidden chest or ark) and within this chest the maiden servants of Pallas found a child with a snake coiled round it. This child became the first King of Athens, and after his death was accorded divine honours in Pallas' temple of the Erechtheum, where a perpetual fire was maintained. Perhaps the egg-and-dart mouldings so beloved of the Greeks are not after all mere sex symbols but represent the *ovum anguinum*, an egg-shaped crystal and the sun's dart?

There is a very beautiful symbolism in the oft repeated legend of the infant, such as Hercules in his cradle or Erichthonius in his ark-chest or Carados Bris Bras, who grasps the serpent in his hands and rends it in two. The material nature of the universe seemed to defy the possibility of light passing through solid matter, and the serpent, as the enemy of the sun's passage, attempted always to defy and deny the sun its path, surrounding and imprisoning the Grail-stone as it surrounded and tried to imprison the sun's path and the sun's rising, but the spirit, the light, the messenger of God, bursts through the barrier from eternity into time, rends time into two, the past and future, and takes possession of man's soul, just as the light issues from the sky to ignite the torch. The messenger of the gods, Hermes in Greece and Mercury in Rome, carries therefore these now divided serpents entwined round the brand or sun-staff which we know as the Caduceus, for Pliny tells us that it was the entwining of the serpents who made the snake-stone that led to the symbolism of the Caduceus.*

In Britain Minerva (Pallas) was not worshipped alone at Bath, but as Sul-Minerva, a combined deity both male and female. In other words Sul is identical with Erichthonius. He

---

* Pliny. *Nat. History* XXIX Ch. 12.

is her fire-child, her perpetual fire which we know was maintained at Bath.

Minerva's Celtic name was Brigit, one of the three Brigits who were daughters of the Dagda. It is not surprising that in the 5th century A.D. a heathen Irish girl should have been called by the name of the goddess. Probably many were so called amongst the heathen Irish. Nor is it to be wondered at that when this particular girl became a Christian and a nun and one of the greatest of Ireland's historical saints, she should have been credited after her death with some of the characteristics and attributes of the goddess. In the Book of Lismore she is addressed as "Brigit, Mother of my High King", as the "One mother of the Great King's Son" and as "The Mary of the Gael". She was represented in painting and sculpture with a cow (the horns of Isis or Hathor) and with a flame over her head. Legend has it that she visited Glastonbury, and her embroidery tools (attributes of Minerva) were at one time preserved in a chapel at Beckery, close to the Abbey of Glastonbury which became a place of pilgrimage for the Irish.

In Ireland at Kildare a sacred and perpetual fire was preserved in her honour down to the time of the Reformation. Giraldus Cambrensis gives an account of the fire.* The Christian nuns who tended it were not nine but nineteen in number. As with the fire at Bath described by Solinus, there was never any accumulation of ashes upon the hearth. Each nun took it in turn to tend the fire at night, but on the twentieth night they left the care of it to St. Brigit herself, who came specially from Paradise for this task. Giraldus was told that in the past a beautiful falcon had frequented the tower of the church. For centuries it had been known as "Brigit's bird" but now, alas, it came no more. The fire itself he could not examine closely, for it was surrounded by a circular hedge or fence of stakes, within which no male might penetrate. We meet with this "hedge of the flame" in the legend of Sigurd (Wagner called him Siegmund) who drew the god's brand from the Branstock and whose son

* *Topography of Ireland* by Giraldus Cambrensis XXV and XXXVI.

Siegfried had to penetrate the hedge of flame to win Brunhilde. And in the story of the Sleeping Beauty the prince must win through a hedge of thorns. The princess slept because she had been pricked by a spindle, perhaps one of the three spindles of the Grail-tree on which the crystal was, so to speak, impaled, and this "tree' was, as we have seen, a hidden allusion to the "Bed of Solomon", in which she slept until the solar light should reawaken and bring her sparkling back to life. One has to keep remembering that the Grail-stone, lens or glass is always a "she" and never an "it".

Fire and water must mingle to mend the broken brand of Siegfried or Perceval, and one has to admit that the tempering of steel does require alternating treatment by fire and water, but light coming through a glass beaker of water can also produce a flame. And Baldr the Beautiful's story is not unlike that of Sigurd (Siegmund), for Mr Lewis Spence assures us that Baldr was slain not by a plant, the mistletoe, but by an enchanted sword, the mistleteinn, *teinn* meaning branch or brand.* Baldr possessed, like Prometheus, the fire-maker's ring. Baldr means the Bright or Shining One. Loki, the fire-god, plotted to have the enchanted brand thrown at Baldr, that is to say to have the brand extinguished; and Baldr dies, just as did Arthur as Excalibur was returned to the water. After which a great funeral pyre was made for Baldr, similar to the one made for another Solar Hero, Hercules, at his death.

There is one further Norse myth worth recording. Both Horus and Odin are one-eyed. The missing eye in both cases had been sacrificed for the welfare of mankind or in battle against evil. Odin had to pledge his eye as the price of wisdom, and it became a vessel to hold mead (Ambrosia). † In Egypt fire was known as "the effluence of the eye of Hor." § It is possible that in both cases a crystal or glass sphere was recognised as the missing eye of the sky-god, though I prefer the association of the crystal etc. with the

* *Druidism* by Lewis Spence. p. 81.
† *Poetic Edda, Voluspa.*
§ *Origins of the Festival of Hanukkah* by O.S. Rankin pp 62-72.

moon; the moon's reflection of the sun, allusions to the moon-goblet, its basically feminine character, the Lunette (a lens) and the Yin principle of the Chinese. On the other hand Thoth, the Egyptian god of wisdom, restored to Horus the missing eye so that with it Horus could bring back Osiris, his earthly father, to life in the Fields of the Blessed as Judge of the Dead.

7 Descent into Hades

Hades is as much a real place as the Grail and sword are real objects. To study the ritual of the Underworld it is necessary to understand the conflicting emotions in man, and also the struggle between a primitive and a more advanced civilisation. The ceremony of lighting a fire from the sun is essentially beautiful, calling up in the imagination the finest ideas of the beneficence and condescension of God.

If the ritual of Hades is repellent, it should be realized that to call down either flame of the sun or the Holy Spirit from Heaven, is to call down power, and power can be used either for good or evil. It is the old story of the fall of Lucifer, the light-bearer, whose light can become the fires of Hell. In very early paintings the head of Satan is adorned with a "glory" of light, similar to that which illuminates the head of Our Lord and the Saints, showing that in ancient times this was well understood. In the Temptation of Christ by the Devil the Scriptures show us that Christ could have used his power for evil had he not resisted temptation. The study of Hades, therefore, is the study of the abuse of power.

Furthermore, as we are going to explore the Celtic Hades, it should be realized that the more mystically inclined and by nature temperamentally devotional a race is, the more it will be in danger of going to extremes, of perpetrating horrors in the name of God. Thus the Greeks and Romans, who were not in the main a race of mystics, very early found excuses for ransoming a devoted victim; whereas the Spaniards of the Inquisition, in whose veins ran the blood of Celts and Moors, committed ghastly atrocities

I. Horus as a Roman Legionary defeating Typhon the Monster. Late
Roman-Coptic. *(By courtesy of the Louvre Museum, Paris.)*

II. (Right) Sixteenth Century Spanish Monstrance from Toro. *(By courtesy of the Victoria and Albert Museum, London.)*

IIIa. (Below) Crown of the Torah – 18th Century Italian.
IIIb. (Below right) A breastplate of the Torah, showing the Tablets of Stone or Torah surmounted by a crown, and placed in the Holy of Holies between the Pillars of Jachin and Boaz. *(From the Gustave and Castle Collections, London.)*

IV. (Above) The Sun God,
Shamash, with his emblem
of the wheel and guardian
serpent. (From a plaque in
the British Museum, London.)

V. (Left) The Seal of the
Abbot of Glastonbury.
(From Dugdale's Monasticon.)

VI. (Above left) The Clach Dearg or Red Stone of the Stuarts of Ardvorlich : a pure white rock crystal set in silver. *(Photograph by J.M. Bremner.)*

VII. Niger, a tame rook, playing with fire. *(By courtesty of Miss Jane Burton.)*

VIIa. (Left) The rook lands in front of a bundle of straw which has burst into flames.

VIIb. (Above) Phoenix-like before the flames, Niger comes to no harm throughout his performance.

VIII. (Right) A large embroidered dragon panel – 19th century.

IXa. (Below) The Talisman of
Charlemagne. *(By courtesy of the
Archbishop of Rheims and the Caisse
National des Monuments Histori-
ques.)* Note that the original central stone was for some reason at
some time replaced by a transparent cabuchon of pale blue
glass. The artistic conception of
'a' transparent stone wearable
upon the breast or alternatively
placed on a 'stand' is what is
important to the study of reliquaries, the Grail or the Urim.

IXb. (Right) A Fifteenth Century
encapsulated reliquary of silver
gilt from Flanders, decorated
with a design of the Baptism of
Christ. *(By courtesy of the Louvre.)*
The Département des Objects
d'Art of the Louvre gave assur-
ance that the hasp or ring, portrayed in Father J. Braun's litho-
graph in his *magnum opus* on reliquaries, did originally exist but
disintegrated, was then badly
restored and therefore subsequently removed after Father
Braun's portrayal of it. The illus-
trator of this book has therefore
marked the ring's original whereabouts with a dotted line on the
modern photograph to indicate
the similarity between this circular capsule and the Talisman of
Charlemagne. To indicate the

general pattern and usage of such reliquaries as being suspendable or separable at will from the foot or 'stand', the Départément des Objects d'Art has kindly contributed a further print of a medallion, **IXc.** (below right), donated by M. le Baron de Rothschild, which originally hung from a chaplet.

X. (Above) Hanging pyx in the form of a dove, decorated with Limoges enamel. *(By courtesy of the Burrell Collection, Glasgow Art Gallery and Museum.)*

XI. (Right) Spanish Monstrance from Toledo, late Sixteenth Century. *(By courtesy of the Victoria and Albert Museum, London.)*

XII. (Left) Crucifixion. Crystal, from the Abbey of Saint-Denis. *(By courtesy of the British Museum, London.)*

XII. (Right) 'Le Feu Sacre à Jerusalem' by Eugene Alexis Giradet – early 19th Century.

often with the purest of motives. The Celt, in his own way, was as zealous a seeker after God as the Jew, but unlike Abraham he had not yet, at the time we are speaking of, heard the word of God wherein the command was given to substitute the ram for the human sacrifice.

With the spread of culture from Egypt in the second millenium B.C. two different rituals came into conflict. A good example of this is to be found in Ireland. The Firbolgs were the primitive men, who worshipped the giant forces of nature – the Formorians. The Firbolgs lit fire from their flint-bags. To them the flame was a living creature, which must be fed with fuel and with a share of their meat, and even on occasions with human flesh. We still talk today of the fire "dying" or of "feeding" it, as though it were a person. To the Ireland of the Firbolgs came the Milesians, bringing Pharaoh's daughter and the Cauldron of their god Dagda. Fire ceased to be the weird "red" animal, and became instead the emanation of the all-pervading sky-god. But unfortunately a new revelation of truth can never at once win free from the old faith. For centuries it remains cluttered up with the more primitive ritual, as is shown so clearly by the Apocryphal and largely pagan legends with which Christianity was burdened until at last one of the Church Councils threw out the Apocryphal New Testament while recognizing some of it as allegorical.

The entombment of the Grail-stone in winter was not itself a bad symbolism. As I have said, all mystery religions seem to have in common the need for a cave, a crypt, a tomb, a blind-folding, to emphasize that man lives in a world of darkness and ignorance before achieving the grade of an Illuminatus. "The people that walked in darkness have seen a great light: they that dwell in the land of the shadow of death, upon them hath the light shined." Thus Isaiah proclaims a deeply psychological truth and a yearning for the fulfilment of prophecy that illumination would eventually come.

Unfortunately instead of abiding in patience in the dark while awaiting revelation, man began to indulge a liking for the weird, the awesome, the awful, almost as children will tell ghost stories to each other in the dark to experience the shiver of fear down the spine, which is a kind of perverted desire to test courage, but can in adults lead to Satanism which eventually declares: "Evil be thou my good", and the flame degenerates into the fires of Hell.

It seems a pity that nearly all books so far written about Druidism are so strictly pigeon-holed into two classes. The first, much favoured in the 19th century, is based on the beauty and mysticism of Welsh Bardic verse, and the belief that all men shared something of the original and pure faith of Noah. Such authors jump wildly to conclusions, and amongst their various errors they fail to realize the very late date at which Gallic or Belgic Druids were officiating, compared with far earlier cultures of which archaeologists now have knowledge. The second and more modern school of thought is a natural reaction from the first. Annoyed by the imaginative flights of the last century, the latest authors see in the Druids no more than the witch-doctors of Gaul, who practised human sacrifice, and whose belief in an after-world was nothing but a primitive totemism. The truth surely lies between the two opinions, in so much as man has never been without an apprehension of God, but has fallen into error as to how best to serve Him.

Several books have been written within the last twenty years in an attempt to throw light on whether Caesar's statements regarding the Druids were correct: namely that the Druid priesthood was peculiar to Gaul and Britain; that Britain was the source of Druidism and the centre of their initiations; and that the German tribes had no Druids, but worshipped the sun, the moon and fire. That Britain probably was the principal centre of initiation because of a particularly impressive "Hades" being situated therein, I shall presently endeavour to show. As to the name "Druid" it seems to me a superfluous question as to what priests were called, for there was no place in Europe where men did not at one time or another practise the cult of fire descending from the sun through a crystal, glass or mirror. It is supposed that the priests of Britain and Gaul took their names of druids from "dru" meaning an oak-tree, because in the territories over which they held sway, the oak provided acorn-flour and fire: it was their Branstock. In southern countries the palm or the pine may have given its name to the priesthood, but the ritual of the fire-cult remained the same.

What then do we know for certain regarding the Druids of the first and second centuries in Gaul and Britain? They were sufficiently cultured to speak and write Greek, and classical references credit them with a firm belief in an after-life of a much happier and more definite kind than the miserable existence of the Shades in Pluto's kingdom. Welsh poetry, admittedly of a medieval period, frequently alludes to the fact that the Druids exhorted the people to be virtuous, courageous, and to avoid unjust and dishonourable dealing. Practically all the classical references assert that the Druids were Pythagoreans, and that they believed in some form of reincarnation. Modern authors have attempted to belittle this claim by arguing that no references to it are to be found in Celtic myth, other than the totemistic reincarnations of a man into a tree or beast. It seems to me unwise to assume that the educated writers of Greece and Rome, who knew the beliefs of Pythagoras, and who had first-hand opportunity of speaking with the Druids, would have identified the two beliefs without very good grounds. Be that as it may, the Druids certainly had a much more cheerful outlook towards death than their Roman neighbours, for Lucan writes: "And ye, ye Druids, now that the sword is removed, begin once more your barbaric rites and weird solemnities. To you alone is given knowledge, or ignorance, which ever it be, of the gods and power of heaven. Your dwelling is in the lair of the forest. From you we learn that the bourne of man's ghost is not the senseless grave, nor the pale realm of the monarch below: in another world his spirit survives still; death, if your lore be true, is but the passage to enduring life."

Those who wish to read all the classical references to Druids, and then to draw their own conclusions, will find Mr T.D. Kendrick's book, *The Druids*, excellent for this purpose. Alternatively, those who wish to study Druidism as

shown by the late Welsh Bards may find The *Mythology &
Rites of the British Druids* by Edward Davies helpful, for
though in his attempts to relate all ritual to Noah have suffered discredit, yet he gives a very good picture of what
ritual was actually practised.

Coupled with this firm belief in a next world, the classical
writers often refer to the barbaric rites of the Gallic
priesthood. The Druids, Caesar tells us, believed that only
human blood could blot out the sin of man.* They read
auguries from the entrails of their human victims, and
sometimes burned them alive in wicker cages. Nevertheless
by A.D. 50, and probably due to Roman influence, human
sacrifice had become, according to Pomponius Mela,
merely a ritual blood-letting.

There is hardly time here to discuss all the significance of
the ritual of the scapegoat. But I take this opportunity to
express my personal opinion that the desire to put sin upon
the head of another, man or beast, argues that man has
never been without a conscience and a sense of failure: a
feeling of guilt so heavy as to demand the forfeiture of his
life. Where he fell into error was in supposing that by
"borrowing" blood from his neighbour he could expiate
his own offence, for such "borrowing" only increases the
guilt, and, like a loan from a money-lender, the interest on
the original sum grows at such an alarming rate as to
become impossible of payment by human kind. The history of the ritual of the scapegoat should not, therefore, in
my view, be used as an argument against the beauty and
potency of Our Lord's sacrifice upon the Cross, for it
needed God Incarnate to make a full perfect, and sufficient
oblation in blood for the debt which mankind had been
laying up for untold centuries by the ghastly practice of
human sacrifice, apart from all other sins.

From the time of the coming of Egyptian culture to
Europe, it is very unlikely that the barbarian tribes indulged
in cannibalism, but it is possible, though not proved, that
the early flint-bag men did. Having said a word about the

---

* *Gallic War* Bk VI Chap. XVI.

scapegoat, it might be as well, therefore, to follow it up with a brief paragraph on this latter subject. Some years ago I listened with some impatience to a public discussion (I think it was on the Radio) talking about the cult of the Great Mother goddess and her dying son. When the speakers had reached a skilful peroration wherein cannibalism and the Eucharistic feast were associated, they seemed to indicate that the last word had been said. In fact they had failed utterly to touch on the question what cannibalism *is*, and what emotions it can arouse in man. It was always ritualistic, and almost never indulged in from appetite. It was no more than an innocent desire on the part of primitive man to take into himself the qualities which he knew he lacked. The great wisdom, courage and fair-mindedness, the prowess in battle or the skill in medicine, which distinguished the chief of the tribe, were qualities which his less heroic brethren longed to possess. It was a man's sense of something lacking in himself, and of a separation from the Fountain of all Being which was the motive behind such practice, and the emotion is a good one; only wrong in that man's ignorance led him to suppose that by eating his chief he could eat the chief's qualities.

As an instance of what I mean, let the reader walk up to the hilltops in spring-time and gaze at a really beautiful sunset. In nine cases out of ten his mouth will open, and a sigh issuing from his lips will bear witness that he has first taken a deep breath in his spontaneous and natural reaction of trying to take all the inexpressible beauty into himself, and to become one with it. In so much as he opened his mouth and breathed deeply, he is a cannibal, for he has shown his desire to absorb and engulf God and beauty; but I do not suppose that this thought will greatly disturb him.

Let us now examine what characteristics are required in an underground cave for it to be used in religious ritual as the entrance to the Kingdom of the Shades. First, its depths must proceed into the bowels of the earth *farther* than a man can follow them, for if at last he comes up against a rock face, his imagination can no longer be terrified by what might lie beyond. Then, if possible, the cave must be able to give out noises: the more awesome, the more will the place be identified with the abode of ghosts and "terrible awfuls". Now the only caves which can supply these characteristics easily are those formed by subterranean rivers. There is a point where the rocky roof meets the water, beyond which a man cannot wade without the certainty of drowning. Furthermore, the air pressure, caught in the channels by the varying level of the flood, will escape at intervals with a clap whose echoes reverberate in the caverns.

Lucan describes such a place and locates it at Marseilles, but it is more than probable that he is confusing the Druid Grove there with the British Hades, for Britain was the centre for inititation according to Caesar. According to Lucan, "A grove there was, untouched by men's hands from ancient times, whose interlacing boughs enclosed a space of darkness and cold shade, and banished the sunlight far above. No rural Pan dwelt there, no Silvanus, ruler of the woods, no nymphs; but gods were worshipped there with savage rites, the altars were heaped with hideous offerings, and every tree was sprinkled with human gore. On those boughs – if antiquity, reverential of the gods, deserves any credit – birds feared to perch, in those coverts wild beasts would not lie down; no wind ever bore down upon that wood, nor thunderbolt hurled from black clouds; the trees, even when they spread their leaves to no breeze, rustled of themselves. Water, also, fell there in abundance from dark springs. The images of gods, grim and rude, were uncouth blocks formed of felled tree-trunks. Their mere antiquity and the ghastly hue of their rotten timber struck terror; men feel less awe of deities worshipped under familiar forms; so much does it increase their sense of fear, not to know the gods whom they dread. Legend also told that often the *subterranean hollows quaked and bellowed*, that yew trees fell down and rose again, that the *glare of conflagration came from trees that were not on fire*, and that *serpents twined and glided from the stems*. The people never resorted thither to worship at close quarters, but left the place to the gods. For, when the sun is in mid-heaven or dark night fills the sky, the priest himself dreads their approach and fears to surprise the lord of the Grove."*

This account certainly does not seem in accord with other classical references that the Druids were Pythagoreans, and as Lucan admits that no one but the priest frequented the place, he may have used his imagination somewhat freely to write a popular "spine-chiller". But I have given the quotation in full to show that terrors were certainly conjured up by such a place and probably with some reason.

In the earlier editions of this book I admit to the temptation of considering the British "Hades" as the prototype of all such initiatory grottoes. Since then I have seen another such cave near Beirut, and I realise that there must be several such mouths of Hell in the Near East, Greece, and also in Crete where I long to see the Idaean cave where Zeus was reputed to be born and where lenses of rock crystal have been found†; also on the various coasts of the Mediterranean there must be other caverns. But it is still possible that the sea-traders were as impressed as I was at my first visit to Wookey Hole, and they could have brought back word that a particularly awful mouth of the abyss existed in the British Garden of the Hesperides, near Avalon, the Island of Apples. Indeed I feel sure that Lucan was describing Wookey rather than any grove at Marseilles.

These caverns are situated within a few miles of Glastonbury Tor, and are formed by the River Axe, as it winds its subterranean way out of the Mendip Hills. Its old name, Ochie Hole (now called Wookey) is supposed to come from an old British word "ogo", meaning a hole. Mr H.E. Balch, F.S.A., spent his life excavating and examining the caves of the Mendips, and his book *Mendip – The Great Cave at Wookey Hole*, published by Simpkin, Marshall Ltd., should be read by every student of the Grail legend.

The cave is approached from a semi-oval cove, a wooded gully not far from Wells and the Cheddar Gorge, which

---

* Lucan, *Civil War* Bk III. 399.

† *Zeus* by A.B. Cook. Vol II Appendix B. p 935 et seq.
Also *Nineveh & Babylon* by Austen Layard, p. 197.
Also *Antiquaries Journal* Vol VIII p. 327.

would have been thickly forested in ancient times. Out of the rock face flows the River Axe, and a little above and to the side of the arch of its exit is the entrance to an earlier river-bed. In the entrance gallery of this old bed Mr Balch found traces of occupation by men of Pleistocene times. From here a very steep, sloping, and narrow passage, known as the Hell Ladder, leads down into the bowels of the earth. You come then into the First Great Chamber, filled with little pools and stalactites, which gleam like crystal or ice in the glow of what is now electric, but of old would have been torch-light. In a central and arresting position in this large cavern is an almost jet-black stalagmite, peculiarly horrible in its resemblance to or caricature of a sphinx. For nature has poured out the features and breasts in lop-sided and misshapen surges of dripping limestone, so that at one moment the resemblance to a hideous female face and breasts is apparent, and at another is mercifully hidden. This natural image has been known since time immemorial as the Witch of Wookey. Mr Balch was of the opinion that it received divine honours in ancient times. To my mind there is little doubt that it is the image of dread Proserpine or her Celtic equivalent.

Beside her crouches the little stalagmite known as her "dog", and here her Cerberus received offerings of bones, which Mr Balch found. At the feet of the witch, steps have been cut down to the river, and here in the water Mr Balch found the human skulls which were probably overlooked by the Christian exorcists when they came to give the place its spiritual cleansing. In the left breast of the goddess, whose name in Grail legend was I think Brandigan, a socket has been hollowed, and the decomposed remains of wood which had been thrust into it, were discovered. This then, if I am right, was how the Celtic Vesta or Proserpine held her torch fastened in her bosom, and her cave, as we shall see, is none other than the Chapel Perilous. Round her have been found in the water coins and pottery dating from 100 B.C. to the 4th century of our era.

From the most ancient times there has existed a local legend of a wicked woman who lived in this cave, and who was changed into stone. Malory gives his account of the transformation in this fashion: "When the king awoke and missed his scabbard (possibly the sheath or golden setting of the sun-sword, the crystal), he was wondrous wroth, and asked who had been there. And they said his sister Queene Morgan had been there, and had put the scabbard under her mantell, and was gone." Arthur pursued her: "And when she saw she might not escape, she rode unto a lake thereby, and said, "Whatsoever becommeth of me, my brother shall not have this scabbard." And then she threw the scabbard in the deepest of the water, and it sunke, for it was so heavie of gold and precious stones. Then she rode into a valey where many great stones were. And when she saw that shee must needes be overtaken, she shop herself, horse and man, by enchantment, into a great marble stone."

It will be seen here that Arthur was credited with taking part in a pagan ritual, but I do not believe this to have been the case. That he was a Christian will be shown more fully later, but the following account gives some evidence of his struggling to abolish the remnants of the heathen cult. In the story of Kulhwch and Olwen from the *Mabinogion:*, Kulhwch is daunted by the task put upon him of obtaining the blood of the black witch, the daughter of the white witch, who lived in a cave at the head-waters of the Stream of Sorrow, on the confines of Hell. Arthur undertakes the task, and hacks the witch in two. Mr Balch found what is probably the skeleton of this wretched creature in the entrance of Wookey cave, with the right femur buried under debris twenty feet away. Beside her were the bones of her tethered goats, her milking pot, her sacrificial knife and, most curious of all, the traditional witch's ball, which had been fashioned by primitive tools from a lump of stalagmite. Thus there are two legends which have become confused: the one of the goddess, and the other of her worshipper. The remains of the latter bear mute witness to the Nemesis which overtakes those who will not accept a new and more spiritual revelation but cling to their out worn ritual, even though they must resort to fashioning a useless "grail" out of grey limestone. For, by Arthur's day, all that was good in the old religion, including the crystal itself, had been transferred to the Church, and all that remained was the black bread of evil magic, which the good Phoenix (one of the many symbols of Christ) strikes mercilessly from the hand of mankind. This head-water of the Stream of Sorrow is referred to in Grail legend as Mount Dolorous.

From the First Great Chamber of Brandigan one proceeds into a cavern seventy-five feet high. This has always been known as the "Hall", not I think of the Fisher King, for the Fisher derives I am fairly sure from a Judaeo-Christian source, but a pagan Hall of Hades, of Pluto, used for initiatory purposes. It is jewelled with gleaming stalactites and stalagmites. Beyond it lies the Third Chamber, a low wide cavern always known as the witch's parlour, whose sandy shore borders the subterranean river. The Axe flows into the Parlour from a low arch, and here we begin to understand the necessity of crossing the Styx in the Ferryman, Charon's boat. For if we are to enter that low arch and penetrate into the inner chamber, we must either paddle a small boat, or wait until the flood levels have subsided sufficiently to show the old stepping-stones. On the other hand, if flood level is too high, our boat will be crushed against the roof of the arched tunnel, and we shall be swept away and drowned in some ghastly black channel beyond the reach of help. Nevertheless, men did enter here and this inner chamber has borne from ancient times the name of the "Holy Hole". I believe it to have been the winter shrine of the talismanic crystal stone or possibly mirror. It will be seen now why the draw-bridge of the Grail castle disappears from time to time, and why so often the Grail hero is either fetched by a fishing boat, or half-drowned by the demon water-horse.

At the present time there is no landing place in the Holy Hole, but Mr Balch thought that there may have been dry channels in the days before modern drainage of land increased the level of the river. No one can now follow the course of the river beyond this inner chamber without diving apparatus, and the attempts at diving have proved the Chapel Perilous worthy of its name.

We now come to Mr Balch's description of the noises that bubbles of air can cause in these awful subterranean hollows. The fame of this phenomenon had certainly spread abroad in the 3rd century, for Clement of Alexandria wrote thus: "Those who have composed histories say that in Britain is a certain cave at the side of the mountain, and at the entrance a gap; when, then, the wind blows into the cave and is drawn on into the bosom of the interior, a sound is heard as of the clashing of numerous cymbals." The same sounds of these clashing cymbals are heard to this day in Wookey, also hammering noises, as though the dwarfs of Niflheim were forging Odin's "Ring". Once Mr Balch heard such strange gurglings, as of a man struggling and shouting in the water, that he rushed to the bank below the Witch's image, fearful that some visitor had been sucked beneath the arch of the river. But there was no one. On the roof of the Parlour the hooves of a galloping horse have been heard, though the distance to the hill-top above precludes all possibility of its being a natural beast. This is important, for the water-horse which the Grail hero unwittingly mounts (the Egyptian Typhonian monster or Celtic Each-Uisg, our old acquaintance, the Hippo of the Nile) plays an important role in nearly every version of the Grail legend. Lastly, Mr Balch gave me personally an account of what he alone of all men then living heard, for his companion was later killed in the Great War of 1914. The two were standing together in the "Hall", when the sound of a confused murmur of voices came to them. Believing the voices to come from a party of tourists, they waited with the kindly intention of adding to the interest of the visitors by describing the excavations at first-hand. The murmur grew to a clamour, then to a roar, and then such a thunderous noise enveloped them, that they were left clinging like little children together. The sudden silence was painful, and no disturbance of water or air ensued to explain the strange occurence. It is hardly to be wondered at that Perceval fainted in the Chapel Perilous!

That at certain festivals the sacra of the Greek Mysteries were hidden underground is well known.* But I think I may be the first to suggest that one particular symbol was commonly and invariably entombed by all the peoples of Europe and the Near East: namely the vessel or cauldron by which fire was kindled from the sun. Hesiod's *Theogony* is the earliest account of the Greek gods, and in it we find that a golden vessel is periodically brought out of Hades, filled with water from the Styx, as a sacred symbol on which the gods take irrevocable oaths. First he describes a terrible female monster in Hades, so like our chimerical stalagmite of Wookey's Witch that again one is forced to wonder from what source the legend of this female monster originated. She is nowise like to mortal gods, he says, but dwells in a hollow cavern: "the divine Echidna – half nymph, with dark eyes and fair cheeks; and half, on the other hand, a serpent huge and terrible and vast – speckled and flesh devouring 'neath caves of sacred earth". Then in another passage he goes on to describe Hades: "There in front stand the *resounding* mansions of the infernal god, of mighty Hades and awful Persephone besides: and a fierce dog keeps guard in front." The three heads of this Cerberus may well have derived their origin from the particular shape of some stalagmite in one or other cavern. Hesiod goes on: "There too dwells a goddess odious to immortals, dread Styx, eldest daughter of back-flowing Ocean; and apart from the gods she inhabits renowned dwellings vaulted by huge rocks; and round about on all sides they are strengthened to heaven by silver column (Stalactites, no doubt in one or other cavern used for initiatory purposes) "And seldom goes the fleet-footed daughter of Thaumas, Iris, on a message over the broad back of the sea, namely, when haply strife and quarrel shall have arisen among the immortals: and whosoever, I wot, of them that hold Olympian dwellings, utters falsehood, then also Jove is wont to send Iris to bring from far in a golden ewer the great oath of the gods, the renowned water, cold as it is, which also runs

* *Prolegomena to the Study of Greek Religion*, by Jane Harrison.

down from a steep and lofty rock... Whosoever of the
immortals that occupy the top of snowy Olympus, shall
have offered this as a libation, and sworn over it a false oath,
lies breathless until the completion of a year, nor ever
comes near the repast of nectar and ambrosia, but also lies
breathless and speechless on a strown couch, and a baneful
stupor overshrouds him."*

Here we have a picture of the defunct son-of-the-Sun
lying upon a bier, perhaps the bier which appears so frequently with the Grail, while the new hero succeeds to
office. Apuleius, in the *Golden Ass*, tells how the cruel
mother Venus makes Psyche descend into Hades to fetch
water from the Styx in a jar of polished crystal. We now
know that the pearl-rimmed cauldron of the Celts was
associated with Hades (Awen), and we come now to the
metrical preface to Chrestien's *Conte du Graal*. Whoever
wrote it, and the preface may not have been by Chrestien
himself, explains that the whole purport of Arthur's gather-
ing together the knights of the Round Table was to
reinstitute the custom whereby a maiden issued from a
grotto with a golden cup. That this is probably a calumny
upon a Christian king need not concern us here. Rightly or
wrongly, legend identified Arthur with a solar cult, and our
task is to study the cult with which legend credited him. The
poet explains the custom as follows: "These maidens dwell
in caverns – which the old tale elsewhere calls grottoes –
hewn out by more than mortal art, in the depths of the
forest." They were accustomed to issue forth with a golden
cup and with food and drink for the wayfarer. "For then, I
trow, there came out of the grotto a maiden – they could not
have wished for one more fair –in her hand she bore a
golden chalice." But once long ago, a wicked king ravished
one of these maidens and took her cup away. (Could this be
a Roman memory of the son of Tarquin who ravished a Vestal? At that early period, Vestals did not serve thirty but only
five years, from the ages of six to ten, and were subsequently
married. Lucretia was happily married when violated by

* Hesiod's *Theogony*, Bohn's Classical Library. 28 et seq.

Sextus, and consequently committed suicide because of the dishonour. Both her shame and her rejection of dishonour became forever renowned in Rome. Whether she had served as a Vestal in adolescence is a matter of speculation). Since when the maidens had never more issued from their caverns. The peers of the Round Table, "when they heard the tale related were at once filled with a desire to win back the grottoes", and they prayed God, "that he might recover the grottoes and restore them to those hands which formerly possessed them."

I will give now my theory as to the disentombing of the symbol of Spring, and we will see whether the various legends support my supposition. As at the grove of Nemi, the man appointed to be priest-king fights with and slays his predecessor, and, using a real sword, he decapitates him. The so-called "Druids" have already extinguished all fires except the one torch, the special brand of the late king, which the stalagmite Brandigan holds in her breast. The new hero lays the head of his predecessor at the Witch's feet (where Mr. Balch found the human skulls) and the late king's torch is then extinguished, either by the hero or the Druid. The hero must penetrate to the "Hall" (I prefer to call it that of Gwyn or Pluto in pagan times rather than that of the Fisher-King of Judaeo-Christian legend), and there enquire concerning the use and symbolic meaning of the talismanic crystal. Having acquired this knowledge he must then penetrate to the inner chamber or Holy Hole, and his journey will not be made easy, for it is a test of his courage. Having gained the inner chamber, he must unveil the talisman and take possession of it; and then at last bear it forth re-veiled from the eyes of the unworthy, and go in procession up the Tor for the rekindling of a new fire.

The local traditions speak of the yearly battle between Gwyn ap Nudd and Gwythr for the possession of a maiden. This might of course mean no more than the celestial battle between Gwyn, who was a Lord of the Underworld, and Gwythr, a hero whose name may derive from "Gwydr" a variant of *vitrine* or glass. The fight might only refer to the glass-holder's struggle to penetrate the obscurities of the

Underworld. In the preface to the *Grand Saint Graal*, the
monk is bidden to seek his lost book about the Grail by first
going to a great stone in the plains of a place called Walescog, which the poet wrongly supposes to be in Norway, for
it is obviously the "ogo" of Wales – Wookey. In A.D. 700 it
may well have been held by Norse settlers, and the story of
Beowulf suggests that it was, for the Danes had settled at
that time along the Bristol Channel, and the fight of
Beowulf and Grendel in a subterranean cavern could
perhaps refer to the ritual of Wookey, whose Witch could be
Grendel herself, demanding human sacrifice. The monk of
the *Saint Graal* is told that he will recognize Walescog by the
Fountain of Tears in the Vale of the Dead, where the famous
battle between the two best knights of the world took place.
And there he will find a strange beast, part sheep, part dog,
part wolf – yet another allusion to the chimerical stalagmite.
It would be pleasant to suppose that the battle took place
between the forces of light and darkness, spring and winter,
only, but there is, I fear, too much evidence to the contrary.
The tale of *Sir Gawayne and the Grene Knight* (who lives near
the Wirral, a small hill beside Glastonbury Tor) is a story in
point. The Green Knight lays bare his neck to Gawain's
sword in return for Gawain's promise to undergo a similar
fate in a year's time.

The quenching of the king's torch signified assumption
of divine and royal honours by his successor, together with
the talisman and a new fire, but alas, brought its conse-
quence of the slayer eventually being slain. The following
account from the *Prose Perceval* shows how gradually there
was instituted a custom of substituting a less valuable member of the tribe for the king who had proved to be a wise
leader (even Grendel could no longer "touch the throne").
The story from the *Prose Perceval* concerns Lancelot. The
reader should imagine a palisade of megalithic stones,
hung with painted hides, in place of the palace and tapes-
tries provided by the medieval poet. And the city which is
all aflame, and whose flames Lancelot has power to
extinguish, if only he will accept the crown, is not of
course a burning city but a sacred fire within a city, whose

king must always perish at the end of the year.

"Up at the casements of the great mansions, noble ladies and damsels give utterance to their joy and thankfulness, saying to one another, "See – they are bringing the new king! Now the fire will die as the year draws to its close." But for the most part "Ah! God! they say, "what loss it is, that so handsome a knight should perish thus!" "Nay be silent," say the others, "there will be much cause for comfort, since by his death this great city of ours will be saved; and from that day forward the whole kingdom will pray for his soul's repose ..." Lancelot found the great chamber draped and carpeted with precious silks, and the lords of the city arrayed ready to do him homage. This, however, he vehemently refused to accept, and set forth that he would never be their king or their lord on such terms. At this moment behold a dwarf... the dwarf calls upon the lords of the city: "My lords, since this knight will not be king, I am willing to reign in his stead..." with that they set the crown on the dwarf's head, and Lancelot took his leave. The noble ladies and damsels averred that he had no wish to be king only to die so soon." Poor Dwarf! Poor scapegoat!

In the earlier editions of this book I quoted fully two stories from the *Poetic Edda, The Lay of Skirnir,* and the *Lay of Day-Spring and Menglod*, but because there was total confusion in ancient times between ice and crystals, the latter being, as was thought, a permanently petrified form of the first, I have decided to pass over these lays, for basically they concern the sun-god wooing the earth to life in spring-time from her imprisonment by the frost giants of Scandinavia and Iceland, and the only point worthy of recording is that the earth, the maiden Menglod, had, like Hathor or Freyja or the third Arthurian Queen to visit Perceval at court, a wonderful necklace to which one of the Queens drew the attention of Perceval and said that it was connected with the mystery of the Grail. Well, mountains such as the Alps, Caucasian heights and perhaps parts of Scandinavia are the sources of the best rock crystals so the identity of the mysterious necklace must remain undetermined until perhaps we meet with another significance in Judaic tradition.

We come now to the account of the Chapel Perilous where pagan and Christian custom mix and are blended, but Christian symbolism triumphs. It will be remembered that Lancelot entered a haunted chapel, and removed Christ's grave-clothes: that is to say the coverings of the chalice, the veil and the corporal (in its burse) which can be seen as representing the grave-clothes of Christ. The vessel thus unveiled is not described, but Lancelot issued from the chapel with a new "sword".

Perceval pays two visits to the Chapel Perilous. On the first occasion he sees a corpse upon the altar, and before it burns one candle and one only.

Devant lui .I. cierges ardoit
Ne plus ne mains n'en i avoit.

Then he beholds a great brightness – "Si vit une moult grant clarté" – but he knew not whence it proceeded. Then came a terrible clap of thunder, as though the place would tumble into ruins:

Uns escrois qui tel noise fist
Que il li samble que caîst
La capele et debrisast toute.

Then from behind the altar came a black hand, which extinguished the candle:

Une noire mains jusqu'al couste
S'aparut derrière l'autel;
La candoile ki ardoit cler
Estaint ensi c'on vit goute n'i.

Perceval full of awe and dread, leaves the chapel. Later when he is riding through a wood, he meets one of the maidens of the Grail Castle. He tells her of how he has seen a *burning tree* and of his adventure in the haunted chapel, and she explains to him that these mysteries concern the Grail:

Ciertes, ce dist la damoisele,
Sire, cou est senefiance
Del saint Gréal et de la lance.

But she will say no more, for she is under pledge of
secrecy:

Mais Dieu ne place que jà isse
De ma bouce nule parole

On the occasion of Perceval's second and successful visit to
the Grail castle, he asks the Rich Fisher concerning these
mysteries. The Fisher-King replies that more than four
thousand men have perished in the Chapel Perilous, which
was built by Brangemore (another name for Brandigan) and
that she is buried beneath the altar. The king explains that
to exorcise the evil and overcome the Black Hand, Perceval
must take the veil from a shrine, dip it in holy water, and
sprinkle the chapel:

Biaus dous amis ki combatroit,
Fait li rois, à cele main noire
Et puis presist en .I. aumoire
.I. voile blanc qui est mis
K'en sa garde a li anemis,
Cele persone maléoite,
Et puis, en l'eve béneoite
Le boutast sans trestour,
Et arrousast tresout entour
Et autel at cors et capele,
Par celui Dieu que on apièle
Jà mais nus n'i aventroit
Mais hardi estre convenroit
Qui à la main vorroit combatre;

Perceval sets out upon the adventure. Through storm and
rain and wind he rides through the forest, ties his horse to a
tree outside the chapel, and enters. The dead knight, and
the candle are there as before, but this time the Black Hand
issues from a window:

Que d'une fenestre se boute
Une mains noire jusqu'al couste,

M. Potvin explains in his writing of the *Conte du Graal* that
"puis" should not be translated as a "well" but as a
"grotto" – that is to say a cave. As soon as the Black Hand
has extinguished the flame, the vault takes on a leaden hue,
and Perceval finds it so dark that he might, says the poet,
have been in a cave – a most significant description, for
there is little doubt that that was just exactly where he
was!

Dès que li cierges fu estains,
Devint li cius torblés et tains;
Il ne vit laiens goute puis,
Nient plus que s'il fust en .I. puis;

Perceval then draws his sword, and the terrible combat with
the Black Hand begins. Awful noises are heard, as though
thunderbolts are being hurled from the vault. The Devil,
for the Black Hand is that of Satan himself, warns Perceval
that unless he withdraws, his body shall lie upon the altar
to-morrow. Each time that Perceval makes the sign of the
Cross, the Devil answers with such claps of thunder as
would have killed with terror a less heroic knight. Perceval
cannot approach the veil, because the Devil will not let him
pass. At last the good knight makes the sign of the Cross
with his sword, and the most fearful noise yet heard beats
him to his knees, half fainting:

Et maintenant lièvé .I. espart,
Et del ciel uns tounoiles part,
En une effoudre perellouse
Si très grans at si mervellouse
C'onques si grans ne fu veue;
À Piercheval tourble le vue,
Et cai, el moustier pasmés;
Mais n'en doit pas estre blasmés.

But the Devil has been overcome by this last Sign of the Cross. For easier reading I will give a translation of what follows. "In the precincts, close by the altar, Perceval lay prostrate a goodly space, bereft of his senses, so sorely had the falling thunderbolt stunned and bewildered him. Returning to his dwelling (the body), he went with all haste to the shrine, drew it towards him, and opened it. There, within the shrine, he discovered a vessel of gold; and without stay or hindrance took out the white veil, just as the king, who had revealed all that was to be, had shown him." He sprinkles the precincts with the veil dipped in holy water, and puts back the golden vessel into its shrine. Then he looks at the dead knight upon the altar, and thinks that no one could recognize him, so black and ugly is his face. Thereafter, exhausted by his initiatory ordeal, Perceval lies down to sleep. "In that place he lay until morning; for no light had appeared there, nor did it, until the very moment when day began to dawn. For on that day was lit the candle which has never since been extinguished, nor shall it be until the world comes to an end. There, within the midmost chapel, the worthy Perceval fell asleep until morning, when the sun's rays appeared therein, clear and ruby red. At that Perceval awoke, bewildered by the radiance, and saw the candle burning. Long he remained thus, gazing upon the lighted candle, and marvelling whence it had been lit; for he was well aware, he knew and saw indeed that it had been kindled by the hand of God".

When Perceval leaves the caverns of Wookey, he has won his name, which means – so Wolfram von Eschenbach assures us – to Pierce-the-Vale, that is to say an initiate who has passed through the Vale of the Dead.

We have in this account two conflicting ideas: an initiation wherein Perceval wonders at the power of the Grail to bring down fire-from-heaven; and the later legend of how Wookey Hole was exorcised by a Christian monk, a local tale which we shall come to in the chapter dealing with Christian times.

It should perhaps be added that Lancelot's adventures in La Doloreuse Garde, described as situated near the River

Humber but more likely to be near the Roman Wall, are yet another version of an initiatory experience. He was led to a chapel in which was a door leading to a cave. The keys of the enchantment were in the cave. As he entered, the earth quaked and noise filled the air. Two knights of copper, holding huge "swords" (almost certainly they were originally the brands held at the entrance of a Mithraeum) were posted at the entrance of the next chamber. In front of another door was an evil-smelling deep well, from which ghastly noises arose. On the opposite side of the water was an ugly monster with a black head and flaming breath. Lancelot was victorious and obtained the keys, wherewith he was able to open the perilous coffer. A whirlwind arose from it, as if all the devils had been freed. The coffer is reminiscent of Pandora's box. I think the original ordeal of Wookey has become confused with a much later Mithraic ritual, possibly connected with the Mithraeum near the Roman Wall.

8 THE ORACULAR HEAD AND THE WOUNDED THIGH

Brandigan, the stalagmite Witch of Wookey, is none other than the Loathly Damsel, who supports the head of a dead knight in her lap, and who reproached Perceval because, on his first visit to the "Hall" of the Grail King, alias in this case Gwyn or Pluto, he had not enquired concerning the mysteries.

We must now face, unpleasant as it is, the question of why the dead knight's face in the Chapel Perilous was black, and what is the significance of all the oracular heads of which legend tells. That of Osiris was preserved at Abydos, and that of Orpheus at Lesbos, both sanctuaries being oracular. King Saul's head was hung in the temple of Dagon by the Philistines. Odin was accustomed to consult the decapitated head of the dwarf Mimir. Bran, the hero of the story of Branwen's cauldron, was decapitated by his followers, but his head continued to utter for many years. Cuchulain's father's head had the same property. In the *Mabinogion* Peredur sees a head carried in a dish in procession in the castle of the Lame King. In the *Grand Saint Graal*, Joseph sees an angel issue from the ark of the Grail bearing a head. In the *Conte du Graal* the head of the Grail King's enemy, Partinal, is placed by Perceval on a pike above the Grail castle's tower. Cernunnos, the stag-headed god of the Gauls, is the Divine youth himself. In Greece he was called Actaeon, and in Scotland the Hynde Knight or Old Horny, meaning the Devil. No doubt some head-dress of antlers was worn by the Divine Youth, dating from the days when the reindeer was man's principal meat and totem beast. Indeed there are still folk-dances where the male dancers wear these horns in some English villages. Christian legend transferred these horns to the Devil, because of their fear and hatred of the old abuses.

All this may not be as sinister as it at first appears. I have heard it suggested that the Celtic vessel known as the cauldron of the Head of Hades, and the cauldron of Branwen, which restored men to life, may have been an iron-cooking vessel in which the Egyptian or Phoenician settlers had taught the flint-bag men to mix the substances necessary for a crude form of embalment. The cauldrons of Celtic myth, which restore men to life, could be of this category, and should not be confused with the pearl-rimmed metal mirror, which supplies inexhaustible riches (of sunlight). The habit of preserving an oracular head seems to have originated in Egypt. But the story of Osiris and his dismemberment will lose some of its horrors if we try to realise the pathetic irony of the tale.

In pre-Dynastic times there arrived in the Nile valley two strangers, Osiris and his wife, Isis, who was later identified with the earth goddess and Hathor. They were reputed to come from the West, perhaps from some lost Atlantis, or more likely from the region of the Sahara in its prehistoric era of fertility and green vegetation. According to Jewish legend as recorded in Genesis, Ham, son of Noah, went to dwell in Egypt and certainly gave his name, Khem to that land. Ham could have been identified at least in legend with the Osiris who taught the prehistoric Egyptians to grow corn, while his wife, Isis, taught them to spin, and he and Isis persuaded the original inhabitants to give up the evil customs of their pre-historic religious ritual. But just *because* he was such a good and holy and wise leader, all the more would his body be powerful, thought the simple folk, to fertilize their fields, and his head would bring them counsel. So they dismembered him; and in tears the queen, Isis, went forth throughout the land to recover the remains and give them reverent burial. I have given the story of Osiris as it is generally understood, but I am not at all sure that we have understood it correctly. The enemy Set or Typhon, who slew him, may have symbolized death in the abstract, and the simple folk may have dismembered his body *after* his *natural* death, and preserved his relics, just as the bones of the saints were dissevered and preserved and distributed around Europe.

The relic of a saint or an Osiris can give the possessor power, and a sense of power is always in danger of being abused by the holder of it. So we must accept that nearly all religious legends include the preservation of oracular heads. The Grail legend is no exception, and heads appear in many of the knight's adventures. Because of the total confusion by de Borron between the adventures of Joseph, the son of the Patriarch Jacob, with those of St. Joseph of Arimathea, it is probable that the head issuing from an ark in the vicinity of Egypt is the head of Joseph in his sarcophagus which Moses carried back to Israel together with the remains of Jacob and accompanying the Ark of the covenant at the time of the Exodus.

The head swimming in blood in a dish is described in the very pagan Mabinogion of Peredur, where the spear with its effluence appears, but there is no mention of the Grail, although snake-stones and Druids can be inferred. It is unlikely to have been a memory of the Baptist's head, as this was reverently interred in a shrine in the Christian church at Damascus (which later became a mosque) and is highly venerated there by Moslems. I have seen a Moslem praying beside this shrine wrapt in silent contemplation for more than an hour, for Islam greatly reveres the Baptist.

To my mind the withered head of St. Catherine of Siena, preserved in a glass case in the church of her Dominican convent at Siena, gives me the shudders and a desire to give it a decent burial. The skulls of human sacrifice in the pool of the Witch of Wookey I find less repugnant for at least they dated from pagan days, whereas St. Catherine of Siena is the intrepid 14th century historical saint who journeyed to Avignon to persuade the virtually imprisoned Pope to return to Rome and his duties there.

Much more important to our quest than the "head" is what explanation to give for the lameness of the Fisher-

King. Robert Graves postulated a theory that all demi-gods were lame and he was acute enough to name a list: Achilles, Vulcan, Adonis, Ulysses, Oedipus, Krishna, all at one time or another wounded in the leg or lower limb. Also, as he pointed out, it is prophesied in Genesis at the expulsion of Adam and Eve that the serpent shall bruise the heel of the woman's seed, meaning Christ. But this theory leads nowhere. I prefer that of Professor Holmes, the Professor of Romance philology in the University of North Carolina. He held, as I have already explained but now wish to repeat here, that Chrestien de Troyes was a converted Jew from the famous rabbinical school of Rashi at Troyes; and that the Fisher-King's Hall, once we swing from Celtic paganism into Judaeo-Christian thought, is a memory, a symbol of Solomon's temple. The Lame King is Jacob, with his black cap and purple fringed mantle (in accordance with Mosaic custom for priestly garments: Num.XV.38). The vital question which all the Grail heroes fail at first to ask at the King's supper, is the still current custom at the Jewish feast of Passover in which the youngest member of the family must ask the head of the family: "Why is this night different to all other nights?". Then the head of the family has the duty and opportunity to explain the whole story of the Exodus: how Israel was enslaved in Egypt and issued forth under God's protection. Failure to ask this question might explain how the knowledge of the Urim and its stand, the Thummim, came to be lost during the Exile to Babylon, so that after the Exile no Jew knew what exactly such oracular objects had been, unless some hidden sect, such as some of the Cabbalists, still preserved the secret in silence.

Far from Miss Weston's theory that the cure of the Lame King was connected with the injured virility of a spring-time demi-god, king of the tribe, whose virility once repaired would ensure the regeneration of the vegetation and corn, is the theory of Professor Holmes, which I support, namely that the land of the Fisher King is the "Wasteland", that is to say Israel, as described by Isaiah VI.11 and LX1.4. and Jeremiah XL1V.22, who both prophesy that Israel shall become a Wasteland.

Again I am in accord with Professor Holmes when he holds that the mysterious old man, father-figure to the Lame King, who dwells in the inmost chamber, of which we never have a sight, is no other than Jacob's father or grandfather, more likely the latter, in other words Abraham. To him the Grail maiden takes the Sacrament, one Host only each day, on which he subsists without other food. An impossible idea chronologically? Not if we believe Christ's words (John VIII 56-58):

"Abraham rejoiced to see my day... before Abraham was, I am". Can one not therefore infer that during Our Lord's period in Limbo between the Crucifixion and the Resurrection, Abraham did indeed meet and rejoice with the long-expected Messiah, and that the old man's reception of the Sacrament in the Grail castle is symbolic rather than actual, for says Grail legend, "he is as one dead". Commentators have concluded that the Lame King's wound concerned injury to his genitals. It is perfectly true that the genitals, being a sign of the Covenant, were considered sacred to touch when taking a solemn oath, for Jacob's son, Joseph took such an oath under the "thigh" of his dying father when he swore that Jacob's body should be taken from Egypt to the family burial cave in Israel (Gen.X-LVII.29). But there has never been any suggestion in Jewish tradition that Jacob's extraordinary wrestling with an angel wounded his genitals or robbed him of virility, though various commentators have jumped to the conclusion that the Fisher King's wound "parmi les haunches" more or less castrated him.

The story in Genesis is a very curious one and worth further examination here. Jacob's wrestling feat takes place beside the ford of the Jabbok rivulet (Gen.XXXII22). Scripture does not say that it was an angel who appeared there to Jacob, for the word in Hebrew means no more than "messenger", and can be interpreted at your choice as either human or divine, but in this case it is stated quite definitely that it was a *man* who confronted Jacob. My own interpretation is this: In his youth Jacob, a possible "sensitive" in the making, but a failure as far as ethics and honour were concerned, did not behave admirably. He cheated his twin brother Esau of his birthright by a rather nasty trick. Then, fearing vengeance, he ran away. Only when he dreamt of the ladder to heaven with the angels of God ascending and descending did he "come to himself". Eventually be became a rich shepherd-king in the north, while his twin established himself as a powerful king of armed forces in the south, in Edom in the locality of Petra. At last Jacob, homesick, wants to return with his wives and his flocks to his old home, but he is conscience-stricken at having cheated his brother, and fearful of the much more powerful army that Esau, now king of Edom, can raise against him. So Jacob sends his wives and flocks to cross the river Jabbok to comparative safety, and himself stays behind to meet his twin brother privately, the twin who was the companion of his childhood, and issues an invitation to a "show down": a wrestling match between the two, who as boys must often have ragged, wrestled, sparred, and "made it up", as all little boys do; a match this time in which honour would be saved and reconciliation effected without loss of face. Only *after* the wrestling did Jacob claim that he had seen the face of God in his adversary. Medieval artists, faced with the difficulty that "no man has seen God", and that the Absolute and Ultimate Godhead cannot be represented in any material fashion, resort to the supposition that Christ appeared out of his time and took God the Father's place, and they portray a repulsive fight between Christ and Jacob reminiscent of an exhibition of Karate in which kicks and fisticuffs are only too evident. But when on the next day Jacob meets Esau publicly for an inter-tribal reconciliation, he greets his brother with exactly the same words he used to describe his wrestling partner: "I have seen thy face as though I had seen the face of God." To me this indicates that Jacob's combatant on the previous night was Esau himself. But Jacob, though preserving "face" and effecting reconciliation, has paid the price of the fight in pain, because forever after he halted upon his thigh, for his hip joint was injured. But no rabbinical tradition has ever existed to suggest that his genitals suffered. This is pure invention on the part of the commentators on the Grail legend.

Before exploring alternative possibilities regarding the lameness of the Fisher King, it might be as well here to complete Professor Holmes studies in his *New Interpretation of Chrestien's Conte del Graal*, with his two further suggestions: first that the Golden Pot of Manna, known to be kept in the Ark of the Covenant prior to the Exile to Babylon, was the Grail. With this I disagree for I do not believe the Golden Pot to have contained Manna. Modern scientific study of species believes Manna to have been some form of edible fungus such as mushroom. Moses expressly forbade the Israelites to retain it for more than a day for it bred worms and stank thereafter (Ex.XVI. 19). So I really cannot believe that a shredded powder of decayed fungus was accorded a golden pot in the ark. I feel sure it is a euphemism for the Urim containing the ambrosia of light, the Grail. Secondly Professor Holmes suggests that Aaron's rod, by tradition passed from Adam to all the Jewish patriarchs in turn, could not be pulled from the ground save by Moses, who knew the name of God engraved upon it and uttered the name. He compares this to Excalibur, and when in a further chapter of my book we meet with the "sun's staff" in Egyptian ritual, it is very likely that the Professor is correct, though he never realised that Excalibur was a brand, a burning brand, nor does he associate, as I do, the Golden Pot of Manna with the crystal Urim, source of the ambrosia of light so beloved of all immortals and of mortals alike.

I have left until last theories which in my earlier editions of this book I did not favour and now favour even less since Professor Holmes published his views: First, The Emperor Justin of Byzantium, contemporary of King Arthur, was historically suffering from an incurable spear thrust in his thigh, and had to depute all authority to his nephew, Justinian. Secondly, as we have seen, the sunbeam of Horus/Rê wounds at dawn the northern constellation of the "Thigh", which we call the Plough. Thirdly, Dionysus, reborn from the "thigh" of Zeus, may have been identical with the fire born from the cylix-type cup, which is similar in shape to the acetabulum of the pelvic socket of the thigh-bone, that is to say, concave. Perhaps the mirror known to be sacred to Dionysus was of silver, cup-shaped and reflective: fourthly, the Rich Fisher might be none other than the Egyptian god Thoth. He was the god of wisdom, had charge of the moon's calendar and of the missing eye of Horus, which just might have been the sun's crystal, and he invented writing. In the Fields of the Blessed he weighed men's hearts in the balance against the feather of Truth and acted as the Recording angel to Osiris, King of the Dead. He became in Greece Hermes, and in Rome Mercury, and was the god of riches, from which the word merchant and merchandise derives. His sacred symbol was the Ibis, and he is portrayed in ancient Egypt as having the head of an Ibis on the body of a man. Now the Ibis is a wader who stands for hours on one leg to do his fishing in the Nile, so it is not impossible that the Rich Lame Fisher, High Priest of the Egyptian mysteries is Thoth.

Nevertheless I prefer Professor Holmes' theory when we remember the words of Jeremiah (XXX) regarding Israel: "Thy bruise is incurable and thy wound grievous. There is none to plead thy cause, that thou mayest be bound up: thou hast no healing medicines." Yet in the day of redemption, "I will restore health unto thee and I will heal thy wounds, saith the Lord".

9 The Fish of the Fisher-King

I have already said that there was a custom of blindfolding before Illumination in the majority of Mystery religions, including the Freemasons. Herodotus gives an account of a Pharaoh, Rhamsinitus, who entered a temple thus blind-folded, and played a game of dice (similar to chess) with the goddess of the Underworld,[*] just as did Perceval in the cas-tle of the fairy lady, where at last he flung the pieces into the moat, perhaps the circular Oceanus surrounding the earth, the "pieces" taking the place of the stars in heaven. The absolute and ultimate Godhead of the Egyptians could not, in accord with Jewish belief, be represented in any form whatever, according to M. Renouf in the Hibbert Lectures in 1879,[†] but it must be remembered that the Egyptians used picture-writing, and would have been forced to write the name of God or his semi-divine angelic servants in pic-tures, such as Horus with the head of a hawk and Thoth with the head of an Ibis. Such symbolism is sometimes more impressive or at least more mysterious than the occasionally banal and uninspiring statues of Apollo, Her-mes, or the Eros which adorns Piccadilly Circus. Quoting from M. Renouf again: "Osiris found the soul of Rê, and they embraced each other, and became as one soul in two souls." As Rê he ruled the visible world from his solar bark and as Osiris, the Pharaoh who had been done to death by Typhon, he ruled the Kingdom of the Underworld, into

* Herodotus Bk II. 122.
† Hibbert Lectures of 1879 p. 113.

which the sun apparently sank at night. Horus, who rose like the bright sun from the crystal lotus-cup, is like Brahma, the dew. The dew itself is feminine, watery, akin to the Chinese Yin principle, but it holds the sunlight, and Horus is both the son of the Sun and also son of Osiris for they form together an almost indivisible Trinity concerned with light.

It was in Hermopolis, the oldest city of Egypt and sacred to Thoth "that light began when thy father, Rê, rose from the lotus." The separation of sky and earth was said to have been effected by Shû who (like Atlas) ascended the "mound" that he might sustain the goddess and uphold the sky.* Is this the memory of a priest ascending a pyramid – (Tor in the Celtic, tower in lingua franca)? One recalls Arthur's Seat in Edinburgh, a small mountainous hill where legend has it that the "silver tassie" is buried, and where many people go up it on May morning to see the sunrise. Did Shû in Egypt uphold a crystal? Guess work! Were the pyramids originally tipped with gold to catch and reflect

Fig 13. TWO EGYPTIAN BENNU BIRDS.
After illustrations in a coffin text and "The Papyrus of Ani", British Museum.

* *Dawn of Civilisation* by Professor Maspero. p. 140.

the first gleam of the dawn? In the *Pyramid Text* the original god, the Complete One, is addressed as "O Atum! when you came into being you rose up as a high hill. You shone as the Benben stone in the temple of the Phoenix at Heliopolis." Taken in conjunction with the illustrations of the Phoenix from the *Coffin Text* (see Fig 13) some belief is lent to the supposition. The Jewish priests were accustomed to ascend to the highest pinnacle of the temple to see if "the sky was lit up as far as Hebron" and, if it was, they could begin the morning sacrifice. Such orientations and sitings were always important in the ancient world, and as it would have been difficult to make a daily climb up a pyramid, it is possible that some shining object was once and for all placed at the tip, for the same reason that sailors used to climb the masthead to see over the curve of the horizon. The placing of such a shining object on high is indeed more than possible; it is probable, for the very greatest authority and one-time Keeper of Egyptian Antiquities at the British Museum, Dr I.E.S. Edwards C.B.E., C.M.G., S.B.A. in his latest Pelican edition of "The Pyramids of Egypt" writes on page 262, as follows: "An inscription found by Jéquier at the pyramid of Queen Udjebten" (6th dynasty) "refers to the gilded capstone on her pyramid, which suggests that these stones were, at least sometimes, overlaid with gold."

As I have already written but wish to emphasize here, Herodotus was incorrect in saying that the Phoenix in Egypt resembed an eagle. It *is* represented as an eagle in the valleys of the Euphrates and Tigris, and he did say that it came from the general direction of Arabia. But in Egypt it was known as the Bennu Bird and was pictured as a grey heron because, like the Logos of Christianity, it spoke the first word, calling the world to life at dawn, and the grey heron does in fact utter the first sound at the break of day on the Nile. However, to support Herodotus, it did come from the Isle of Fire bringing with it that vital essence Hikê, a kind of Ambrosia, the everlasting light and life-force desired by mortals and immortals alike. It was the soul of Rê, first appearing in darkness and putting darkness to flight at dawn, and the *Coffin Text* shows it perched on something very like a pyramid. Herodotus was quite correct in saying that the principal sanctuary of the Benben was Heliopolis, the City-of-the-Sun, and he was equally correct in connecting it with the fire from which it issued.

One of the repudiations of sin which the soul was supposed to declare at the Judgement of the Dead was considered by Sir Flinders Petrie as very strange: "I have not quenched fire in its moment", i.e. when beginning to burn. Sir Flinders says: "Possibly fire was looked on as a portion of the sun-god, who would be offended at being thwarted." As charred linen was used as tinder in ancient times* and particularly in Solomon's temple, it is possible that the words of Isaiah (XL.ii.3.) concerning the expected Messiah, "The smoking flax shall he not quench," were inspired by the same line of thought, meaning that in the spiritual sense Christ would never quench the birth of the spiritual flame struggling to establish itself in a man's heart. Prometheus was reputed to have carried the fire of the gods, stolen from Olympus, in a fennel stalk, a pithy reed, and Isaiah also prophesied of the Messiah in the same verse that "a bruised reed shall he not break." Both flax and the pithy reed of fennel can be used as tinder; and tinder is of the greatest importance when lighting a fire either from the sun or from iron and flint.

It may be of interest and amusement to the reader to know that in the Spring of 1985, a scientifically-minded friend and I† lay at length on a lawn in Tuscany to prove that Pliny's assertion that fire could be ignited by a globular glass beaker filled with water was true and not fanciful. It was fairly easy to focus the sun's rays (albeit the sun was extemely cold that Spring) to a glowing point, but how to arrive at the "flash point" was more difficult, because we have in this generation lost the art of the "tinder-box" on which our ancestors depended, and which they used regularly. Then I remembered reading that Highland

---

* *Bab. Talmud* trans. by Rodkinson, Tome 4 Vol. VII Succah. p. 77.
† My brother, the Earl of Halsbury, F.R.S.

shepherds in Scotland carried the spark in a metal box all day, by first igniting a type of fungus which grows on birch trees or deciduous trees, and particularly on rotten tree trunks, and in which the spark will remain for hours at a time. The fungus is of the Bracket type (shaped like a bun) and two well-known types are the Pine Fire Fungus and the Hoof or Tinder Fungus. Luckily, there was just such a bracket type growing on an apple tree right beside us,* and by focusing the water-filled beaker's rays on this fungus we achieved "flash point" and with a few wooden shavings to "feed" the fire we achieved a cheerful if small blaze. Much blowing and puffing is needed and the use of breath is most important to arrive at "flash point", but we had only a very cold sun. As will be shown in a later chapter, in the Near East with a really hot sun there is no problem, though, as I have said, charred linen (flax) was the favoured tinder in the Eastern Mediterranean, where perhaps bracket fungi do not grow, but fennel stalks do, which Prometheus is reputed to have used. According to the British Encyclopedia, Neolithic man used saltpetre on his firewood, and Herodotus describing the oil lamps at Sais, when he says salt was added (presumably to the wicks) probably meant saltpetre, which *is* a salt, and when mixed with sulphur (both substances lie encrusted on the shores of the Dead Sea) is highly inflammable; and indeed the Chinese are credited with the invention of gun-powder by a spark acting on these chemicals. They are furthermore, in all probability, the "earth" which the Jewish Mishnah prohibits the fire-maker to use on the Sabbath.

In the Hermetic literature of the 4th century a man was deemed emancipated from the grip of earthly matter if a ray from Rê penetrated his soul. Sir Flinders Petrie continues with a quotation from the Hermetic books: "He (God) is essentially not manifest, but only manifests himself through his works. Pray therefore to catch a single ray of thought from the unmanifest by contemplating the ordering of nature." †

---

* *The Book of Mushrooms* by Roger Phillips, Pan Books 1981.
† *Personal Religion in Egypt before Christianity* by Sir F. Petrie p. 140.

Plutarch says* that "on the eighth of the waning of (the month) Paophi they keep the Birthday of the Sun's Staff." This seems singularly like the tradition of Aaron's staff being, like Excalibur, extremely difficult to draw out, and then only by him who knew the Sacred Name. It seems probable that the Egyptian Sun's staff was the fiery brand. Plutarch also tells us that after the priests had celebrated the mourning of Isis for her murdered husband, they "carry out the sacred chest, having within it a small golden vessel, into which they take and pour fresh water." Since the Ark of the Covenant is generally accepted as a direct borrowing from the Egyptian custom of processing with a chest containing the *sacra* of the gods, it seems doubly likely that the Golden Pot of Manna was also either a crystal (the Urim) or a globular vessel capable of being filled with water – dare one say, shaped like the gourd or pumpkin of a particular fairy tale? — of which more later.

The great successor to Egyptian religious ideas was the cult of Orpheus in Greece. He began life as a priest of Dionysus, and like all heroes of mystery religions he descended into Hades to bring out a maiden. One cannot help wondering if Eurydice, the maiden, is a euphemism for the virginal talisman, the pure crystal. Orpheus is often depicted as a fisher with rod and line, or else like Dyctis, who drew up Danae, he holds a fishing net. The temple of Thoth at Hermopolis was called "The House of the Net" for the Ibis is also a fisher. †

Taking gold from the mouth of a fish is a legend that goes back to Solomon. The fallen and mischievous angel, Asmodeus, stole the king's ring, thus robbing him of power, threw it into the Sea of Galilee, and himself assumed the throne and the likeness of Solomon. It is the legend from which must stem Longellow's wonderful poem, "King Robert of Sicily" (a character who never existed historically, but was possibly confused with Robert le Diable, father of William the Conqueror). The legendary Sicilian King, bored by attending vespers and suffering from hub-

* Plutarch *On Isis and Osiris* LII.2.
† *Orpheus the Fisher* by Robert Eisler.

ris, asks the monks for the translation of the Latin and is told: "He hath put down the mighty from their seats, and hath exalted them of low degree." Whereupon he vows that no one shall so abase *him*. Thus his pride tempts God to send an angel to take the king's place and teach him humility, and for a year the wretched Robert goes unrecognised as the Court jester with an ape as his only companion, until as last he learns humility, and God reinstates him on his throne. This is exactly what happened in legend to Solomon, who at last recovers his ring from the mouth of a fish.* The Greek, Polycrates, also recovered his ring from the mouth of a fish.†

Cabbalistic legend held that when Jonah in the fish's belly prays to be delivered, and says, "I went down to the bottom of the mountains; the earth with her bars was about me forever," he is describing "the halls of a palace," and "inside was a precious stone which illuminated all around." In other words the belly of the fish was a euphemism for a ritual cave of Hades. Let us continue to remember that gold (and presumably royal rings were of gold) was a periphrastic word for flame or sun, for thus we shall find out exactly what it was that issued from the fish's mouth.

St. Kentigern, afterwards called Mungo the Beloved – patron saint of Glasgow – was born in a circle of flaming sparks. He is reputed after he entered the church to have kindled flame from the frozen bough of a tree; and St. Patrick in Ireland brought fire out of an icicle. Both these occurences were regarded as miraculous, but we know from Pliny that ice and crystals were regarded as identical, the latter being a petrified form of the first. When the wife of King Roderick of Strathclyde lost her ring in a river, Mungo recovered it from a salmon's mouth.

So we return to the question of what exactly it is that issues from a fish's mouth, and we find that the clay lamps for burning oil, used by all the olive-bearing countries in

---

* *Zohar*, Trans. by H. Sperling & M. Simon. Vol III. p. 146.
† Pliny *Nat. History* Bk XXXVII. Ch. 2.

ancient times, were roughly fish-shaped. The oil is poured into the hole on the back of such a "fish", and the wick issues from the fish's mouth. Candles were really only used in the north, where the olive trees would not grow, but oil was the fuel for lamps throughout Mediterranean countries in days of old. Now when we come to Christian times, we find that there is a twofold meaning in the fish-like clay lamp for the Greek for a fish is *ICTHUS*, and the initials can stand for "Jesus Christ, Son of God, Saviour". Thus the early Christians, in the days of persecution by the Roman Emperors, would draw a fish on the sand, gravel or paving stone to indicate by a secret sign to a fellow Christian that they were brethren of the same faith.

When Christ bade Peter hook a fish in the Lake of Galilee, in the mouth of which fish he would find the much needed tribute money, he may have been indicating that he was the heir and of the same blood as Solomon. Miracle or legend, it is a mystery into which one cannot justifiably explore.

But with regard to fire (light) issuing from a fish-lamp a point of great interest is this: when Ian Wilson wrote his magnificent book about the Holy Shroud of Turin, he gave the earliest known version of how the shroud, promised by Christ to the King Abgar of Edessa to cure his affliction of arthritis, was taken by a disciple. Thaddeus, one of the Seventy and an evangelist, who travelled with it from Jerusalem to Edessa via the city of Hierapolis on the Syrian/Turkish border, where he spent the night. Classical references assure us that Hierapolis, where the mother goddess was worshipped under the name of Atargatis or Semiramis, indulged not only in horribly orgiastic sexual excesses,* but in a yearly fire-feast of vast proportions and celebrations: just as did Sais in Egypt,† and as Jerusalem did also at the Jewish Feast of Hanukkah, though not of course with any orgies in the latter. The account states that because of the holiness of Christ's shroud being hidden with Thaddeus in the city of Hierapolis, a "tile" in the city also received the

---

* Lucian's *Goddess of Syria*.
† Herodotus Bk II Sec. 62.

impression of Christ's face from contact with the shroud. Then all the other "tiles" in the city caught fire until the town seemed ablaze. We shall meet presently with the confusion in Greek and Latin between ceramic "tiles" and ceramic pots or vessels. They were both ceramics, i.e. made from earth's clay. In Sais in Egypt Herodotus tells us that the oil for the lamps of the fire-feast was held in saucer-shaped vessels, and in Phoenicia Dr G. Conteneau, the French archaeologist tells us that such clay lamps were "d'abord une simple galette en terre dont les bords sont repliés,* easily therefore confused with a "tile". However, certainly by the time of Our Lord clay lamps would have been roughly fish-shaped, with a mouth for the wick. It seems therefore to confirm the veracity of the early account of the travels of Thaddeus and the Shroud that he arrived in Hierapolis at the time of the famous fire-feast, when all clay lamps would have been sparkling on every

Fig 14. AN ICHTHUS LAMP OF EARLY CHRISTIAN DATE. Published by the National Society.

door step, and that Thaddeus, who resided overnight with a fellow Jew, may have been one of the first to convert some of the Hierapolitans to realise that Christ is "The Light of the World", and perhaps persuaded them to begin the manufacture of the Ichthus lamps which represented Christ's initials and often bore Christ's monogram, Chi-Rho, between the letters of Alpha and Omega.

When, therefore, in the *Grand Graal* Alein le Gros (Alias Brons) is bidden by St. Joseph of Arimathea to place a fish

* *La Civilisation Phenicienne* by Dr G. Conteneau.

on the altar of the Grail, he may in fact have been placing the lamp (generally lamps) necessary for the celebration of Mass.

10 The Flower of Light

In previous editions of this book I devoted two whole chapters to folk-tales illustrative of my theory, but later researches have provided so much more material and of so much greater interest that I have cut drastically such fables to make way for what is more important. In any case Medieval Lays can be turgid and boring reading to anyone not specialising in Romance Literature, and students who want to specialise can do their own detective work, always bearing in mind that certain clues will lead them through the maze.

The clues to watch out for are:-

1. The crystal is always feminine and is often the heroine of the story.

2. A magic ring is generally the regalia of a fire-making solar hero such as Prometheus.

4. Eggs, either of the Phoenix or some other creature can be either the World-Egg surrounded by the serpent-sea of Oceanus or a crystal embedded in its traditional setting of a serpent formed of precious metal.

To be as brief as possible then:- In the story of Ortnit the eggs of the Abrahamic toad provide the beacon fires which protected the shores of Britain from invasion by Angles, Saxons, and the Spanish Armada by means of warning signals from one hill-top to another.*

In the *Lay of Yonec* by Marie de France (c.1175) the "win-

---

* *Epics & Romances of the Middle Ages* by Dr W. Wagner and M.W. MacDowell.

dow" of the heroine had metal bars across it which dashed
and wounded the Hawk Knight who was trying to approach
his love secretly. In the *Chevalier de la Charette* by Chrestien
the "window" is similarly barred and injures Lancelot. In
both these stories we may have come up against the royal
orb. Pythagoras was the first to teach that the world was
round, though his reasons for so supposing were never
clearly given. Curiously enough he was the son of a gem-
engraver, whose work would have presumably included the
polishing of cabochon precious stones, crystals etc. and
some knowledge and experience of splitting the spectrum
with a transparent splinter like a prism which gives "all the
colours of the world." According to legend, Pythagoras
was given the very dart of Apollo by a Hyperborean
Celt.*

Amongst the educated Romans a rather vague idea existed that the earth was a globe, nevertheless by the beginning
of the 6th century it was a punishable offence and heresy for
a Christian to believe that the earth was globe-shaped. The
Church had by then decreed it to be flat and square with
four corners, as in the Old Testament scripture. How comes
it then that both pagan and Christian Emperors carried an
orb, generally of crystal, as a symbol of the earth over which
they ruled? The later Roman Emperors held a crystal orb
inside a metal crossing (probably of gold) which therefore
enabled the orb to be surmounted by the Cross. The metal
crossing would therefore prevent the focusing of sun-rays.
Thus Horus, the Hawk Knight, could no longer enter the
"window" of his love, the earth. In Austria the royal orb of
the Hapsburg Emperors was known as the Reichs-apfel, the
State-Apple, and if I am right such a crystal is identical with
the golden apple of Hesperides which was enshrined in its
'tree" and was guarded by a serpent. It was stolen by Hercules who had been guided to the "tree" by Prometheus,
the first fire-maker, who alone knew the whereabouts of the
apple-tree.

That the legend could also concern "The World Tree",

* *Life of Pythagoras* by Diogenes Laertius.

whose leaves are the stars with which Hercules is concerned
as a solar hero, labouring through the twelve constellations
of the zodiac, is equally possible; for symbolism (also
colour and sound) repeats itself at the higher without dis-
counting the lower levels – just as on the piano if the dam-
per is down the harmonics vibrate from the "Do" of an
octave in the base up to the next "Do" and to all the other
harmonics in the scale, until the highest "Do" is ringing
out. The vibrations can presumably ring in reverse order,
for Jacob saw the angels ascending and descending on the
scale, the ladder, the scala. Let no one therefore assume that
the Virgin Mary is merely a translucent crystal. On the contrary, her purity is prefigured on the lower symbolic level of
the ascending scale.

In the collection of Marie de France, the *Lay of Graelant*
tells of the fairy lady who is discovered while bathing naked
in a stream by the hero, and in the *Lay of Sir Launfal* by the
same authoress the heroine is likewise discovered, and her
attendants carry a basin of pure gold and a towel of white
linen. In Greece, Actaeon came upon Artemis, the moon
goddess, unclothed and bathing in a spring, and she exac-
ted vengeance. Callimachus in an *Elegy of the Bath of Pallas*
describes the dangers of seeing the goddess unclothed, and
Tiresias is struck blind for daring to behold her unveiled.
Both the fairy ladies in the lays written by Marie de France
seem to represent either the moon's reflection in water or
the "moon goblet" filled with water and held hidden from
the uninitiated; and both are described as "slender". No
doubt a slender figure was in the 12th century considered
very attractive; but here we are brought sharply up against
the pun transmitted by the Provencal, Kyot, to Wolfram,
who declares that the Latin name for the Grail stone was
lapis exilis, meaning the "slender stone", for *exilis* is "slender" in Latin. Unless you understand the punning, this
simply does not make sense, and no commentators have so
far been able to understand the meaning of it. But Grêle is
the French for slender as well as for a hail-stone, a spherical
piece of ice, and we know that ice and crystals were regarded
as identical substances, and that to focus sun-rays a crystal

must be spherical unless cut into a lens. In Hebrew the two substances are also identified: *Gavish* meaning a rock crystal, and *El Gavish* a hail-stone which was not yet petrified into a permanent crystal as the ancients believed possible, according to Pliny.*

In the Lay of Gugemar, also by Marie de France, the hero finds the "bed" of Solomon. In the *Epics and Romances of Middle Ages* by Dr Wagner, the hero Dietrich, like St. George or Horus, defeats the dragon or Typhonian monster, and wins his way to the virginal Elfin Queen who lives amongst the glaciers and snows. This, like the tales from the Poetic Edda, may concern one of the chief sources of rich crystal, the Alps, and the lady had a huge "red" stone in her diadem – (the Clach Dearg?). Dietrich is believed to be identical with the Gothic king Theoderic, who did cross the Alps to invade and conquer Italy.

The story of *Pretty Goldilocks*, as told by Andrew Lang, includes caverns similar to Wookey, and a crystal vase which Prince Charming has to fill there with water – a direct borrowing from the story of Psyche's task inflicted on her by the cruel Venus (Aphrodite), the jealous mother-in-law and mother of Eros.

In several of these stories the raven plays a part. A raven-stone was believed to exist in its nest, a stone which was a magic talisman if obtainable. These birds figure in the story of the Flood, of Elijah and of Wotan; and "raven" was a title for a degree of initiation in the cult of Mithras. On plate VII is reproduced a photograph of a rook (close kin to the raven) playing with fire, which appears to have a great attraction for these birds. The one in the photograph is taken from the London Illustrated News of July 1957. It was a tame bird kept by Dr. Burton, who considered playing with fire a trick of behaviour common to some birds, and this particular pet went into ecstasy when allowed the treat of what is known as 'anting'. Such behaviour may have given rise to the idea of the Phoenix, the hawk and to the "pecking bird" of the Chinese to which we shall come overleaf.

* See Jewish Encyclopedia under Precious Stones.

If the ritual of the Grail was so widespread in the West, one would suppose that it spread equally to the East. Indeed it did, and may even have originated in the Far East. Travelling gradually eastward then, we come first to the *Arabian Nights* and the story of Aladdin and his wonderful lamp. The young and simple lad is led by a magician to a cave, and there given a magic ring. The youth enters the cave and gathers the fruit of the jewelled trees within it. (According to legend both Solomon and Prester John possessed jewelled trees, and moreover in the *Queste del Saint Graal* Galahad fashions a tree of gold and precious stones to cover or enshrine the Grail.) Aladdin then emerges from the cave with the magic lamp and the fruits (jewels). He sees the Sultan's daughter on the way to her bath, and falls in love with her. By the power of the magic ring he miraculously transports her "bed" to his house, and because he can provide unlimited gold (always a periphrasis for fire or sun) the Sultan agrees to the match. Aladdin thereupon builds for the princess a fitting palace, reminiscent in its splendour of Solomon's Temple. But the twenty-fourth window remains unfinished, in compliment to the Sultan who is invited to expend his wealth beautifying it. But not all the Sultan's wealth can fill this "window". Why? Because I guess that only the light of the sun-god, alias the genie, can fill it. But, alas, the evil magician obtains the lamp (extinguishes the year's torch) and carries the princess away to a desolate place. Thankfully the days of human sacrifice are ended. So the Moslem hero recovers his flame, and they all live happily ever after.

Today the Parsees and the Brahmins both light their sacred fires by means of the oldest known method, the rubbing of two sticks together (the fire-drill). But long ago, if we are to believe Apollonius of Tyana in his journey to India in the 1st century A.D. he was received in Kashmir where the mystics bore a ring and a wand, and on the summit of a hill were accustomed to worship fire extracted from the sun's rays, probably by a burning glass.*

---

* *Life of Apollonius of Tyana* by Philostratus Bk.III.14 and 15.

In April 1985 his Majesty Bhumibol Adulyady, King of Thailand, lit the funeral pyre of the Dowager Queen, Rambhai Bharmi, widow of King Rama VII, by means of focusing the sun's rays through a crystal. The cremation of the Dowager Queen was carried out with the same reverence shown at the burning of the late Indira Ghandi. But this subject of funeral pyres brings me back for a moment to the Near East. It was the custom for the ancient Phoenician kings of Tyre to be cremated, but their god, Melqart, was the antithesis of the usual kindly sun-god. He demanded the sacrifice of little children by burning alive, and was regarded by the Jews as an abomination, against whose customs and demand they had to fight hard even in Jerusalem, which was often contaminated by such abominable practices, which infiltrated their holy city through their heathen neighbours. The Jews knew this Satanic sun-god as Moloch, and exactly why the Greeks identified him with their solar hero, Hercules, is a mystery, for the Greek fables about Hercules (Heracles in Greek) though dealing with his connection with the sun, his twelve labours and his voyage in the solar bark, contain nothing of an abominable nature. What I would ask the reader to remember for the purpose of fully appreciating the last page of this, my book, is that although the Greek Heracles, like the Tyrian kings, was given after his death a right royal funeral pyre, he did not die a natural death. His jealous wife sent him a *shirt* impregnated with poisonous chemicals which burst into flame when he donned it, so that he died in agony, scalded, roasted,skinned alive.

After this interlude, which if unpleasant is important for the reader to remember, particularly the word *shirt*, let us return to the East and this time to the Far East. The lens was familiar and used in China, and they have a myth that it was a "pecking bird" who first brought fire to man. If we look again at Plate VII and the tame rook which so delighted itself by playing with burning twigs, this myth may have originated in a possible truth. The first man to take possession of fire was, according to the Chinese, a certain Suy-Jin. "Suy" can mean either fire-drill or the speculum. We have

seen that ice, crystal, and glass were all regarded as more or
less identical substances by the ancients, and that dew can
contain sunlight. All these transmit light to a greater or
lesser degree. But objects that *reflect* rather than transmit
light were equally venerable, for instance the concave metal
mirror; and to the Chinese there was confusion between a
pearl which reflected a certain amount of light, and the crystal which transmitted the sun's rays to flash-point. When
they wished to refer to the crystal they called it "The Flaming Pearl", while still confusing it with the pearl which rose
from the sea. If Chinese porcelains and their embroidered
dragon robes are examined closely, it will be evident that
the fire issues from the "flaming Pearl", and that the attendant dragon or twin dragons are blowing and puffing away
at the spark in the tinder in order to kindle the blaze. Unless
of course they are evil-minded and trying to blow it out
altogether, but dragons in China are not evilly disposed but
are royal escorts and guardians. However it be, no flames
issue from the mouths of the dragons, but only the all-
important breath to blow the flame to life; the flame issues
from the pearl itself.

I once had a very interesting conversation with the
greatest authority on Byzantium, Stephen Runciman, and I
told him that I had just seen a very well produced French
film about the notorious Empress Theodora. "Were the
costumes correct?" he asked, and I answered in the affirma-
tive: "Just like the Ravenna Mosaics". "You know", he said,
"why the Byzantines gave up the Roman toga and took to
wearing those stiff robes? It was because the caravans were
for the first time crossing Asia to bring Chinese porcelains
and embroidered Dragon Robes to Byzantium." I was fas-
cinated, and when, years later, I was asked by a very critical
Protestant why the Catholic priests wore such odd outland-
ish vestments, (the customary clothing of any Byzantine of
the 4th century onwards) I was able to reply: "Would you
abolish the Beefeaters' uniforms at the Tower of London
because they date from Tudor times, or the cuirasses of Her
Majesty's Life Guards which date from the early 19th century and would give no protection whatever against a

machine-gun bullet?" Continuity in religious custom and
the memory of man's history are very important for main-
taining a sense of time and a steady outlook. Stephen Runciman's information was very apposite, for even the black
biretta of a priest, now alas no longer worn, is extremely like
the hat of a Mandarin. Whether or not it derived from
China like the embroidered robes of all Byzantine gen-
tlemen I do not know.

All this brings me to the legend of St. Margaret, whose
name has always meant a "pearl". She was repudiated by
Pope Gelasius in 494 A.D. but her popularity persisted and
the Pope never managed to have her struck from the list of
saints, though her saint's day is no longer celebrated.
According to legend she was the daughter of a pagan priest
of Antioch (fairly near Byzantium or at least to the borders
of its Empire). Being of delicate health, she was brought up
by her nurse in a wild and lonely part of the country. The
Governor of Antioch glimpsed the damsel, and desired her.
She refused his advances, so he seized and confined her to a
dungeon, where was a terrible serpent-dragon. The little
maiden held aloft her cross to defend herself, but the serpent swallowed her entire. However, the power of the cross
burst the serpent in twain, and the saint was delivered by no
less a person than St. George, slayer of the Typhonian monster, alias Horus the god of the sunny sky. On plate VIII will
be seen a picture of the Dragon Robe of China, suddenly
fashionable in Byzantium, which gave birth to the legend of
the apocryphal saint, who is none other than the "Flaming
Pearl", the crystal of the Chinese, encircled and blown
upon by the dragon-like priest whose duty it was to bring
the sacred flame to birth.

To return to the West: it was the Breton Lay of *Peronnik
l'Idiot* which first led M. Potvin and other French authorities
to realise that the Quest of the Holy Grail had a Celtic and
pre-Christian origin. Peronnik is the simple lad, the young
Fool of folk-legend, as was Perceval and Aladdin: an innocent who has much to learn and far to go. A magician had
charge of the Golden Basin and the Lance of Diamond
which shone like flame. They were placed for safety in a

dark underground pit below the magician's castle. In front of it stood a dwarf with a fiery sword to guard an apple tree. Peronnik could only gain access to the talismans if he picked the "Flower which Laughs". Blindfolded by his cap (pulled down in fear of dreadful sights) he at last rides to the castle of Kerglas (perhaps Carnac?). A loathly damsel called Pestilence promises to help him kill the wicked magician. He opened all the doors of Kerglas with "The Laughing Flower" and possessed himself of the Golden Basin and the Lance of Diamond.

What was this Laughing Flower, which can unlock the gates of Hades? It is the very flower which the Madonna carries; for the Fleur-de-Lys was originally spelt "Fleur-de-Luce" and meant "the Flower of Light", the flame of Horus and Brahma filling the dew within the lily or lotus in which the dew-drop lay.

Just as St. Catherine of Alexandria carries her virgin-crystal at the hub of her wheel, and St. Margaret of Antioch is no other than the "Flaming Pearl", so Our Lady carries the most ancient symbol of the Incarnate Light. Thus in all Apocryphal stories and in pictures of her, she bears a pot of lilies or just one lily to a fountain at the moment of the Annunciation. According to the Rev. W. Greswell in his book *Chapters on the Early History of Glastonbury* the monks claimed to have amongst their relics the very vase of lilies which the Blessed Virgin held at the moment when the Archangel saluted her. If the monks did indeed make this claim it would show that they had inherited a knowledge of the ancient symbolism, and were referring to a particular crystal which they undoubtedly possessed, and which in turn gave rise to the somewhat ridiculous fable that the Virgin herself is buried at Glastonbury. It is a strange coincidence or perhaps an intentional artifice that the seal of John Chinnock, Abbot of Glastonbury (see Plate V) portrays St. Catherine of Alexandria with her wheel and St. Margaret of Antioch with her dragon on either side of Our Lady who carries the vase of lilies. I will not repeat here my correspondence with the Keeper of Manuscripts at the British Museum regarding the lettering on the seal as it is recorded in earlier editions of this book, but the Museum agreed that whereas at first sight the Latin inscription is taken for granted to read, "There is at Glastonbury as witness to this document the Holy Mother of God", the usual term for whom is "Genetrix", the seal, although slightly damaged, appears more likely to give room only for the word "Matrix", of which the "A" is clear. *Matrix*, as I have written in an earlier chapter, is a very unusual word to describe the Virgin Mary, and is used customarily to signify a mould, cavity or cup, or the ore or rock in which a jewel is found embedded. That the Abbey did in fact possess such a jewel I shall show later in a tale about King Arthur of which one of Glastonbury's monks bore written witness.

Mr Harold Bayley in his *New Light on the Renaissance*, after spending a life-time studying paper-marks, gives his reproductions of 16th and 17th century portrayals of the Flower of Light (see Fig. 15). He came to the conclusion, as I

Fig 15. 16TH-17TH CENTURY WATER-MARKS, SHOWING THE FLOWER OF LIGHT: HOW IT RISES FROM THE HOLY VESSEL: AND SPRINGS FROM THE HUB OF A WHEEL.
From "A New Light on the Renaissance", by Harold Bayley.

have already explained, that as paper-making first flourished among the heretical Provencals and Lombards of the early Middle Ages, their water-marks were nearly all symbols of a religious character and constituted a secret language between one sect and another of such heretics. His theory fits perfectly with that of Professor Leonardo

Olschki*, which was published subsequently to my own book's previous editions. Professor Olschki found that the one common denominator of all the appearances of the Grail is the accompaniment of blinding light, which other interpreters have consistently ignored, or so he complains. Such light "streams from the vessel and distinguishes it from every other liturgical object." To overcome the old difficulty that a female was never allowed to bear the Christian chalice or Sacraments,† he suggests secret rites of Gnostic and Manichaean tradition, and that these sects over-emphasized the import of Christ's being the Light of the World. He suggests that such a group of heretics was led by Tanchelm of Antwerp and Éon de l'Étoile, and that they adopted a female figure to represent (as in a charade) Gnosis, or Sophia (Wisdom), later called Sapientia or Maria, who bore the light or the symbol of the *Lumen de Lumine*. Sophia and Sapientia are both feminine nouns, as is the Hebrew *Shekinah*, and even the Cabbalists were criticised by the more orthodox Rabbis for apparently allotting a female spouse to God the Father in their abstract conception of Wisdom, Sophia. This is simply a language trap. Professor Olschki is at pains to make clear that the later appellation for Gnosis, Maria, has nothing whatever to do with the mother of Our Lord. For the convenience of students there are far too many Marys in the Gospel for one to grasp quickly which Mary is which, and if the joint authors of *The Holy Blood*, Messrs. Baignet, Leigh and Lincoln, had ever studied the Apocryphal Ethiopic texts they would find confusion even worse confounded. The name of course in Hebrew is Miriam, and the first so named to be mentioned in scriptures is the sister of Moses, reared in Egypt, and, according to Sir Alan Gardiner, the famous Egyptologist,§ the name probably derives from the hieroglyph MRY, feminine MYRT, which by adding IMN, gives "The Beloved of Amūn, i.e. God": it is therefore a lovely and satisfying and

---

* *The Grail & its Mysteries* by Professor L. Olschki translated from the Italian by J.A. Scott.
† By special dispensation an Abbess was occasionally allowed to do so.
§ *Egyptian Origin of English Personal Names*, by Sir Alan Gardiner.

poetic name for Our Lady if we are prepared to substitute *Javeh* for Amūn. It is a pity that Professor Olschki is so adamantine in his refusal to accept any association between the Fisher King and the Ichthus, the initials of the Christian secret sign during the days of the persecutions, for he has failed to appreciate the existence of the Ichthus lamp, the light which would have strongly supported his theory regarding the Gnostic preoccupation with the *Lumen de Lumine*. If the Maria, alias Sophia, i.e. Wisdom, whom he believes bore the Grail in its procession through the Fisher King's hall, represented any particular individual in such a charade, it is likely to have been a representing of Mary the Jewess, the first historical Alchemist, who lived in Alexandria (a hot-bed of Gnostics) in the 1st century and invented the Bain Marie. I cannot on this page enlarge on Alchemy, which deserves examination later on, but we can now enquire into who were the Gnostics, what they believed and why the Church regarded them as heretics. Gnosis only means knowledge, and the pursuit of it would at first appear innocent. But it was tied up with the study of astronomy, which we know from Wolfram was studied by the Jew, Flegetanis in Toledo, from whom the story of the Grail seems at least partly to stem. Before the discoveries of Copernicus, it was assumed that between the sun and earth there lay tier after tier of curved, glassy parasols one above the other, on each of which rolled a different planet. Above all such glassy transparent floors reigned the Absolute and Ultimate Godhead, before whose final glassy "sea" the sanctified would one day cast down their crowns in homage (Rev. IV.10). But the Gnostics could not conceive that the Ultimate and Absolute Godhead could ever descend directly onto our planet, as did Christ. They had to invent a demi-urge who would take the first step downward, and after the demi-urge various belittlements of God had to be invented until his representative could pierce all those glassy barriers to reach earth. The ascent of man through such spheres of planetary obstructions was equally complicated, so that it is little wonder that the Church set its face against ideas which were in direct contrast to the simple message of the Gospels and teachings of Christ.

To return to the support of Professor Olschki's theory, the appearances of the Grail invariably include the manifestation of descending light. In the *Prose Perceval* a hermit bids the knight ride on until he finds the holy chapel of the vessel: "La ou la flambe del Saint Esperit descent chaucun jor, por le seintime Graal et por le pointe de la lence." In the *Queste* when Lancelot approaches the sacred talisman, he sees in the chamber "si tres grant clarté comme se li solaus fust descendus." *Y Seint Greal* describes the manifestation thus: "And then they saw a ray of the sun shining a hundred times brighter than if it had been midday, and everyone's face was brighter... after a time there came unto them the glorious vessel called the Greal, covered with white samite." In the *Grand Saint Graal*, a ray of fire enters the mouth of the beholder, and this is an example of man's desire to absorb into himself the essence of the Holy Spirit, just as did Esdras when he drank from the angel's cup of fiery water in order to light the candle of understanding in his heart.

Of the sword Excalibur, Malory says "it was so bright in his enemies eyes that it gave light like thirty torches", and Chrestien describes it "com uns brandon de fu espris."

Truly before the days of electricity there was no brighter light than Peronnik's diamond lance, the beam of the sun upon crystal or glass, and it can be a blinding if an impermanent light.

Thus we come to the historical study of optics, and here we must salute Islam and acknowledge the debt we owe to a very great scientist, a Moslem. While burning glasses have been found in Crete dating from as early as 1500 B.C., and while Archimedes set the Roman fleet on fire with mirrors, and sacred fires were lit by crystals or water-filled glass spheres, these may have been haphazard occurences by adventurous men. The Greeks preferred dialectical arguments and metaphysical discussions to scientific experiments. Aristotle, however, made a tentative beginning, and Claudius Ptolemaeus, a Greek of Alexandria, living between 127 to 151 A.D. studied astronomy (which entailed study of the spheres) and began to be interested in the behaviour of light. He wrote a book on optics, but there was still great uncertainty as to whether the image seen was received into the eye or emitted from it.

Then after a long period of doubt and ignorance during the Dark Ages comes the great Islamic scientist, Ibn Al-Haytham (known in the Latin translation of his work as Al Hazeni). He was born in Basra, now Iraq, in 965 A.D., and came to Egypt to Cairo during the Caliphat of Al-Hakim, and lived there between 996 and 1021 A.D. dying in 1039. He borrowed from Ptolemaeus and Euclid, but was the first to deal with light as an observable substance, and thus with questions that could not be raised in the Ptolemaic context.

His work on optics was first translated from Arabic into Spanish by a Jew, Abraham of Toledo, and again by Jacob ben Mahir Ibn Tibbon in 1271. In Arabic, therefore, it would have been available earlier to Flegetanis, the Jew of Toledo, whom we are told by Wolfram wrote in Arabic, as did most Jews in Spain at that time. Wolfram's Flegetanis, he tells us, studied astronomy and the spheres, and read the secrets of the Grail in such studies.

Al Haytham almost discovered magnifying lenses, and why he did not (or did he?) is curious, for he was experimenting with spherical segments and glass vessels filled with water. His work influenced Roger Bacon, Leonardo da Vinci and John Kepler, and also the great Sir Isaac Newton. Al Haytham wrote a separate monograph on the Burning Glass, but though he wrote in it of "glass" his actual instructions are concerned with how to prepare steel concave mirrors so as to focus light; perhaps for "burning glass" one should read "burning device".

His *Optica** was translated into Latin by Gerhard of Cremona in 1572, but alas, my Latin is of elementary standard, and the foot square volume two inches thick in 16th century print is beyond my ability to read it. Moreover if one wished to study optics today one would turn to a mod-

* See Al Haytham's *Optics* by Saleh Beshara Omar, and the proceedings of the thousandth anniversary of Al Haytham's life and works in Pakistan edited by Hakim Mohammed Said.

ern English scientific publication. But what I long to know is whether Al Haytham, who first acquired learning from the traditions of Baghdad, had inherited any knowledge or legend deriving from Solomon's day. In a study of a cult that was world-wide, such as the conjuring of fire from the sun, one cannot hope to be an expert in every branch of every variety of the cult. But the Hamdard National Foundation of Pakistan held within the last year or two a centenary celebration in honour of Ibn Al-Haytham's thousandth anniversary, and I am greatly hoping that the Foundation will contribute any knowledge it may have regarding any ancient traditions or legends Al Haytham may have learned in Baghdad where he first studied, and particularly if any such legends derive from Solomon, for it is with Solomon and Jewish ritual that the next chapter is concerned.

11 GOD'S PRESENCE IN THE BURNING BUSH

So far Grail legend has shown at least three possible links with ancient Jewish history, quite apart from the many very important links which Professor Urban Holmes has made in his thesis and which I have already given. The manuscript* tells us that the name of the Grail King, Brons, was short for Hebron, the place which the writers assert was the locality where the Phoenix stone was to be found (actually iron pyrites are inferred and can be found there). It was the tribal territory of that very Hebron, son of Kohath, to whom the charge of the Ark, the table, the candlestick, altar and vessels of the sanctuary was given. (Num.III.19 and 31).

Next there is the claim that the magic sword was taken by Solomon from the Temple and sent in its ark-like chest (the bark) to Britain.

Thirdly, there is the legend of the Perilous Seat. It has been suggested that because at Jewish family feasts for a circumcision a seat is always placed empty and ready for the expected return of the prophet Elijah, the empty seat at Arthur's Round Table, awaiting its rightful owner, might be that left empty for the prophet. The stone of the seat split in half when Perceval, not yet worthy, tried to seat himself on it. That the Stone of Destiny of our Queen Elizabeth's throne, taken from Scone, is supposed to have been that on which Jacob laid his head when dreaming of the ladder to heaven, and was originally transported by the Egyptian Princess Scota's Irish descendants to Scotland, is I think,

* *Roman de l'estoire dou Graal* by Sire Robert de Borron (Metrical Joseph).

pure fable. My own suggestion regarding the Perilous Seat is this:– The early poets definitely declare it to have been the thirteenth place at the Round Table, kept empty in memory of the traitor Judas (Iscariot). As the authors and poets invariably confuse Old and New Testament history, and regularly confound the adventures of Joseph, son of the Patriarch Jacob, with both Joseph of Arimathea and the historian Flavius Josephus, I believe there is here confusion between Judas Maccabeus and Judas Iscariot. Chrestien tells us definitely that Gawain (all the Hawk Knights are really identical one with another and undergo exactly similar adventures; their names are really merely local renderings of the same Celtic solar hero who originated as Horus) received the sword of Judas Maccabeus, that great warrior and hero of the Jews. The split throne, I think, is an allusion to the division of the kingdoms of Israel and Judah after the death of Solomon. At last in the 2nd century B.C. Judas Maccabeus united the two kingdoms once again, and established his own, the Hasmonean dynasty, until the time when the Idumaean Herods, who were not really Jews at all, but lived south in Ishmael's country, usurped the throne. Alas, the land was split again under the Romans; broken up into Tetrarchys, while the Zealots waited for a Messiah, longing for the appearance of another warrior as brave as Judas Maccabeus, the Messianic Galahad-figure who should once again make war to rejoin the fragmented kingdom. Nowhere in Grail legend is the word Iscariot used, but only the prefix Judas, though he is described as the traitor. But we have seen how the poets confused Bible characters. That the Perilous Seat awaited the Galahad of Solomon's seed, a Messianic figure of purity and rectitude, who at length claimed and sat in it without peril and the split stone was joined again, seems more likely than the retention of an empty seat for Iscariot. It must, moreover be remembered that the memory of the Maccabean hero was commemorated by Gawain being presented with the sword of that hero – which was not in fact a weapon of war at all, but the visionary appearance of a golden sword given to Judas in a dream wherein the prophet Jeremiah presented it to him as a sign of his mission. It could well have been a fiery sword in such a vision (see II Macc.XV.15).

We come now to the subject of fire. Do we know of any special veneration of it by the Jews? It will be best to begin our enquiry at a period for which detailed historical records exist, and then work backwards to the beginning of Israel's traditions. The *Mishnah*, which records all the Jewish memories of the Temple, and which was written down shortly after its destruction in A.D. 70 states that amongst the various gate-houses of the outer court was one known as the Gate of the Flame and another as the Gate of the Hearth.* In the chamber above the former was preserved a perpetual fire. In the chamber of the latter was a simple hearth to which the priests, like the monks of the Medieval age, might come to warm themselves. The perpetual fire in the Chamber of the Flame received no divine honours, as it would have done in a pagan temple, and the purpose of it is not entirely clear. It probably constituted a source of "pure fire" for use in burnt offerings, for it would not have been considered reverent or fitting to take fire which had been kindled for a secular purpose and use it for God's service.

Indeed, there is evidence to show that the proper dedication of the altar depended upon the kind of fire which sanctified it. The altar of burnt offerings was first initiated to use by Moses and Aaron when fire came down from heaven and consumed the sacrifice (Lev. IX.24). Thereafter the flame was theoretically supposed never to go out, but to be kept perpetually burning (Lev.VI.13). But in practice it must have suffered extinction in war or other violence, as did the sacred fires of Delphi and Athens. On the occasions recorded of the re-dedication of the altar it is shown that only "pure" fire could legitimately sanctify it. When Solomon built the Temple and dedicated the new altar, fire came down from heaven and consumed the burnt offering (II Chron.VII.1.) When, after the return from exile in Babylon, Nehemiah rebuilt and re-dedicated the altar, he

* *Mishnah* (Middoth 1.5 and note on p. 59) of Dr Danby's translation.

used the old fire sacred to the altar, but it had been kept privily in a pit and had turned to "thick water". This may refer to some easily ignitable liquid, for we know that the Jews possessed naphtha which was some form of refined oil product, possibly a type of petrol gushing from the earth around Babylon. But it had been kept too long to be effective. However, "after some time had elapsed, and the sun, formerly hidden in the clouds, had shone out, there was kindled a great blaze." (II.Macc. I.. 22,23.) When in the days of the Maccabees the Temple was once again purified and re-dedicated, cleansed of the filth the pagans had intentionally cast into it, the priests then kindled a pure flame by striking iron and flint. They had lost their Urim and perhaps also the art of refining naphtha. Whether or not the altar fire did thereafter burn continuously in practice as well as in theory is uncertain. The *Mishnah* (Tamid 11.4) refers to the priest kindling the faggots. No doubt there were occasions, as in the case of the Vestal fires, when the flame died, and perhaps it was from the perpetual fire in the Chamber of the Flame that a new brand was then brought. Moreover, at this date it is doubtful whether the Jews, with their advanced and spiritual concept of the Deity, would have cared greatly if the flame on the altar did die, any more than a Catholic priest to-day would be perturbed by the failure of the sanctuary lamp. It would simply be relit.

As to why the flame no longer descended from heaven to the priests of the Maccabees, but had to be struck from iron and flint, I repeat that the Urim was lost because the Ark of the Covenant itself was lost together with the holiest things. It had been hidden by Jeremiah in a cave at the instigation of the good King Josiah,* who foresaw the coming destruction of Jerusalem, and, as being with it and specifically mentioned was the altar of incense, and probably the original candlestick, the Menorah. But, alas, on the return from Exile in Babylon no one could find the cave in which Jeremiah had hidden these precious things.† And any§

* Yer Skek. VI.I.
† II Macc.II. 1 et seq.
§ Nehemiah VII. 65.

treasure subsequently taken to Rome by Titus in 70 A.D. to be carried in his triumph would almost certainly, therefore, have been facsimiles of the originals, copies made by Nehemiah or more likely by Herod.

That the Jews at the time of Our Lord were nevertheless well acquainted with the phenomenon of lighting a fire from the sun is shown in the *Mishnah*, where, amongst various prohibitions against labouring on a festival day or Sabbath, it is forbidden to light a new fire by any of the known means: either by wood, stone, earth (probably some form of sulphur) or *out of water*.* The Feast of Hanukkah was in this latter period the season at which fire played an important part in Jewish ritual. The purpose of the celebrations was to record for all time a grand episode in Jewish history. The pagan king, Antiochus, had sought to persuade the Jews to idolatry; he had despoiled and purposely defiled the Temple. Then Judas Maccabeus led a successful revolt against the tyrant. As soon as the insurgents had won Jerusalem back into their own hands, they set about cleansing the defiled precincts of Mount Zion. They cast out all unclean rubbish and whatever had come into contact with idols. Then, when all was once again pure, they prayed God to re-enter His Holy Place. The Feast was therefore known as the Feast of Re-dedication or of re-entry of the Lord into His Temple, and one of the songs ordained for this occasion was, "Sing and rejoice, O daughter of Zion; for, lo, I come, and I will dwell in the midst of thee, saith the Lord." It is significant, therefore, to find that the re-entry of the Lord was in fact celebrated by the re-entry of fire into the Temple. Hanukkah (meaning re-dedication or inititation to use) was commonly spoken of as the Feast of Lights, and in commemoration of how the priests relit the altar fire and the seven-branched candlestick (or copy of it) in the Tabernacle, every Jewish family still lights the Hanukkah lamp (a special type of candlestick), which in old times was placed a handsbreath from the door-opening so that all might see it.

* *Mishnah. Betzah* IV.7 See note in the translation by Dr Danby: "A glass vessel is put in a hot sun; the glass emits flame which will kindle a wick brought near to it." (Bert).

It is probable that Our Lord had this very custom in mind
when he said: "No man, when he hath lighted a candle,
covereth it with a vessel, or putteth it under a bed; but set-
teth it on a candlestick, that they which enter in may see
the light."

The Rev. O.S. Rankin in his work *Origins of the Festival of
Hanukkah*, says that the *Habineu* prayer which is repeated at
this time, makes petition for "the preparation of thy lamp
for the son of Jesse, thine Anointed". In this latter period
the Lamp of the Messiah was, according to Mr Rankin, symbolic only of the Law, the Torah, or as we Christians might
phrase it, the Word of God or Logos – "The commandment
is a lamp, and the law is a light" (Prov. VI. 23). In both
Jewish and Christian thought, therefore, the lamp is symbolic of something which *proceeds from God*. In the synagogue
it is hung before the scrolls of the Law, and in Catholic
churches it hangs before the tabernacle in which the Sacrament is reserved. Despite this late spiritualised concept of
lighting the Hanukkah lamp and putting it outside the
door, Mr Rankin finds its origin in the rite described as
practised throughout Egypt. "At Sais, when the assembly
takes place for the sacrifices, there is one night on which the
inhabitants all burn a multitude of lights in the open air
round their houses. They use lamps in the shape of flat
saucers filled with a mixture of oil and salt, on top of which
the wick floats. These burn the whole night, and give to the
Festival the name of the Feast of Lamps." * Plutarch, *On Isis
and Osiris* infers that Hierapolis held a fire feast at the
autumnal equinox, but it was not at the same time of year
that Jerusalem held its Feast of Lights, but at the winter
solstice, whereas in Europe the pagan bonfires were lit on
the eve of Midsummer, and in Christian times had to be
associated with the Feast of St. John the Baptist. It seems a
fairly common instinct to have a yearly fire-feast, even
though we in Britain descend to commemorating Guy
Fawkes!

The Samaritans held that "The Law came forth from

* Herodotus Bk II. Sec. 62.

fire",* which seems to imply a belief that God manifested Himself in fire before revealing Himself in the Word. The orthodox Jews, who would have no dealings with the Samaritans, would no doubt have attempted to deny such an assertion. Nevertheless in Deut.IV.24 it is stated that "the Lord thy God is a consuming fire". But, there again, the post-exilic Jews would have held this to be a poetic metaphor, indicating only the wrath and jealousy of Jehovah.

To sum up the situation as it was from the days of the Maccabees until the final destruction of the Temple: There was an annual Feast of Lights (Hanukkah) and also the Feast of Tabernacles, which will be described in the paragraph devoted to the Solomonic period. On both these occasions the outward appearance of the city at night would have presented as sparkling a spectacle as any feast of Sais, Hierapolis or Beltane; there was an instinct to use "pure" fire for God's altar; yet nevertheless at this period of history the use of the flame was as innocent of idolatry as the present use of candles in a Christian church. All of which proves that not even the Jews and Christians are able to dissociate entirely the ideas of God and light. The two really are inseparable in a finite world, in which we can only argue and think by analogy. At the present day the Jewish morning service includes a prayer which is supposed to have come down from the Essenes of the 1st century B.C., who daily greeted the sun: "O Lord, be thou praised, thou great in wisdom, who hast ordained and created the rays of the sun." †

We have, however, from the Samaritans a hint that once long ago fire played more than a symbolic role in Hebrew ritual. And when we remember that Solomon "went after" strange gods, and that the boast of the post-exilic Jews was: "Our fathers, when they were in this place, turned with their backs towards the Temple of the Lord and their faces

* *The Origins of the Festival of Hanukkah* by O.S. Rankin p. 271.
† *The Essenes* by Christian D. Ginsberg.

towards the east, and they worshipped the sun towards the east, but as for us, our eyes are turned towards the Lord,"* it becomes more than probable that in the days of Solomon the manifestation of the sun descending to earth in the form of fire was as sacred to the Hebrews as to any other race. "The sun and the moon stood still in their habitation," writes Habakkuk (III.XI) "at the light of thine arrows they went, and at the shining of thy glittering spear." The Jews were therefore well aware of the traditional equipment of the sky-god, including perhaps lightning.

It will be remembered that after Solomon had built the Temple, the priests carried the Ark into the Holy of Holies. "And it came to pass, when the priests were come out of the holy place, that the cloud filled the house of the Lord, so that the priests could not stand to minister because of the cloud: for the glory of the Lord had filled the house of the Lord (I Kings VIII.10). This account is strangely like the kindling of fire-from-heaven and the resultant smoke from the sacred flame.†

The Feast of Hanukkah had not yet been instituted, so the only occasion on which fire was particularly used at this Solomonic period was at the conclusion of the Feast of Tabernacles. This ritual persisted down to the time of the final destruction of the Temple. Professor S.H. Hooke in *Myth and Ritual* supposes that the building of booths and the waving of willow branches and palms was originally a fertility rite, and that the Feast of Tabernacles celebrated the wedding of the passive earth with the active powers of creation. At the culmination of the festival-week a great candelabra was lit in the Court of the Women, from which the people lit their brands and vied with each other in tossing and juggling them. This was followed by a procession of torch-bearers up the fifteen steps to the Temple itself, and

---

* *Mishnah.* Sukkak V.4.

† It has been suggested that the cloud which drove the priests out of the Temple was due to an over-generous use of incense. But there must *first* be a fire, because incense has to be ignited, and the pre-Vatican II Roman rite emphasized this by the priest's words when incensing the altar: "May the Lord enkindle within us the fire of His love, and the flame of everlasting charity."

on each step was sung one of the fifteen psalms appointed (Psalms 120-134). According to Professor Hooke a particular lamp was displayed at the celebration, and this is referred to in Psalm 132: "I have ordained a lamp for mine Anointed."

Pliny tells us that in Persia a certain lentil (lens) shaped stone was considered necessary at the consecration of a king.* It seems very probable that the lamp displayed in Jerusalem was that which had been lit at the king's consecration by means of such a lens or spherical crystal, and that it was extinguished at the king's death. We have seen in a previous chapter that David's men of war besought the aged monarch to go no more out to battle, "that thou quench not the light of Israel." We can guess that in the case of the Jews, if a special flame were lit for the king, it would be no barbaric torch such as Shane O'Neill's fire-bearer carried, but rather a beautifully wrought lamp, such as hangs in Jewish synagogues or Christian churches to-day. Nor, I think, would it have accompanied the king either into battle or into his palace. For the special genius of the Jews and also of the Christians has surely always been not so much the institution of a new rite as the borrowing of an already existing ritual from other races and re-dedicating it to the one true God. The lamp of the Messiah, therefore, would have been treasured in the Temple, rather than in the palace, for, while it may have been a symbol of the ancient king's life, it would certainly have been a symbol of a life dedicated to God, or so it was hoped, though, alas, many very evil anointed kings succeeded to the throne of Israel.

Sir Norman Lockyer in his *Dawn of Astronomy* has shown what an important part the orientation of temples played in all religions. The old buildings were so designed as to act as long dark telescopes, pointing towards a particular spot on the horizon at which the sun rose on a particular day of the year. With the aid of such "telescopes" the priests were able to check their calculations of the solar calendar, for only

---

* Pliny, *Nat. History*, XXXVII 53.

once or twice in the twelve months would sunshine enter
the holy place at dawn. The pylons and obelisks which flan-
ked the entrance to Egyptian temples acted like the sights of
a rifle to help the calculations. Such were the pillars of the
temple of Hercules (Melqart) at Tyre, and the famous pillars
of Jachin and Boaz, which the king of Tyre's architect built
for Solomon, were no doubt constructed for the same purpose. According to Professor Hooke, Solomon's Temple
was orientated due east, so that the dawn-light would have
entered the Tabernacle at both the spring and autumn
equinox, probably on the night before the sun was due to
shine into the Holy Palace, and perhaps the torches were
then extinguished just before the king's lamp was kindled;
such a practice could be related to the Birthday of the Sun's
staff in Egypt.

Mr Rendel Harris says that both Dionysus and Apollo are
concerned in the production of fire, and the vegetable symbols – ivy sacred to Dionysus, Laurel and oak to Apollo –
may each be "described as a fire-stick", i.e. as sticks capable
of giving out the sacred fire concealed or hidden in them.*
The birthday of this "staff" was held in Egypt, according to
Plutarch, at the autumnal equinox. In Jerusalem the solar
orb would on this day rise directly over the Mount of Olives,
where it was believed that the feet of the Messiah would
tread, and the rays would leap across the dark and pre-
cipitous gorge of the Kedron valley, the abyss where it was
said that the Last Judgement would take place, and would
enter the Tabernacle to ignite the lamp. It is tempting to
identify the Sun's "staff" with the rod of Aaron, which
legend says could not be drawn out of earth but was immov-
able, like Excalibur, except by one who was pre-ordained
for the task or knew the name of God. This is mere speculation because of a particular Jewish legend; it does not fit
entirely with Aaron's use of the rod in scripture, though it
did "bud", and may have budded with the Flower of Light.
i.e. fire, for it yielded blossoms, and was a staff of
almond wood.

---

* *The Origin of the Cult of Apollo* by Rendel Harris, p. 19.

All this is no doubt poetic and appeals to the imagination, but have we any real evidence that Solomon did in fact employ a crystal to bring fire from the sun? We have seen that an old German manuscript written by Alchemists or Cabbalists and transcribed by "Raphael," claims that Urim and Thummim (Perfect Light) was a crystal set in gold; and that the old Celtic and Medieval Lays claim that the crystal pommel (i.e. apple) of the fiery brand was kept in the Temple at Jerusalem. But this, by itself is not very weighty evidence. Is there no allusion to the talisman in the Old Testament?

There is certainly no direct allusion, but we have seen that in no country was it permissible to speak of the crystal save by periphrasis, a periphrasis so important to the Icelandic skalds, and we should also remember the frequent injunctions to secrecy regarding the Grail. Then we can perhaps deduce – and the matter is speculative – that the "vessel", the crystal, is always feminine, always alluded to as "she" and never as "it"; and that St. Barbara, St. Catherine of Alexandria, the Princess Scota, who in legend came to Ireland to beget all Scots, and Helen Dendritis, bound to a tree, were all from Egypt or connected with it; and that Solomon married Pharaoh's daughter, for which he was anathematized by the Orthodox Jews (and later Rabbis of Spain). So he removed her from the Holy Place of the Ark, and built at a discreet distance from the Temple a special "house" for her.

Leaving now the question of the crystal and coming to that of the "Strange Girdle" of the Grail-sword: it is tempting to compare it with the "Curious girdle of the ephod" mentioned in Exod.XXVIII.XXIX and XXXIX and Lev. VIII, as worn by the High Priest. The word *Cheshebh*, which the Authorised Version translates as "curious girdle", was not, however, so translated in the Aramaic Targum, Septuagint or Vulgate, having in these versions respectively the sense of ornamented, woven work and golden texture. It is not easy to see, therefore, how a 12th century poet could have used any translation of the Old Testament which could have led him to transcribe the girdle of the ephod as

"Strange" unless, as he claims, he was transcribing from a most ancient manuscript now lost to us.

The ephod was the linen garment of the priest (the Medieval equivalent could be white samite) and over it the High Priest wore the breast plate, (of which more later) and above the breast plate, probably from around his neck, hung the Urim. The only sword of David mentioned in the Old Testament is that which he took from the giant Goliath, but, when weaponless, he fled from Saul and came to Shiloh, where was the Ark and where he ate the Shew-bread, and where the sword of Goliath was laid up, the priest took this "sword" from behind the ephod, unwrapping it from its cloth and presented it to David. Was it a fiery brand such as was given (in vision only) to Judas Maccabeus by the prophet Jeremiah?

There is a possibility that the torn and shredded hangings of the Grail-sword, reputed to have been kept in Solomon's Temple, may be a memory of the Jewish custom whereby the cast-off linen belts of the ordinary priests, (not the embroidered girdle of the High Priest) were torn into shreds for wicks which they lighted at the great fire-feast of Tabernacles. In fanciful language one could therefore say that the fiery brand issued from an old and shredded girdle.

So far the evidence of sun-worship is strong but the existence of a crystal in Israel is inconclusive. When, however, we turn back the pages of history to the days of Moses, the Grail legend is blazoned forth with a clarity which is astounding.

Let us remember first what is the true meaning of being "drawn from water". It will be remembered that in the numerous cases previously quoted a hero who is drawn from an ark of bulrushes or a lotus flower is "twice-born" or "illuminated" or consecrated as a son-of-the-Sun. I have kept until now two other examples of how such heroes were found, because of their bearing on the story of Moses. First Lancelot, because Tennyson's words might have been composed for the great Hebrew leader himself: "Lancelot, whom the Lady of the Lake caught from his mother's arms

– the wondrous one." The lake from which this lady took her name was called the lake of Diana, and she herself is described as a fairy. Was her lake identical with the lake at Nemi, known as the mirror of Diana? She caught up the infant from the place beside the water where his distressed and persecuted mother had laid him, and took him to dwell in her fairy halls below the lake until he should have attained manhood.*

Secondly there is the tale of Taliesin. It will be remembered that this hero and poet had gained wisdom from the Cauldron of Inspiration. He had sucked his thumb (like Horus), and had become endowed with supernatural insight. After some tribulation he was reincarnated as a son of the goddess Ceridwen, who put him in a leather bag and cast him into the sea. Now when Elphin, son of Gwyddno Garanhir, known as the Lofty Crane and as Priest of the Ship (the crane is akin to the Ibis of Thoth and nested in Britain until the 16th century) went down to net salmon in the weir on May Eve (the night of the Beltane fires) he came upon the bag. He opened it and found the infant within. And they named the child Taliesin, which means "shining face" or "radiant brow". Taliesin can therefore tentatively be compared with Moses, who was renowned for an occasion when his face shone so brightly that he was forced to veil it from the multitude. I believe that Moses was experiencing the radiance of the true God, which manifested itself at Pentecost, the Transfiguration and the baptism of Christ. But the prosaic explanation of Taliesin's shining face is this: there must always be a "bag" floating in the water if you are netting a river for fish, because the net must be attached to floats. What Elphin found was the "floating stone", a glass coracle sealed and confined in a network of leather thongs, and it sparkled in the sunlight amidst the rippling water. Such hollow spherical glass floats were used in the first World War to support anti-submarine nets, as at the time Britain was unable to import cork. The Admiralty informed me that they believed such floats to have been

* *Vulgate Lancelot* edition Oskar Sommer Vol III pp 8-22.

used previously by fishing drifters. I am not suggesting that the Celts of the 6th century would have commonly employed glass floats for fishing (they probably used inflated bladders) but it is very likely that they knew such a means to be feasible, and it is even possible that after the introduction of Christianity some of the "glassy globes which Merlin made" may have found their way into the hands of the common folk. The story of Taliesin then shows that he is identified with the sparkling light of the sun on glass. He becomes a poet and artist, inspired; and his name, Taliesin, means in Welsh 'Shining Face'.

In view of all these stories of heroes who were drawn from water, and particularly of the Indian Karna, who was specifically named as a son of the sun-god, Surya, can we really doubt but that the story of how Moses was drawn from the Nile water by Pharaoh's daughter is a description of the infant Horus, rising from the lotus amongst the bulrushes and nursed by the daughter of the "Great House" which is the hieroglyph from which Pharaoh (He-of-the-Great-House) derives, and could just as well mean the Great House of the Goddess? She was on her way to bathe, and we have seen how goddesses and fairy ladies take ritual baths. Mr Cyril Aldred, Egyptologist, tells me that the story of an infant found among the bulrushes was an Egyptian folk tale centuries before any possible date postulated for Moses. We know from Acts VII.22 that "Moses was learned in all the wisdom of the Egyptians", and he could not have learned wisdom except through some form of temple-training, the equivalent of a University in those days.

I am not for a moment suggesting that Moses was an idolater, but rather that God was carefully training and orientating him towards the eventual revelation of Himself. According to the historian, Flavius Josephus, Moses was not only learned in wisdom but also in warfare, being sent by Pharaoh to command a military expedition, a punitive force, against enemies in the area of what is now called the Sudan, though Josephus calls it Ethiopia. Later, after having to flee from Egypt because he had slain an Egyptian who

was smiting a Hebrew, the people of Midian with whom he
sought refuge, took him to be an Egyptian, so he must have
conformed to the customs and dress of the Nile valley,
although by that time he knew himself to be a Hebrew and
his sympathies were with them. If he had lived in Goshen,
the Delta – that was where the Hebrews lived – he could there
have learnt to love his own people. If in his youth he learnt
wisdom in the temples, then the Egyptian hierarchy who
would have taught him would have been centred in
Heliopolis in the Delta (close beside the modern Cairo),
chief seat of the worship of Rê; the very place to which the
Phoenix brought its egg, and identical with the City-of-the-
Sun, *On*, of which the Patriarchal Joseph's father-in-law was
High Priest.

The story now takes us to the manifestation of what is
commonly known as the Burning Bush. Let us study what
Moses actually saw. "The angel of the Lord appeared unto
him in a flame of fire out of the midst of a bush: and he
looked and, behold, the bush burned with fire and the bush
was not consumed."

In the adventures of St. Brendan, the Abbot reminds the
Saint that the answer to the Mystery of how the candles light
themselves is to be found in the Burning Bush. Lucan's description of the Druid grove at Marseilles includes an
account of a tree from which came the glare of conflagration, although it was not on fire. Nonnus speaks of a tree
from which fire, self-made, issued but the tree was not consumed. Perceval beholds a tree which seems to burn with
candles, and he is told that it concerns the mystery of the
Holy Grail. Finally, we have the astonishment of the
ancients that a crystal which could *cause* fire did not itself
grow warm. The Orphic Book of Stones remarks this
phenomenon. It could cause a torch to ignite, but it was *not
itself consumed*. There is no doubt in my mind that Moses
must have stood at some time during a temple-training
before the little golden tree in which the crystal shone. Such
a talisman is unknown to Egyptologists, but could it have
been kept secretly at Heliopolis, the City-of-the-Sun to
which the Phoenix brought its egg? It seems more likely

that it came into Egypt with the Hebrews or the Shepherd Kings and into the Delta only. Such a crystal can throw a white spot of light upon a hand, the focal point of which could resemble the dreaded white spot of the onset of leprosy, a phenomenon which Moses, and in Grail legend Vespasian have to experience. The theory that the ritual of the crystal could have entered Egypt (to which it was foreign) from the direction of Canaan is borne out by the legend of Abraham's visit to Egypt, given in the Zohar recorded by the Cabbalists.* His sister-wife Sarah was so beautiful that, fearing the lustful desires of the Egyptians, "He brought her in a box", but the customs officers at the border insisted on opening the box and "When it was opened a light like that of the sun shone forth." They reported her beauty to Pharaoh, who straightway desired her. The *Shekinah* (later thought of as the radiance denoting the presence of God) was constantly in the abode of Sarah†; and the *Zohar* continues "Abraham called the name of his son that was born unto him, whom Sarah bore to him, Isaac: to wit, the son that was born to him as fire born from water."

Sarah therefore probably had a double identity. She was a real woman who gave birth to Isaac, but was also the "abode" of sunlight, i.e. the crystal. According to legend she was not yet the real wife of Abraham on his arrival in Egypt, for legend says that he had not yet consummated the marriage, and gives the rather feeble explanation that his failure to have conjugal relations with her was due to his being so chaste that he had not ever observed how beautiful Sarah was, nor looked at her, until he saw the reflection of her beauty in the water of a stream through which they waded on their way to Egypt; then he first beheld her beauty like the brilliance of the sun.§ The reflection of light on water is all part of the true God's picture-writing to draw man to wonder and reverence at the beauty of God's creation and in particular the beauty of light; also to wonder

---

* *Zohar*, trans by H. Sperling & M. Simon Vol I. p. 64.
† *Legends of the Jews* by Louis Ginzberg Vol I. p. 162.
§ *Legends of the Jews* by Louis Ginzberg.

when a primitive man beholds the reflection of his own face and first questions himself: "Is that really me?" I shall presently show how this legend about Sarah's reflection is repeated, I believe, in a pre-Christian writing about Our Lady.

Let us then adopt as a hypothesis that Moses was already acquainted with the fact that fire can come from a crystal, a stone which is not itself consumed, and was probably enshrined in a little golden tree. Where does this lead us? *Not*, I repeat *not* to any denigration of the vision of the Burning Bush and the reality of Moses' experience of the true God. But God chooses to use the furniture of a human mind to convey messages and visions. If a mind is over-furnished, there will be no room, no time, no place for God to use that over-busy mind. If the mind is totally unfurnished, it may be difficult for the true God to convey any messages at all, though He has been known to use the almost empty minds of little children, as at Lourdes or Fatima. But such children are rare and are pre-ordained saints, whereas Moses, although the greatest of prophets, was not exactly a saint. He had killed a man, and according the historian, Josephus, had commanded an Egyptian army in a punitive war, and he was to prove harsh to rebels and to the heathen in the days of the Exodus. But if my hypothesis be accepted, he had exactly the right furnishings of the mind to receive a vision, and the symbolism of the crystal, about which he already knew, becomes the medium through which the true God can communicate to a human being who is undergoing a visionary or trance-like state of mind, the all-important message of what mission God has appointed him to undertake.

The *Grand Saint Graal* gives an account of another such Burning Bush. St. Joseph of Arimathea, preaching to a certain heathen, Duke Gaanort, exhorts him to believe in the miraculous conception of Christ. Joseph reminds the Duke that when he (Gaanort) was a lad of fifteen years old in Galilee, he had been, like Moses, employed as a shepherd. While keeping his flock, he saw a bush of "Fleur-de-Lys", which, Joseph says, is a symbol of Eve. From out of this tree

of Fleur-de-Lys (Perhaps tree of candles) grew another tree
of roses. The roses which grew in the place of the seven
Fleur-de-Lys (lights) correspond, says Joseph, to the Hebrew prophets. But one after another they faded and fell.
Until at last a bud appeared (the Rosa Mundi) and although
the bud never opened, nevertheless from its closed petals
sprang a man, issuing from his mother's virginity *"as sun
that shineth through glass so bright"*, and he slew a serpent and
picked up the fallen roses. There is confusion here between
Rosa and the Latin *ros*, meaning dew, and dew is very
important, as important as crystals, for it can contain sunlight. The Rosicrucians presume to alter the meaning of the
initials above the crucifix, INRI, meaning "Jesus of
Nazareth King of the Jews" as in the writing of Pilate himself and pinned above the Cross, to IGNE NITRUM RORIS
INVENITUR its meaning being "the baptism or cleansing
power of dew is only discovered by fire."* I shall have a lot
more to say about dew very shortly now, but in the mean-
time let us return to Moses. If we accept that he was in a state
of visionary trance, that he beheld in his mind the liturgical
object of which he already knew, but beheld it in such a way
that the true God could speak to him through this particular
symbol which the mind of Moses provided, then would he
after such a soul-shattering experience have regarded the
mere liturgical object in greater or lesser respect?

The answer, I think, is to be found in Martin Buber's
inspiring book on the prophet, and his interpretation of the
meaning of God's name as revealed from the Burning
Bush. "I AM that I AM" is not merely "I exist", nor is it a
refusal by God to disclose his true nature: rather it is a promise. "I shall be as I choose to be. I shall always be with you,
but I shall choose in what manner to manifest myself." This
is a very different idea of the Deity from the pagan conception as held by ordinary folk at that time. In the imagination
of ordinary men, as distinct perhaps from a few of the
highest initiates, rain and thunder were produced by one

---

* *Secret Societies and Subversive Movements* by Nesta H. Webster. p. 89 and also Mac-
key's *Lexicon of Freemasonry*. p. 150.

celestial being, fire by another, the fruits of the earth by another, and so on. It was theoretically admitted that all these principalities and powers were ruled by the Creator, but fortunately for sinners, or so men thought, the Creator was far removed from the affairs of mankind. Meanwhile such angelic beings could be tidily arranged in departments, and, *most* important, they could be *confined* to a particular department: shut, as it were in a box or tabernacle under lock and key, and only liberated at the command of man to do his behests; then conveniently banished again by an evil conscience – in fact the genie of an Aladdin contained in its glass bottle. But here is the Creator, even though he has for the moment chosen the glass vessel or crystal as a symbol in which to appear, declaring that He will not be so confined or banished. He will *always* be present with Moses and with mankind, but He will *choose* in what manner to reveal Himself, and He has all his creation from which to choose. God keeps his promise. He is the sea which engulfs Pharaoh; He is the dawn upon Mount Sinai; He is the thunder; He is the consuming fire. He is whatever causes man to experience a sense of abiding wonder. Yet this is not the pantheism of the Egyptians. God does not say He *is* in everything, but there is nothing in which He cannot appear, *if* He so chooses. He can come upon a man in the beauty of the sunset, or meet him amidst the lilies of the field.

Nevertheless, in the nature of things, certain men must be more or less prone to receiving this sense of abiding wonder through one medium rather than through another. Some find it in the beauties of nature, or in music, or in the Creator's ordering of the animal Kingdom, and perhaps Moses was particularly prone to receiving it through the sight of light, for there is reason to suppose that the little golden tree, the liturgical object which perhaps Abraham brought in the chest of Sarah in legend, may have been treasured in the Tabernacle under the name of the "Golden Pot of Manna". Considering the frequency with which archaeologists dig up everything of value, such as Tutankhamun's tomb, Viking settlements at York, Macedonian

and Bulgarian gold etc., one cannot but hope that the cave
in which Jeremiah hid the Ark containing the Tables of
Stone, the Pot of Manna and probably the original
Menorah, will one day be discovered. One might pray that
it will be found in the land of Israel and not on Mount Nebo
where, according to one tradition, the lost cave is situated,
because Mount Nebo is now in Jordan. If found there it
might cause conflict for possession of the trophy as it did in
the time of King Saul when the Philistines captured it.
However, Islam with its regard for Bible history would
without doubt venerate and preserve such a treasure.

If my theories prove correct, would the golden tree of the
Israelites be very similar to the illustration of the Babylonian seal on page 74 (Fig 2.)? We must not forget that a
branched candlestick shows in its very name that the artist's
design was originally based on a tree. It seems probable that
in Jewish hands the Babylonian design (or should I say the
original design which came from Ur of the Chaldees with
Abraham?) underwent certain alterations. It will be
remembered how often in Grail legend a seven-branched
candlestick was present at a manifestation of the holy vessel.
Before Perceval comes to the Grail castle he sees a tree on
which burn candles, and he is told that it concerns the mystery of the Grail. In the account of Duke Gaanort's Burning
Bush, there are seven Fleur-de-Lys in a row upon the tree. It
seems probable that the famous seven-branched candlestick which Moses had made for the Tabernacle was in some
way combined with a crystal. Now the well-known candlestick which Titus seized at the fall of Jerusalem and which is
portrayed on his triumphal arch, may not have been a
replica of the original. The one seized by Titus would have
been made after the return from the Jews from Exile in
Babylon, for amongst the vessels listed as restored by Cyrus
the candlestick is not mentioned, whereas the Altar of
incense is specifically mentioned as being lost in the cave
with the Ark, and the inference is that the Mosaic candlestick was with it. It appears, therefore, that the post-exilic
Jews only had their memories on which to rely when
attempting a copy of the lost original.

If the accounts of the candlestick as ordained by Moses in Exod.XXV 31-40 and XXXVII 17-20 be read carefully it will be seen that there is an extraordinary likeness between it and the tree on the Babylonian seal. The "knops" are the "spinning whorls" on Solomon's "bed", the six bowls are the upward pointing leaves, and the flowers those which point downwards. It can be noted briefly here that in the Koran, Mohammed, borrowing as so often from the Hebrew scriptures, not only gives an account of the Burning Bush, but as the Burrell Collection (recently opened) shows, many Persian rugs decorated with what the catalogue calls "Flaming Palmettes" were evidently a favourite motif for rug-makers. The buds on all the branches of the palms are flames, and probably derive from the Islamic account of the Burning Bush.

Fig. 16. 17TH CENTURY WATER-MARK SHOWING GRAIL AND BRANCHED CANDLESTICK COMBINED.
From "A New Light on the Renaissance", by Harold Bayley.

So far we have dealt with the six bowls only. No mention of a central or seventh light is made until the very end of both Hebrew accounts, when there is a sudden reference to the total number of flames as seven. Zechariah (IV.2.) refers to the candlestick as having *a* (i.e. one) bowl upon the top of it. This may be no more than a careless or poetic use of the singular, but he does employ a different word for "bowl" than that hitherto employed to describe the hollows for the oil lamps. If the reader will glance at Fig.16 he will see the attempt of the heretical paper-makers to record in an old water-mark a confused memory of the Grail and candlestick combined. The famous Hebrew work, the *Zohar*, says of the *Menorah* or seven-branched candlestick: "These lamps, like the planets above, receive their light from the sun."[*]

The Hanukkah lamp, which the Jews still use for their festival of the re-dedication of the Temple, may provide a possible clue to the original combination, for it is plainly derived from the same source of symbolism. A cross-section of the relative position of the candles is given in the accompanying diagram. The number of candles is increased

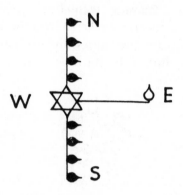

to eight because the Feast lasts for eight days. The candle at the East, known as the Master Candle would no doubt have originally represented the rising sun, for from it the other candles are lit in turn on the successive days of the feast. Directly opposite the Master Candle in the East is a point which is generally surmounted either by a heraldic flame in metal or more often by the "Star" of David. If the crystal Urim were interposed between the East and the point, then the Morning Star of the Messiah would light itself.

A word here about the so-called "star" of David with its six points. This is a misnomer. The Jews know it not as a star but as The Shield of David, probably because it was considered a magical protection against evil, being the acknowledged symbol in other Near Eastern religions of the

---

[*] See *Jewish Encyclopedia*, under "Menorah".

interlacing or fusion of the human and the divine triangles.
Because it was a protection against evil it may have been
painted or embossed on the circular targe of King David.
William of Malmesbury writing about St. Joseph of
Arimathea (in a side-note of the manuscript which may be a
later interpolation) says not only did the Apostles James
and Philip accompany St. Joseph to Britain but Galahad,
that Messianic figure, received, presumably from Joseph, a
certain shield which no one else could bear without great
loss of strength. The so-called "star" encircled by a gold
circle is often worn by a Jewess as a necklace in present
times. One cannot help wondering (if Galahad did indeed
possess a shield with the Star of David painted on it)
whether the queen who pointed to her necklace as a clue to
the Grail was wearing that same symbol. Certainly Hathor's
necklace carved on the temple at Denderah is a much more
elaborate affair, and so for all I know was the necklace of
Freyja, but the Arthurian queen may well have worn the
simple six-pointed "star" of Israel. I share with the Sufis a
great reverence for this symbol because, as the Sufis hold,
the triangle representing the Divine, has its apex pointing
upwards indicating that everything proceeded from the
One, i.e. God. While the triangle of humanity points in the
opposite direction. I was dissatisfied with the position of the
equilateral triangle of the Divine which in Christian church
embellishments represents the Trinity: three equal Persons
in One God, each being equal with the other two; though I
delighted in the interlacing of the two triangles to form one
star – a splendid illustration of what theology calls the
Hypostatic Union – union of the divine and human in
Christ who is both man and God. But my dissatisfaction
with the triangle of Divinity arose because I felt that it
aspired, as does a pyramid or a church-steeple or Durer's
"Praying Hands". Then all at once the message came
clearly to me from the direction of the altar where a trick of
light was creating the symbol on some metal work: "You are
gazing on a star, and the nature of heavenly bodies such as
stars is to revolve." Suddenly it was clear to me. The revolving of that "star" would bring the Divine to earth and the

human would automatically ascend to the throne of the
Divine. This illustrated perfectly the almost incomprehensible creed of Athanasius, known as the Quicunque Vult, –
which says: "Not by conversion of the Godhead into flesh;
but by taking of the manhood into God."

That St. John was well acquainted with the original
association of the crystal and the candlestick is, I think,
shown very clearly in his Revelation. He sees the Christ "in
the midst of the seven candlesticks," that is to say taking the
place of the Star of David or Morning Star. (The stem of
Jesse and the branch of the Messiah are all symbolized on
the Hanukkah lamp). And these lamps were burning before
the throne of God, and before the throne was "a sea of glass
like unto crystal" a sea mingled with fire. Admittedly this is
a vision of the final sphere above the sphere of the sun and
planets, but the use of the word "sea" is interesting because
as we shall find on the next page it was a word which the
Jews used for a very large vessel such as the laver of the Temple which could, like a lake, reflect light. Compare the Cabbalists' description of Paradise: "And the righteous put on
their crowns and feast themselves on the brightness of the
pellucid mirror – happy are they to be vouchsafed that
celestial light! The light of the mirror shines on all sides, and
each one of the righteous takes his appropriate portion,
each according to his works in the world."

That the crystal was in some way connected with the
branched candlestick, the *Menorah*, and at the same time
was the Urim which the High Priest must wear when entering the Holy of Holies could perhaps be explained by a
jewel being interchangeable in different settings. That this
is possible I shall presently show when we come to the Carolingian preoccupation with crystals.

My reason for supposing the Urim to be a crystal and the
Thummim the metal support, shaped like a tree, on which
it hung, the combination meaning "Perfect Light", is not
only the German Alchemical manuscript illustrated on
page 79 by a certain Raphael, a pseudonym, but certain
Cabbalistic passages in the *Zohar* such as: "Other prophets
beheld visions in a glass that did not illumine, and even so

they did not venture to lift up their eyes . . . nor was their message given to them in clear terms. Not so was Moses, the faithful prophet: he saw his vision in a luminous glass, and still stood upright . . . for even while he was in that exalted grade he did not lose his faculties, and straightway after gazing on the brightness of the heavenly glory he returned to the camp . . . and his mind was as clear as before."* Admittedly the *Zohar* is full of such allusions to a luminous glass, and they are to be taken symbolically rather than literally. But the following passage, beginning "The secret of the Lord is to them that fear him", has a more precise terminology. "The term "Urim" signifies the luminous speculum, which consisted of the engravure of the Divine Name composed of forty-two letters by which the world was created. Whereas the Thummim consisted of the non-luminous speculum." If we admit that the writer regarded the letters of the Divine Name as the source of light, it must still be asked from what ancient rites did this symbolism devolve, why are Urim and Thummim connected in ancient Jewish thought with a speculum (i.e. mirror) and why is this particular symbolism so rooted in Judaism that St. Paul uses the analogy of a speculum on two occasions to describe God's revelation of Himself? "For now we see through a glass darkly; but then face to face." I Cor.XIII.12 and "We all with open face beholding as in a glass the glory of the Lord, are changed into the same image from glory to glory." II Cor.III.18.

We have so far accounted for the contents of the lost Ark awaiting discovery in its cave: The Tables of Stone, the Pot of Manna, Aaron's rod, Urim and Thummim and presumably together with it the *Menorah* and the golden altar of incense. This latter was, I think, revealed to Parzival (figuratively) as a table of jacinth in the Fisher King's hall.

Now we come to the most astonishing and most interesting part of the legend of the Grail – the ship which de Borron describes as having been sent by Solomon to Britain.

---

* *Zohar* translation by H. Sterling and M. Simon. Vol V. 363 and Vol IV. p. 300.

It is without doubt and in truth the very Ark of the Covenant. His description, which I have kept until now because of
its significance, would not have been fully appreciated
earlier. It states that at the head of the "bed" (the Grail tree)
Solomon had put a testimony to explain the history of how
the "ship" was made and prepared for Galahad, and over
this "testimony" he had placed his crown. Now it is the custom of the Jewish synagogue to place a crown over the
scrolls of the Law. It is called the Crown of the Torah, and an
example will be found on Plate III. On the breastplate
beside it (a nostalgic memory of a breastplate worn by
Israel's High priests) are figured the pillars of Jachin and
Boaz and the lost Ark is replaced by a similitude
of the Two Tables of Stone which were inscribed through the
powers of Moses with the Ten Commandments. Therefore
the *Grand Saint Graal* describing the "ship" of Solomon in
which is placed a "testimony" surmounted by a crown *can*
only mean that the ship was meant to describe the Ark containing the Tables of the Law. From *no* other source in the
Near East save only Jerusalem could this particular symbolism derive.

How does it come about that the Celtic and probably
pre-Christian legends of Glastonbury have preserved an
accurate memory of the Ark of the Covenant and its real
contents?

1. If de Borron knew that he was transcribing a description
of the Ark, then why the secrecy? Why call it a ship and why
use such veiled language that its identity has remained
largely unrecognized?

2. Again, if de Borron was not, as he claimed, transcribing
from a secret and ancient account, but was simply using his
familiarity with the Old Testament to describe the Ark in an
ultra-poetic way, he could have obtained from the Jews the
knowledge that a crown was usually placed above the
Torah, but he could *not* have obtained from either the Old
Testament or the Medieval Rabbis a knowledge of the crystal
and brand. Because from the time of the Exile to Babylon
the Jews seem to have lost all memory of what Urim and
Thummim were. They were probably as mystified as the

modern scholar is today. Moreover, if a few rabbis, such for example as Nicodemus, knew the real nature of the Pot of Manna and Aaron's rod, would they have transmitted the secret to a Christian?

3. The mystery might be explained if de Borron was a member of some secret cult, but it is believed that he was very much under the influence of St. Bernard and the Cistercians, and may even have been a Cistercian.

4. If the Medieval poet was transcribing a purely Celtic lay, and was himself ignorant of its import, then knowledge of the crystal and brand might possibly have derived from Egypt, Heliopolis in the land of Goshen, but an Ark from Heliopolis would have had no Tables of Stone nor crown of the Torah.

5. One possible explanation is that St. Joseph of Arimathea, who would no doubt have received a full interpretation of the Scriptures from the Resurrected Lord, did really come to Britain, and that the Celts carefully preserved a memory of his teaching them about the Old Law of Moses, just as they did in fact carefully preserve his thatched church down to the days of St. David.

Let us return for a moment to that particular Burning Bush in the *Grand Saint Graal* which budded first of all the prophets and finally the Rosa Mundi, because we shall find that the dew, the "Ros" probably has a connection with the Ark, with the Song of Solomon as well as with Our Lady and with Sarah, and thus can be placed fittingly in a chapter devoted to Jewish traditions.

Long before men learnt to light a fire through a spherical crystal or lens, they must first have noticed, as Shelley did, the beauty of sunlight caught in dew. The dawn was personified as a female goddess in pagan times: Aurora or Eos. Milton in *Paradise Lost* wrote:

"Now Morn her rosy steps in the earthen clime
Advancing sow'd the earth with oriental pearl."

The ancients in fact believed that it was the moon which spread the dew, seeding tiny facsimiles of herself, but it was

dawn who traditionally trod the dew. "The Morn," wrote
Shakespeare, "walks o'er the dew." May I repeat yet once
again that the ancients confused the various substances
which transmit light (crystal, glass, ice) and that they held
the dew in veneration as a container of light.

Beginning with Pandora (The Eve, the First Woman of
Greek theogony) who was given charge of a chest: she was
ordered by Prometheus (Before man thought) who was the
stealer of fire and thereafter became Epimethius (after
thinking) and was a type of Adam and her husband, never
to open the chest. She did so and brought disaster by her
disobedience. From Pandora we come next to a legendary
King of Athens who had three daughters, one of whom was
named Herse, meaning "dew". Her two sisters were jealous
of her beauty – the triple goddess again – and they became
the two ugly sisters of Cinderella. The three of them had
charge of cult-secrets in an ark or chest. The meaning of
Cinderella's name is Elen or Elaine, the Celtic goddess of
the ashes (Elaine is daughter of the Grail King and mother
of Galahad by Lancelot). She is found amongst the cinders
of the fire which she (the crystal heroine) had lit and is identified with Elen who imprisoned Merddin, the sun-god in a
house of glass.

Of the three hundred and eighteen accounts of the Cinderella story collected by Marion Roalfe Cox in the Folk
Lore Society in 1893, eighty-three speak of a tree as the
source of her magic gifts; twenty-three describe it as a tree of
golden apples; twenty-six say that her clothes were hidden
in a cave; and in fifty-five she is called Wooden Mary"
because she or her clothes are hidden in a magic box. If her
story is compared to I.Sam.VI.3. her adventures are very
similar to those of the Ark of the Covenant. After a battle
and the defeat of the Israelites, the Philistines took the Ark
as a trophy, but it brought down the curse of a plague upon
them, so they decided to return it humbly and as an act of
penitence that would remove the curse. It was therefore put
on a new cart to be drawn by kine, and with it went jewels;
and as a guilt-offering they put with the chest five pure
golden mice or rats, a possible source of the plague and

possibly used as a magical antidote when offered. Thus the carriage of "Wooden Mary" could become in fairy story a carriage drawn by rats and mice transformed by magic into coachmen and footmen. According to Marion Cox she meets the Prince at religious festivals more often than at balls, and her dress for such occasions must be trimmed with bells and made from the sun and the moon, the manufacture of which can only be accomplished by a Jew. Those very "dresses" will be shown to the reader in the next chapter and with illustrations. Meanwhile I will resort, not to real poetry but to a little versifying of my own in honour of a certain verse in the Song of Solomon and in honour of Herse, the Athenian lady.

The moon upon the earth doth strew
Her orient pearls, her seeds, her dew,
But must be gone ere dawn can pass
Dew-shod across the embroidered grass.
She in her turn must shortly fly
Before the sun can mount the sky,
Leaving her tiny shoe behind
Along the path which he will find.
The glassy slipper fills with gold.
When the sun's beam doth it enfold.
How beautiful are thy feet thus shod,
O Prince's daughter, for thy God
Thy Bridegroom hath thy chamber filled
With sparkling light; and thus has willed
That every microcosmos shine
In image of the Light Divine.

I discount the claim of certain Romance literature scholars that Cinderella's slipper was of *vair* (fur) rather than *verre* (glass), since fur stretches, making the size variable and the testing of it pointless. Besides, the story was current in Egypt* long before it reached Europe in the tale of

---

* Egyptologists have speculated whether that enigmatic sign of immortal life held by all the gods, the Ankh, is derived through punning and similarity with the Coptic word for the straps of a sandal.

Rhodopis and Pharaoh Menkaura, where the hawk (Rê, the sun) drops the slipper (sandal) into Pharaoh's lap just as the sun lifts and drops the dew. *Tal* is the Hebrew for dew, and *talisman* the Arabic for a magic stone.

If the Song of Solomon celebrates the love of Light (God) for dew (earth) then we have an almost exact repetition of the story of Sarah's beauty reflected in water in an Old Testament Apocrypha called "The Twelve Patriarchs" written down in the 3rd century *before* Christ in the days of the Maccabees. In this is recorded the vision of the writer seeing a virgin clothed in all the colours of the world. She is in a pool surrounded by twelve bulls, and within this circle of bulls this virgin gives birth to a lamb. Commentators have suspected a later Christian interpolation here, but the Apocryphal writing as a whole is admitted to have existed a century or more before Christ; so away with all the cynics who doubt prophetic visions! Now the twelve bulls, representing the twelve tribes, obviously refer to the great bronze circular laver which Hiram, the builder, constructed for Solomon's Temple. It was almost as large as a small swimming pool, being seventeen and a half feet across with a circumference of fifty two and a half feet; and it was, and still is, referred to as a "sea" even in the most modern translations of the Hebrew, e.g. the Jerusalem Bible. Its purpose was to provide water for lustrations and purifications, and had to be itself purified with the herb Hyssop (Num.IXX.18 and Psalm 11.7.); hence the phrase in the prefix to the Mass "Purge me with Hyssop and I shall be clean." It was water which was called "purification from sin", and such clean water was very necessary when cleansing utensils after a bloody sacrifice or for the washing of the priest's hands. The bronze bulls on whose backs the circular "sea" rested represented, as I have said, the twelve tribes of Israel. Such a figuration approved by Solomon was much criticised by the later Spanish Rabbis as idolatrous, but in the Sinaitic script (the very first alphabetical as opposed to the picture-writing of hieroglyphs) the first letter is Alpha, and represented the bull of Osiris, Apis, and I regret to say the Golden Calf. It was therefore written in what we would call an "upside down" way, i.e. with its horns in the air thus ∀ . There are six triangular designs in the star (Shield) of David and the points can be doubled to twelve as on a clock-face. If the star revolves, the Alpha eventually comes to the position it holds to-day (the manhood is taken up into God and man's original place on earth is occupied by the Holy Spirit.) St. John, writing his Revelation for the Greeks, makes Omega the last letter of the alphabet, whereas in Hebrew the last letter is "Tau", the sign of the cross, but the Omega is appropriate when written in the earliest Sinaitic form as a circle, for it can represent the revolving. The second letter of the Sinaitic script is Beth, a square meaning the house of man □; and from Alpha and Beth derive our word "Alphabet". There is a charming Apocryphal New Testament story of Christ's infancy when he gently rebukes his teacher, a Rabbi, saying why teach the "beth" before you know the truth about the "Alpha"?

So the visionary in the Apocryphal *Testament of the Twelve Patriarchs*, who sees in his dream the circle of bulls, is seeing the bronze laver; and the pure water represents the Virgin who reflects in the water purified from sin, all the colours of the world. Regarding her title of 'Star of the Sea,' I have consulted every Encyclopedia, Catholic, Judaic, Islamic, Britannic, and Hasting's Religious Encyclopedia, and at last three priests in my efforts to disassociate Our Lady from the planet dedicated by the pagans to Hesperus (we call it Venus and, when Hesperus was forgotten, the pagans associated it with Aphrodite). Finally Father Noel Donoghue, Lecturer in Theology at New College, Edinburgh was kind enough to do some research into the origin of the Virgin's title, *Stella Maris*. It appears that St. Jerome tried to derive the name Miriam from a "drop of water". I do not think any philologist to-day would accept such a derivation, and the Egyptian origins given on page 194 is much more likely, but it shows that St. Jerome was probably aware of the feelings for dew as a container of light, about which I have already written on page 226. Nor does it explain how a "drop of water" became the Star of the Sea. Only the Pole Star was used by mariners to navigate. The planet

Venus is known as both the Morning and the Evening Star, but it has nothing to do with navigation. The Morning Star is identified with Our Lord by St. John in the Revelation. So we come back to the question of why the mother of Christ is called the Star of the Sea. I prefer the derivation from *The Testament of the Twelve Patriarchs* where the pool is obviously the laver of the Temple in which the Virgin appeared in that "sea", the water of purification from sin. Just as Sarah in Jewish legend reflected the light of the sun in the water of a stream, so did the pure water of the laver or bronze "sea" reflect the light, and thus Our Lady's "star" is the dazzling point of sunlight like a star shining in the water. The Sufi poet, Jami, wrote:

Beware! say not "He is All-Beautiful,
And we his lovers. Thou are but the glass,
And He the Face confronting it, which casts
Its image in the mirror. He alone
Is manifest, and thou in truth art hid.
Pure love, like Beauty, coming but from Him,
Reveals itself in thee. If steadfastly
Thou canst regard, thou wilt at length perceive
He is the mirror also – He alike
The Treasure and the Casket. "I" and "thou"
Have here no place, and are but fantasies
Vain and unreal. Silence! for this tale
Is endless, and no eloquence hath power
To speak of Him. 'Tis but for us to love
And suffer silently, being as naught.*

To sum up: the *"Fiat"* of the Virgin Mary is not just a supine acquiescence, nor the shrugging of shoulders to which ordinary Moslems are prone when they say, *Inshallah*, but rather the transcendental love of Christian, Sufi and Oriental mystic alike for the utterly beautiful ultimate Godhead, who rewards the devotee with Himself.

---

* *Transl.* by E.G. Browne.

12 ALCHEMY, THE EVOLUTION OF THE MONSTRANCE, AND WOLFRAM'S DOVE

From the moment of the experience of Moses at the Burning Bush, man's search for God takes on a different pattern, for whatever man is able to control, he can no longer worship. Once light and fire are his servants, he must look more deeply within himself to search and hope to find the presence of the True God, a presence which hereafter will be denoted by radiance: a radiance no longer associated with the sun, but given by the Jews the name of the Shekinah, and later by the Christians thought of as the celestial fire of the Holy Spirit, manifested at Christ's baptism and Transfiguration and at Pentecost, as also in the haloes of certain saints. But to recognise that sunlight and fire are merely part of the material world, necessarily implies that men have begun their scientific examination of all that exists in the material creation around them.

So far we have only touched briefly on the subject of Alchemy, but now we need to see it as one of the first steps in such a scientific exploration of the world. In certain Islamic sects Elijah is known as the "Father of Alchemy", but while this shows that the prophet may have had an enquiring mind, his date in the 9th century B.C. is far too late for him to have been the originator of the science of metallurgy. Chemistry seems to have derived from Egypt; at least it took its name from Khem, the name of that land. The Israelites called it the land of Ham, son of Noah, which is only another pronunciation of Khem. The knowledge of colouring glass to imitate gems shows that Assyria in the 7th century B.C. must also have been acquainted with chemistry.

Thus, hand in hand the formulation of the study of metallurgy, chemistry and astronomy began. Following Aristotle in Greece and Euclid's school on the Nile Delta, it was in Alexandria that scientific discovery really started. There was no way of dividing true astronomy from astrology and Gnosticism (with its inevitable planetary spheres which was all that could be postulated before the discoveries of Copernicus) and alongside the study of the stars there went Euclid's geometry and Aristotle's four elements of earth, air, fire and water and observations about the natural world. Claudius Ptolamaeus in the 1st century was involved in all this, as well as with geography and his erroneous if ingenious ideas about optics. He had his observatory at the famous light-house, the Pharos of Alexandria, deemed to be one of the Seven Wonders of the World.

Alongside and at the same date the study of metallurgy began and it was called Alchemy. Most of it was founded on false premises. As I have already said, the first historical alchemist, a contemporary of Ptolemaeus, was Mary the Jewess, who invented the Bain Marie used in our kitchens to-day. The Alchemists must be given credit for being the first to discover distillation (which required glass vessels, beakers, retorts and piping in glass as in a modern laboratory) and they began to distinguish clearly between various types of metals and chemicals. Where the majority of them fell into error was to suppose that by mixing gold, silver, mercury and a corrosive acid or sulphur, they could fabricate unlimited gold, and this excited a desire for much wealth. Such mixtures were sealed in a glass vessel and sealed hermetically. This word derives from Hermes, the Greek name for the Egyptian god Thoth, god of wisdom and inventor of writing. The mixture when heated over a fire turned black and stank, and instead of producing the Philosopher's Stone, which the Alchemists believed would have converted all it touched into real gold, produced only a disappointing, messy and evil-smelling result. Amongst the Alchemists, however, there was a minority who believed that the search was not for what they despised as "vulgar gold" but was the cloak for a hidden cult which sought spiritual excellence. The union of the gold (the sun) and the silver (the moon) was likened to the union in man of divinity and humanity, and was pictured as the king and queen united in a marriage bed. The blackening and the stink of the elements by the addition of the sulphur and Mercury (the Roman name of Hermes or Thoth) was pictured as death, and after death came the resurrection. The glass vessel in which all this was effected, was identified with the hoped for Philosopher's Stone of immortal life, and was often pictured as embraced by a serpent, who represented the sealing tightly and hermetically of this vessel, but it could still, presumably, not only admit sunlight but in certain positions split the spectrum, because the alchemical pictures often show a peacock inside the glass to denote "all the colours of the world" as seen in Solomon's sword-pommel. A series of symbols for planets, metals, materials etc. existed for writing the secret recipes for the Alchemists to follow, and the sign for gold was the circle of the sun with a dot in the centre, and the sign for fire *was a sword*.

Inevitably such semi-scientific, semi-spiritual explorations were taken up by the Jews from Alexandria to Spain, and then to Spain's Moorish conquerors, spreading at the same time eastward to the Caliphs of Islam. It was suspect by the Church just because it was practised chiefly by both Gnostics, Jews and Infidels. But curiously enough the Catholic Litany of the Virgin acclaims Mary not only as the *Vas honorabile* but as the Home of Gold and Ark of the Covenant.

Remembering that Alchemists could provide innumerable pictures of glass vessels, let us turn now to the evolution of what the Catholic church calls the Monstrance – known in Italy and Germany as the Ostensorio and in Spain as the Custodia. I began by explaining on a former page that the Sacrament (the Holy Bread) was not originally displayed, but was kept hidden but handy in a jewelled box for speedy administration to the sick or dying. In*DiuCrône* we have an example of the Grail maiden carrying just such a box to the sick Fisher King. There then grew a desire among the laity to *see* the evidence of the Real Presence, for the people rarely took communion themselves because they feared their own unworthiness, dirty and tired from their work in the fields and probably aware of some worrying sin. So the Church first introduced the simple glass cylinder which when placed on the altar allowed the people to behold the Host. This became slightly more embellished when mounted more safely in metal, but was still a cylinder, as portrayed in Fig. 10 and it gave rise to the legend of St. Barbara's tower with its three windows when supported by three metal staves to balance such a container. Thus it became the source of a pagan legend, but of use in church.

We come next, after the fall of Rome to the Goths and other Germanic tribes, to the age of Charlemagne, who became the first Emperor of the new Holy Roman Empire, was crowned and anointed by the Pope in Rome in 800 A.D., and was not only a fervent Christian but anxious to succeed to the Christian traditions of the later Caesars and to become a world power. His relationships with other states and realms were therefore very important to him, and thus he entered into communication with the Patriarch of Jerusalem. The Patriarch, in compliment to the great Christian Emperor, sent him a very precious gift, known as the Talisman of Charlemagne. (See Plate IX left side). It consists of two lenticular (cabochon) stones, both transparent, mounted in precious metals and adorned with small jewels to encapsulate pieces of the true Cross. The transparent stone (probably crystal) which displayed the relic has at some unknown time been replaced with a cabochon of pale blue glass smaller than the original. The reason postulated for the change by modern thinking is that the glass displayed the Cross more clearly, but all that is certain is that the talisman, the relic, was found around the neck of Charlemagne at his exhumation in 1166. He is reputed to have always worn this reliquary suspended by its chain over his heart, just as the Jewish High Priest wore the Urim over his heart. But when the Emperor retired to bed, he must have removed it from his neck. He would hardly have cast such a precious treasure carelessly down on his dressing-table. In the last century a gentleman with a valuable golden watch hung it, on retiring, upon a small porcelain stand constructed for the purpose, where the clock-face remained visible if the gentleman wished to see the time from his prone position in bed. So did Charlemagne do the same? Yes, almost certainly he did, for on Plate IX right is shown a reliquary to encapsulate a relic and it is for wearing, as evinced by the hasp from which it would have hung, but it is now fixed to its "stand" for display upon an altar. Such encapsulated relics were worn by Christians at an early date and were termed phylacteries, meaning in Greek 'a guard' or talisman against evil. They should not be confused with the Jewish *Tephillin* which contained words of the Torah that had to be bound on the head and arm when praying, though Proverbs III.3 & VI.21 suggest that some such Jewish phylacteries were tied round the neck just as Charlemagne tied his. Compare Plate IX with Fig.3 of the Alchemical drawing reproduced by the so-called Raphael. As was promised, I show here how a large crystal could either be hung from the neck as a necklace or put on a "stand" so that a Seer could gaze into it. Thus the Jewish Urim could either be worn over the heart (when entering the Holy Place) or used as an oracle. It is necessary here to stress that the Carolingian kings were obsessed with a love of crystals and were buried with small crystal balls. Moreover at the same time a figure was constructed by the Carolingians of St. Faith at Conques, a Christian martyr who suffered death during the early Roman persecutions for her belief by being burned alive on a pyre, and her throne is decorated by the Carolingian monarchs with four enormous orbs of rock crystal. Clovis was buried at Tournai with such a crystal ball, and there are two more small ones from Carolingian graves in the Ashmolean Museum at Oxford. Why were they buried with such objects?

The answer, I think, lies in the phenomenon known as "Fairy Fire". The trick was taught me by a Highland gillie as

I was fishing. "De ye ken," he asked, "how to make Fairy Fire?" Obviously he had inherited the knowledge from ancient folk-lore. You take, so he taught me, two largish pebbles of white quartz from the river-bed where they have been polished smooth by the flow of water, and then in the dark of a cupboard or cellar you rub them hard together. The friction creates a fluttering light as though a luminous butterfly was beating its wings within your hands, a phenomenon known to scientists as triboluminescence; it is due to an electron breaking away from the nucleus, like a dancer scampering off and out from a circle of Highland reel-dancers and doing a little jig on its own – very egotistical and reprehensible behaviour. Eventually the electron gets cast into outer darkness until it finds another group to join up with which may be less pleasant than the first! You can never ignite a fire by this means, so it forms a safe and delightful game for small children who can hide in a dark cupboard to perform this "magic".

When I described the phenomenon to my friend, the late professor Stuart Piggott, the famous archaeologist, he was most interested because, as he told me, so often in neolithic graves he had found the human remains of individuals crouched in the pre-natal position, as though anxious to be born again, and their bones were surrounded by a circle of pebbles of white quartz, as though they sought for light in the darkness of the tomb. I feel sure that this is the reason that Carolingian kings and princes were buried with transparent rock-crystals – a kind of prayer for resurrection into celestial light.

We can digress here for a moment to remember that in Wolfram's Parzival the Host is laid on the stone from which the Phoenix rose periodically, and this stone is called the Grail and also Latinised as *Lapis Exilis*. The name of any knight who achieved the Grail was to be found miraculously inscribed on this stone. We can deduce that it was white, because it is a direct borrowing from the Revelation of St John, wherein the author promises "to him that over-cometh" all the various contents of Solomon's Temple, to wit: The Pot of Manna; the white raiment of the priests; the prophecy that the victor shall become a pillar in the Temple and shall share Christ's throne, and that Christ will give him a white stone, and in the stone a new name written, "which no man knoweth saving he that receiveth it." If this white stone is one of the furnishings of Solomon's Temple, what can it be but the lost Urim? But Wolfram misunderstood the significance of the words in the Revelation of St John (III.12) for it is not the name of the recipient that is to be written on the stone, but the new name of God, that is to say that the Tetragrammaton on the metal surround is to be replaced by the name (or image) of Christ on the stone itself, and we shall see in a later plate that Christ's image did in fact appear on the White Stone eventually.

So far we have arrived at an encapsulated relic in a reliquary very similar to the alchemical illustration of the Urim (Fig 3.) but it is not yet used to display the Host.

The next stage in the evolution of these liturgical objects is all-important to students of the Grail legend. It will be remembered that when Parzival, lacking or having forgotten all knowledge of Christian custom, visits his uncle the hermit, Trevrezent, the holy man shows him the chapel of his hermitage, and great stress is laid on the fact that, the day being Good Friday, the altar is stripped bare. This, if nothing else, proves that Wolfram was writing a purely Christian story (that is to say Christianity by his day had taken over almost completely from Judaic or pagan origins) for it is the custom of the Catholic Church to strip the altar on Good Friday, and to leave no consecrated Hosts (the priest has to consume the last Host).* This is in order to emphasize symbolically that the Real Presence has left mankind, Christ has died, and there will be no Sacrament until the reconsecration of the Bread and Wine at midnight, the Easter Vigil, when Christ rose again from the dead, at which moment new bread and wine are consecrated to celebrate the Resurrection.

Now it was on Good Friday that in the church of the

---

* Since the introduction of the New Rite by the Vatican Council II, the Host is no longer banished on Good Friday but it is removed to a darkened "Altar of Repose" until Easter morning.

Fisher King a dove was supposed to descend with the sacred Host. No commentator to my knowledge has ever realised that the "dove" is not a metaphorical and poetic term for the Holy Spirit, but was an actual liturgical object. I should never have realised this myself if it had not been for the recent opening in Pollokshaws, Glasgow, of the magnificent collection of art known as "the Burrell Collection." There, staring me in the face, was Wolfram's "dove" (see Plate X) It is a hanging pyx. Between its wings is a little sliding door to admit the Host. It is of Limoges enamel work, and would have been hung above the altar on chains. So *of course* it had to descend on Good Friday, just as Wolfram tells us, not metaphorically but very prosaically by a monk, priest or Templar working the pulleys to lower it, so that the consecrated Host might be removed and consumed by the priest at the last Mass on the evening of Maundy Thursday. Wolfram ignores the time-lapse between the descent of the dove and the appearance of the Host on the White Stone on Easter morning.

I have since seen two such doves, one in the Cathedral at Leon in Spain, and another at Burgos, and the Catholic Encyclopaedia asserts that there is one at Amiens and another at Valois, all now consigned to Cathedral treasuries and no longer used since the institution of the Monstrance as known to-day. For all I know many more examples of such doves may exist in Europe for it appears that they were commonly used in the 12th and 13th centuries. The one in the Burrell Collection is dated 1225 to 1250 A.D. – just the correct date for Wolfram's writings.

I have always found it puzzling as to why the dove became the symbol of the Holy Spirit. It was a bird sacred in Greece to Aphrodite, goddess of love, and in Syria to the licentious fertility goddess, Atargatis of Hierapolis. Indeed the Jews accused the Samaritans of worshipping a dove. There is no authority in scripture for the custom of artists to paint the scene of the Annunciation with the Holy Spirit which "overshadowed" Mary represented as a dove.

On the other hand the dove brought a sign of peace and reconciliation to Noah when it returned with the olive branch (incidentally, Noah's ark was in Jewish legend lit by one precious stone only which shone night and day*).

The Turtle Dove, mentioned in the Song of Solomon and known to us as the Collared Dove makes a very attractive coo-ing noise. It has lately invaded Europe from the Near East, and I had two in my Edinburgh garden. They were extremely timid, though we scattered various types of grain, dried peas and lentils, which they found most acceptable, they nevertheless retreated and flew upwards however quietly we approached them. Their behaviour was quite different from the greedy city pigeons of Trafalgar Square or Venice. The Cabbalists took them as symbols of extreme feminine beauty and gentleness, as shown in personalities such as Sarah or Ruth or any other good-looking Jewish mother-figure.

Why such a dove should have been seen at the Baptism of Our Lord is a mystery. Scripture never seems to me to make it quite clear whether the Baptist or Christ or perhaps both together, saw the dove and heard the voice of the Almighty declaring, "This is my Beloved Son in whom I am well pleased." All that we know is that either to the Baptist, or to Christ, or to both simultaneously, the heavens "opened", and what takes place in the mind of a Seer or an artist or poet or prophet is inexplicable to those whose minds do not happen to be "open" to mystical experience. We must just accept that the message came to them in such and such a way. Later on the Holy Spirit descends as the Shekinah, the radiant sign of the presence of God at Pentecost, so we are not forever tied to the dove.

So far we have seen that the metal dove was used as a hanging pyx, and may have continued to be used as such even after the visions of Saint Juliana, the Augustinian nun who in 1209 A.D. received a direct command from the Almighty to institute a Feast wherein should be publicly displayed the consecrated Host. First the local Bishop and then the Pope acceded rather slowly and grudgingly to the divine will, and at first gradually and finally very colourfully

---

* *Legends of the Jews*, by Louis Ginzberg, Vol I. p. 162.

the Feast of Corpus Christi was instituted. At this Feast a "container" holding one single consecrated Host is carried in procession round the city or village. In a village the procession can be most affecting, because the priest carries in his hands a relatively small liturgical object, known as the Monstrance, because it *demonstrates* the Host, the Real Presence, to the gathered villagers in, for instance, Spain. In the procession walk the children who have taken their first communion, the tiny girls in smart white frilly frocks, and the boys proudly wearing their first long trousers, white ones. And the Monstrance is generally followed by an image of the Virgin carried by the strong men, while the proud matriarchs, mothers of the children, are dressed in sober black.

For large cities the 16th and 17th centuries devised, by the skill of their gold and silver-smiths, huge towers to be born on rococo chariots, decorated with gilded cherubs, and the Monstrance, relatively small, was almost lost in these over-grand towering edificies, which I personally, find vulgar and rather idolatrous, although the workmanship is on a par with that of Benvenuto Cellini; the excuse for such overpowering constructions is the problem of "crowd-control". If people have turned out to see from the pavement the procession pass by, they want to be able to see the Monstrance, which they could never do from behind a packed throng if it was borne by hand by the priest as in small villages. In 1209 or thereabouts it would have been impossible for any priest to walk in any procession carrying a metal dove, and in any case the Host would not have been visible inside such a metal container. The effect, moreover, would have bordered on the absurd. It was probably at this point that the Church took a reliquary intended for encapsulating a relic (see Plate IX) and used it for processions such as that of Corpus Christi.

What happened next? The Council of Trent in 1545, had as its main object to counter the Protestant Reformation and reunite the churches. It was at this period that the use of the hanging pyx, the dove, seems to have gone out of use, and the beautiful 16th century Monstrances were adopted, most of them originating in Spain. One can imagine that the members of the Council were attempting any and every reform which would rob the ultra-Calvinistic Protestants of criticism of the Church, and a metal dove hanging above the altar is approaching idolatry and could shock the consciences of wavering Catholics or Protestants.

In my youth there was an old "chestnut", as we called a joke too often repeated, about a Chinese who claimed to know all about Christianity. "They worship," he declared, "an old gentleman with a grey beard, a young man with a brown beard, and a bird."

I hope I shall not be accused of blasphemy if I give a more modern turn to this old joke, but because one is a believing Christian does not necessitate the loss of all sense of humour. The French are not given to limericks, so that the very few they do write are memorable, and the latest is this:-

Il y avait un Jeune homme de Dijon
Qui se moquait de toute la religion.
Il disait une fois
"Ils m'agacent, tous les trois,
Et le Père, et le fils et le pigeon."

Enough said! And pardon any unintended blasphemy, but it underlines my point that at the period of the Council of Trent the "pigeon" was banished to the museums and treasuries of Cathedrals.

What was to take its place? At certain times, such as Feast days or at Corpus Christi, the Church and the people wanted to *see* the Host as witness to the Real Presence. The old reliquary for encapsulating relics was relatively small and very unspectacular if seen from a distance by some one at the back of the congregation. To whom to turn for ideas? Well, artists of whatever religion speak a common language. Look now, please, at Fig. 17 where the Alchemists display their sun-tree and moon-tree, the union of which will provide, so they hoped, the immortal elixir, a design obviously derived from the ancient Urim and Thummim, the crystal on its golden tree. What better method to display the con-

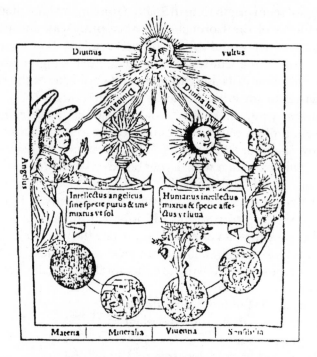

Fig 17. GOD, THE ANGEL, MAN AND NATURE.
From the "De Intellectu" of Bovillus, 1510.

secrated Host than to adopt such a liturgical object, a union
of sun and moon, to contain the sacred Host. Observe now
how these 16th century Spanish Monstrances were made.
The spread of golden rays (Plate XI) shows the sun. Within
is a small crescent of silver, (the moon) which holds the
Host steady, and is known as the Lunette. Like all Jewish
liturgical objects it is decorated with bells, similar to those
which decorated the garments of the High Priest and
warned the Almighty of the approach of his trembling
servant if he was about to enter the Holy of Holies in
Jerusalem. Often the Cherubim on other types of Monstrances resembling sun-rays repeat the memory of the
cherubim who spread their wings above the Ark of the
Covenant to denote the Real Presence of the Almighty.

To protect the Host in the Monstrance a crystal
(nowadays glass) is placed in the midst of the sun-rays. Is it

any wonder that only a Jew could manufacture the sun-and-the-moon dress, trimmed with bells, which Cinderella (the crystal) was to wear to meet the Prince? It is significant (a prohibition due perhaps to painful experience) that whereas the chalice for the wine must be lined with gold, and silver must be used for the crescent of silver, (the Lunette, which holds the Host steady in the Monstrance) the Host itself must never be allowed to touch the glass. (In olden days it was not of glass but of crystal and could be slightly lenticular, if you observe the polished cabochon stones in some of the Italian Ostensarios illustrated in the Catholic Encyclopedia.) Some one must have known that scorching might take place. I myself have caused a deep scorch mark on a valuable antique table by carelessly leaving a spherical glass paper-weight upon it in the sun.

More puzzling than the sun-rayed Monstrance is the 16th century Spanish version on Plate II. It does not appear to have any association with the Alchemical tradition, and is more likely to have derived from Cabbalistic symbology, for it is strangely like a four-poster bed, "the bed" of Solomon in Grail legend. In Chrestien's *Conte du Graal*, Gawain has to achieve the adventure of the Perilous Bed. It was of gold, veiled with white samite, and had four posts, and bells were attached to the lower part of the "bed". The bed of Solomon referred to in the Song of Solomon III.7. was, according to Cabbalist tradition, a code word or traditional periphrasis for the radiance of God, which they called the Shekinah.* It will be remembered that Gawain was attacked in this bed by the magic lance, the point of which was ablaze, a lance of light from the sun shining through the crystal centre. As this Spanish Monstrance (Custodia) dates from the 16th century, the early poets writing of the Grail from the late 12th century must have borrowed their description of the "bed" from a Cabbalistic source, or even seen a secret liturgical object used by the Cabbalists. It could be argued that Plate II is reminiscent of the Baldaquin and pillars of the High Altar in St Peter's,

---

* *Zohar* translated by Sperling & Simon Vol III pp. 13 and 15.

Rome, which did not exist in the 12th century, but, if a prototype altar existed such a design equally would derive from the Jewish Holy of Holies with its pillars of Jachin and Boaz, beyond which the Tabernacle is the abode of the Real Presence. In no case could either a Monstrance or an altar be described as a "bed" except in code-language by some secret cult such as for instance the Cabbalists or Gnostics.

If I have seemed to criticise (perhaps too harshly) the use of the metal dove as idolatrous, let no one scoff at the sun-rayed Monstrance as idolatrous who has not first read *The Secret of the Golden Flower* with its commentary by C.G. Jung, for the Monstrance can induce a state of true meditation and contemplation, almost of trance. In his commentary Jung enlarges on the ability of a Mandala to bring an intuition of the true self. He illustrates in this book the various types of Mandalas drawn by his patients quite spontaneously, and furthermore holds that perfectly normal persons of average intelligence will tend to "doodle" on a telephone pad while, for instance telephoning, and in the majority of cases draw something very like a multi-petalled flower with a *centre*. To quote Jung: "I succeeded in polarizing the whole of the convergent rays of my consciousness into the desired focus." If by such convergence we come to an intuition of the true self, we are almost on the threshold of being able to say with the Indian mystics concerning what they call the Self (meaning God) – "That art Thou". That is to say an at-onement with God, or as St. Theresa of Avila would have described it, entry into "The Interior Castle". Such entry into the deepest part of the self to meet and be at-oned with God requires quiet and silence. "Be still, and know that I am God," says scripture, and unfortunately the Church in its new rite gives little opportunity for being quiet, silent and still, as it is determined to make us into busy-bees at every moment. And I therefore plead with the Church to retain the sun-rayed Monstrance, and to help understanding of its importance, quite apart from its sacred contents of the Sacrament and Real Presence. Some examples of the Mandalas drawn by Jung's patients are shown in Fig. 18 depicted by the artist, Joyce Hargreaves. These drawings were efforts, albeit unconscious ones, to enter the "Interior Castle" of St. Theresa and to meet the true Self, the Christ within.

Fig 18. SKETCHES OF MANDALAS DRAWN BY JUNG'S PATIENTS.

13 THE LORD'S JEWEL AND CANDLEMAS

If it is granted that certain crystals hitherto used in pagan Fire-from-the-Sun rites were used by the Church in the Monstrances dating from the Council of Trent onwards, what happened to the many crystals, such as the Clach Dearg, which must have been treasured since pre-Christian times throughout Europe and the Near East? The answer, I think is that they were gradually surrendered to the Church for embellishing and beautifying its edifices and vestments; for instance, only a Bishop might fasten his cope with a crystal clasp in Medieval times, and we have seen that the throne of St. Faith at Conques has four magnificent crystals on its arms and back.

For the student of Romance Literature and to avoid boring those who are not specialists in such subjects, I suggest that the *Lay of the Ash Tree* and the *Lay of Eliduc*, both by Marie de France, describe heroines laid out upon the altars of churches. In the romance of *Yvain* by Chrestien de Troyes, the heroine, named Lunette, is seized from a fiery death on a pyre (a death similar to that suffered by St. Faith) and Yvain having tamed a lion (symbol of fire or sun) because he freed it from the coils of a serpent, employs the lion as his ally in the adventure of rescuing Lunette from the pyre. Ethne, a fairy lady in Ireland – she was fifteen hundred years old – was baptised by no less a person than St. Patrick.

All these heroines suggest that the crystals of the sun worshippers were given to the Church. There is only one legend of such importance that I must give it in full. Because Henry de Sully, a cousin of our King Henry II,

became Abbot of Glastonbury in 1189, it has been suggested that the history of the Holy Grail and of the coming of St.
Joseph to Britain was an invention on the part of the English
monks, who wished to compete in importance with their
brother monks of the same Order at Fécamp. Nothing
could be further from the truth, for the legend of the Holy
Blood at Fécamp is in reality the history of the surrender of
the golden tree and its crystal to its Abbey, and both legends
derive independently as far as the crystal is concerned from
a common pre-Christian source.

The legends about Fécamp are to be found in *Essai
Historique et Litteraire sur l'Abbaye de* Fécamp by M. Leroux de
Lincy:-

Nicodemus helped St. Joseph to wash the wounds of Our
Lord in the sepulchre. He scraped away the congealed
blood with a "blade". The blood hardened into a crystalline ball. His son, Isaac, then went to Sidon (centre of
Phoenician glass-blowing) and hid the ball and the blade in
a fig-tree. The fig-tree quickly enveloped the relics (just as
the tree-pillar of Byblus enveloped the dead body of Osiris
while Isis was searching for it). Then this fig-tree floated
miraculously to Fécamp (Field-of-the-Fig) where it no
doubt became a pillar in the Abbey. An ancient king,
Ansegis, went hunting, and a white hart led him to the holy
tree. In the days of Lothaire, Carolingian King of the
Franks, a certain nobleman, Wagnen, built a church round
the tree, and gave the building into the charge of the Abbess
Childemarca and her nuns. In A.D. 990 Richard Duke of
Normandy, grandfather of our Conqueror, enlarged the
church for Benedictine monks. He built the tree-pillar into
the church wall, but the Holy Blood (the crystalline ball)
was first taken out of the "tree" and put under the foot of a
pillar near the altar. A very muddled account, but one gets
the gist of it.

Now it so happens that Henry de Sully, Abbot of Glastonbury, which was a Benedictine Abbey, had been reared in
the tradition and under the direction of the famous Abbot
Suger of St. Denis, a fellow Benedictine and a patron saint of
Paris; and St. Denis was wrongly indentified at that time with

the disciple of St. Paul, whereas in reality he was that Dionysius the Areopagite who wrote a whole treatise, *The Divine Names* about absolute light being identical with God, and held that all nature had the possibility of reflecting that light. His writings (4th or 5th century A.D.) so influenced Abbot Suger that he made a point of decorating the church of St. Denis with every type of jewel or precious stone which could reflect the brilliance of the Creator, and he was largely responsible for the introduction of stained glass windows throughout Europe.* Treasured by the Abbey of St. Denis was the enormous 9th century lenticular crystal of Carolingian times, engraved with a representation of the scene of the Crucifixion. It can now be seen in the British Museum. Thus the prophecy of the Revelation of St. John was fulfilled, in that the "White Stone", the Grail, bears the new name (image) of Christ. See Plate XII. That Henry de Sully, Abbot of Glastonbury treasured a similar jewel I shall hope to show presently.

If the Church did not use the Grail for lighting a sacred fire, it seems at least that the Early Fathers must have been well aware of how the behaviour of light could symbolize the operation of the Trinity, for the very words of the creed show that its formulators were thinking in such terms: I believe in one God, the Father . . . and in one Lord Jesus Christ . . . begotten of his Father before all worlds . . . God of God, Light of light, begotten not made, Being of one substance with the Father . . . who came down from heaven and was incarnate by the Holy Ghost of the Virgin Mary." How many church-goers repreat the words "Light of Light" Sunday after Sunday without considering what they really mean?

It is an interesting study to compare the beliefs of different denominations and other religions which have lost the understanding of God's fore-ordained symbolism, and have therefore failed to understand how there are three persons in One God. The reader will remember that de Borron

* *The Age of Cathedrals* by Georges Duby.

prophesied that when the mystery of the Grail was known:

Lors sera la senefiance
Accomplie et la demoustrance
De la Benoite Trinite,
Qu'avons en trois parz devise.

In plain English: "Then shall the significance be accomplished and the demonstration (same root as the word Monstrance) of the Blessed Trinity, which we have divided into three parts." By inference we have been wrong, infers de Borron, to think of the Trinity as divided into three parts, for God is One.

The following diagram will help to fulfil de Borron's promise. The numbers denote (1) the Father, (2) the Son, and (3) the Holy Spirit.

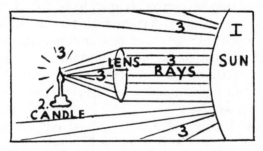

The Buddhists believe in (2) and (3), but not in (1). Englightenment can come to a man, but there is no source of energy from which it proceeds. Life must be an unsatisfactory business if one is to emulate the virtue of a nonexistent God. This may be too swift and sharp a dismissal of Buddhism, but I have picked on what seems to me to be its inherent weakness.

The Mohammedans seem to believe only in (1). To continue speaking in terms of analogy: of what possible benefit would the solar orb be to Man if waves of light did not proceed to earth? We should be entirely unconscious of the sun's existence. In fact we should be in the dark.

Actually, however, the Muslims have accepted the analogy illustrated in my diagram and have come as near to knowing the unknowable as any of us, though the Koran gives a slightly different twist to the symbolism. In the 24th Sûra entitled "Light" it is written, "God is the Light of the Heavens and Earth. His Light is like a niche in which is a lamp encased in glass – the glass, as it were, a glistening star. From a blessed tree is it lighted, the olive neither of the East nor of the West, whose oil would well nigh shine out, even though fire touched it not. It is light upon light."

The Jews believe in (1) and (3) – if I have understood properly the significance of the Shekinah, a kind of divine radiance emanating from God and proclaiming His immediate presence on certain important occasions. But since the loss of their Urim they have refused to admit that the candle can light itself in a Son of Man.*

The Christians of the Western churches have preserved the symbolism with perfect accuracy in the Creed, but have forgotten whence they derived such knowledge with the result that generally speaking the common man, as distinct from a theologian, thinks only in terms of (1) and (2), which leads to forgetfulness that the Holy Spirit issuing from the Christ-candle, can transfer its light to the candles of common men.

The Greek church failed to understand that the Holy Spirit proceeds from Christ, just as light proceeds from the Christ-candle. By coincidence it was in Toledo, the source of Wolfram's *Parzival* that the *Filioque* clause of the Creed was first recited: the clause which split the Eastern and Western Churches, for in the West it is held that the Holy Spirit proceeds from the Father *and the Son*, whereas in the East the Orthodox churches will not admit that the Holy Spirit proceeds from Christ, but only from the Father. But

---

* According to Louis Ginzberg, *Legends of the Jews* Vol VI. The likening of Moses to a burning candle from which many others are kindled occurs not only in the Midrashim and Jerusalem Targum, but also in Philo De *Gigantibus*, 6. from which Theodoretus Num.11.17 may have borrowed it. But there is no hint from Dr Ginzberg as to how the candle of Moses came to light itself; no symbolic medium is postulated, such as crystal, glass or water.

as will be seen in the diagram, once the candle has been lit by the sun of course it gives forth light, a radiance which is of the same substance as the creative power of the sun. The lens is the pure Virgin, fashioned of earth, but transparent so that she can transmit that light.

Curiously enough, although the Greek and Orthodox churches disagree about the Holy Spirit issuing from Christ, nevertheless the Greek and Armenian Patriarchs still to-day hand out fire from the Holy Sepulchre at Easter. According to H.V. Morton in his book "In the Steps of the Master" the people still in 1934 believed that this fire descends from heaven into Christ's tomb, and became ecstatic, almost hysterical, as they lit their candles and torches from the flame and then lit each other's candles in turn. The Holy Fire was carried specially from the tomb to the Tsar in Russia before its revolution. The people have been told time and again that no miracle takes place but they prefer to believe, as they have always done, that the fire descends from heaven. The Catholic Church forbade this ceremony from early times as pandering to superstition. But the Greeks and Armenians still continue the ceremony. Plate XIII portrays that ceremony as painted by Eugène-Alexis Giradet in 1901.

St. Gildas, a British pupil of the so-called hereditary keeper of the Grail, the Welsh St. Iltud, had evidently learned his theology from a teacher who understood the symbology of fire-from-heaven, for in his *De Excidio Britannicae* he upbraids the lethargy of the Celtic church and deplores that the priests have not the courage to go out against the proud gentiles (presumably he means the heathen Saxons) as Gideon went forth, "showing the mystery of the Trinity as was said above, with men holding in their hands the extraordinary pitchers (he means the earthen fire-bowls which the men of Gideon carried) waving also the pitchers in the night with brightest light of fire, which are understood as the bodies of the saints joined to good works and flowing with the fire of the Holy Spirit." St. Paul's verse completes such teaching: "that the excellency of the power may be of God and not of us."

"Light of Light", (or Light *from* Light since in Latin it could be translated either way) – where do we get this phrase from? The creeds were not just composed on the spur of the moment by some priest with a creative urge and a liking for formulae. Every word was carefully and painstakingly chosen to refute some heretical mistake which was at one time or another threatening the Church.

The words "light from light" already formed part of the very early Jerusalem creed when the Bishops were summoned by the Emperor Constantine to Nicaea to a Council in 325 A.D. which was to end the bitter controversy between the followers of Athanasius and of Arius, and to formulate a more explicit definition of faith, to be known thereafter as the Nicene Creed. The Jewish knowledge of the meaning of "light from light" had probably been forgotten, although it was preserved in the Jerusalem creed. If forgotten, I fancy the assembled bishops were brought dramatically back to a full awareness of its significance by the Bishop of Tremithus, St. Spiridon, who, according to legend and art, brought fire out of water at the Council.

Imagine to yourselves the long disputes in the Council chamber as the opposing parties argued about the exact relationship of Christ to God. Was Christ the first of all created creatures, as Arius held, or was he one with God the Father, as Athanasius believed? Spiridon, whose bishopric lay in Cyprus, was regarded by his fellow prelates as a very simple old man, without much education or any gift for elegant rhetoric. He was originally a shepherd, and has been compared to the Patriarchs Abraham and Jacob because of his pastoral life. He was married and had children, and he believed it right and proper to satisfy sex within the marriage bond, which was an unusual attitude for a bishop in his day. This, and his Christian acceptance of pork-eating when necessary, but only when necessary, suggests to me that he perhaps had had some Jewish blood through possibly mixed parentage. Tremithus is the district to which St. Paul and Barnabas made their visit to Cyprus and to its synagogues three centuries earlier, but their converts would have been chiefly Jewish.

Spiridon had suffered greatly in the persecution of Christians prior to the Emperor Constantine's conversion. He had lost the use of one eye when working as a slave in the mines to which he was sent as punishment for his faith. He was eventually to be proclaimed a saint and also a wonder or miracle worker (thaumaturgist). He certainly was a "sensitive" for he could heal the sick and he once received a message from his dead daughter concerning his honour as recipient of a deposit of treasure belonging to and confided to him by a friend, which had got lost but, due to the "message", was duly found.

The other bishops hoped that he would not make any speech at the Council, lest he betray his lack of dialectical skill to the opposition; but his simple reiteration of his faith immediately converted one of his Arian opponents. I fancy that his recorded words were conjoined with his wonder-working, for he began: "God is one, who made heaven and earth and all things. He it is who formed man from the earth." His biographer says that he took a "ceramic" in his right hand from which burst forth fire from water. Because in the North-west of Europe we tend to think in terms of candles, it can be easily forgotten that in the Near East olive oil was the fuel for a light, and it was most usually contained in a small earthenware jar with a hole in it, through which the wick was drawn up. When St. Spiridon seized in his right hand a *keramion* he was holding up the potter's vessel which has always represented Man. The ancient Egyptians told how the god Chnum had made Man out of mud on a potter's wheel, just as in Genesis Adam was formed or modelled from earth. Throughout the Old Testament God is the potter and Man the earthenware vessel, which can be dashed into pieces if found displeasing to the deity (Ps.11.9 and Isaiah LX111.8).

There is confusion in both the Greek and Latin between a "tile" and earthenware pot, i.e. lamp, but if we remember Herodotus' account of the Feast of Lamps in Egypt and that he says the oil was held in flat saucers, and relate this to Dr. Conteneau, the French archaeologist who says that such lamps were "d'abord une simple galette en terre dont les bords sont repliés", we can understand that St. Spiridon's "tile" was a lamp ready and trimmed for the action of the sun.

Today St. Spiridon lies buried in Corfu in a tomb of silver (because his biographer was a native of Corfu living under Venetian domination and he seized the relics from Byzantium). But I see Spiridon in my imagination, his white hair flowing and his age and disability adding to the weariness of listening to men's disputes. So on a sudden he turns to his servitor, and sends for a globular glass flask. He fills it with water and sets it on the balustrade in the full glare of the hot sun. Then he seizes the earthenware lamp. Man has this task - to make the oil and so be ready for the Bridegroom, for the sun "is as a bridegroom coming out of his chamber (Ps.XIX.5). "The Sun of Righteousness" is the metaphor used to prophesy the coming of Christ (Mal.IV.2.) I believe that Jesus was aware of all these old symbolisms when he gave us the parable of the wise and foolish virgins who had no oil in their lamps, and who were not therefore ready for the Bridegroom, the Sun of Righteousness, to arise and Himself ignite their lamps. The more ordinary interpretation of a Jewish wedding party is of course, also valid. Nearly always the parables have at least two levels for understanding to those who have ears to hear.

Spiridon's lamp is ready, however, full of oil and the wick trimmed, and now the sun shines through the water to a focal point, bringing the baptism of fire and igniting Spiridon's lamp. His biographer, Nicolas Bulgaris, a native of Corfu, writing in 1681 and quoting earlier sources confuses, as I have said, earthen jars and tiles, for the Greek word *ceramic* can be used for either artefact, but he declares that the fire, coming through water and then bursting out of the earthenware demonstrated the threefold nature of God. So once again - as with the Grail and also as explained in the work of St. Gildas - we are told that a certain object or phenomenon can show forth the mystery of the Trinity. So it can! The flame is begotten of and of the same substance (energy) as the sun, and the rays which proceed from the SOURCE of energy to the LAMP can represent the Holy

Spirit; and this same energy or light proceeds in turn *from* the lamp once it is ignited.

Very often at this date small earthenware lamps such as Spiridon probably used were modelled, as I have already explained, to represent a fish (symbol of Christ because of the Greek initials) and were therefore called *Icthus* or Fish-lamps. Whatever the shape of the lamp the saintly old man used, he helped to defeat the heresy of Arius. That his demonstration neatly brought together the four Aris-totelian elements of earth, air, fire and water is one of those coincidences which would have held great meaning for his contemporaries at that date. He was subsequently called a miracle or wonder-worker (Thaumaturgist) but, if he had any links with Jewry, the Jews apparently knew all about bringing fire out of water and no longer considered the phenomenon as miraculous.*.

It is not to St. Spiridon but to St. Birgitta of Sweden, however, that we owe the analogy of the glass vessel itself being likened to the Virgin Mary. The people of the Middle-Ages were greatly concerned with the same question which occupied Our Lady at the Annunciation: "How shall this be, seeing I know not a man?" Because it is so important I repeat here what was written on a former page. In the revelation which she received, Birgitta's doubts were reassured by Christ Himself, who appeared to her and told her that, "he took a body without sin or lust, entering the maiden's womb as the sun shining through a clear stone . . . For as the sun entering the glass hurteth it not, so the maidenhead of the Virgin abode incorrupt and unsoiled in taking of my manhood." As the *Harley Lyrics* give the same

---

* The spelling of this Saint's name varies in different hagiographies and early accounts from Spiridion, Spyridion and Spiridonis. Some hagiographers believe that he was not present at the Council of Nicaea in A.D. 325 but at the Council of Sardica in 347 A.D. where the controversy between Athanasius and the Arians reached new heights of acrimonious dispute. Amongst the Bishops (approx-imately 300) who signed at Nicaea Spiridon's name does not appear. The old man may have been too exhausted to endure to the end! The philosopher, Eulogius, is the Arian he is supposed to have converted. All the biographers and early accounts agree on Spiridon's powers as a thaumaturgist, and in the tradition that he brought fire out of water at "a" Council, thereby demonstrating the Trinity.

analogy, it seems that a crystal was in common use as a symbol of Mary in the past. Certainly the Monstrance with its disk of glass is considered sacred to Our Lady because it holds the true body of the Saviour, just as she cradled the Holy Child in her arms.

For those who greatly desire to see women take a more active part in the Catholic Mass, and even advocate female priests, I would suggest that, because the priest represents Christ at the Last Supper, the representative of Christ must be a man, but it would be very fitting for a dedicated nun to carry the Monstrance in processions such as that of Corpus Christi, thus taking the part of Our Lady carrying the Holy Child, even as the Grail maiden carried the Grail.

Returning for a moment to the earthenware vessel which God will shatter in pieces if it displeases him: not only in the Old Testament is Man likened to this earthen pot, and not only does the Egyptian god Chnum make man out of mud on a potter's wheel, as in Genesis God models Adam from clay, but in various books dealing with "magical diagrams" there is figured a square within the six-pointed Shield or Star of David, and within the square is a palindrome in Latin, which may denote the possibility of the Star revolving to transpose Christ to the divine throne and the Holy Spirit to earth. The Latin is not very grammatical but pardonable when composing a palindrome which is very difficult to do. For the words must read identically, horizontally and vertically. The "Arepo" is an ablative A-repo. The meaning of the Latin is roughly *Sator* – the Creator, literally Sower-of-the-seed, *A Repo*, by moving slowly and steadily round, *tenet* holds, *opera*, the work, *Rotas*, on the wheels.

Let us now see how the Church partly preserved and partly altered the ancient symbolism. Excalibur became the "sword of the spirit which is the Word of God", and, just as the Jews hang a lamp before the Torah, so the Christians hang one before the Word made flesh. Just as the Jews celebrated the re-entry of the Lord into his Temple by lighting lamps, so the Christians chose the feast at which Christ was first brought into the Temple in his mother's arms to celebrate Candlemas. A great candle, known as the Candela

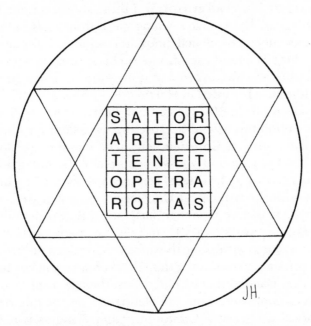

Rotunda, is specially consecrated and then lighted, while the cantor used to begin the antiphon: *"Venit lumen tuum"*. Small candles are then distributed to the congregation who ignite them from the king-candle.

In the great majority of cases men will turn readily towards the light, when once the lamp is offered to them. But there do, alas, exist those whose lives are a firsthand witness to the existence of an evil principle – Satan – in that they can find their pleasure only in perversion. Their greatest moment of joy is to extinguish the lamp; their only bodily fulfilment, to abuse nature; their only triumph to tread what is holy into the mire. While men had no choice but to remain in ignorance of the true God, there was nothing essentially perverted in the ritual of a horrible dark cave, a Hades. But once the new revelation had been given, then only those who had purposely devoted themselves to evil could indulge in such practices. This desire to pervert the truth and extinguish the lamp, which took the form of witchcraft, black masses and the like, presented the Church with a terrible enemy. That such an evil influence was at one time centred in Wookey Hole is, I think almost certain, for local legend has it that a young clerk from Glastonbury Abbey went there with bell, book and candle to exorcise the evil. There he found a witch and, on his sprinkling her with holy water, she was turned into stone – the black stalagmite. The legend is recorded in Harrington's poem of 1748, and is given in full in Mr Balch's book on Wookey.

I mention this legend because there is a faint possibility that this nameless Christian hero, who dared to go alone into Wookey Hole and whose story is plainly bound up with that of Perceval in the Chapel Perilous, may be the very man responsible for making the Grail legend known in Medieval Europe. It is a very strange fact that within a period of roughly fifty years, A.D. 1180–1230, so many poets suddenly began to write upon this subject. Chrestien de Troyes, who pre-dated Wolfram, although Wolfram's sources may be older, claimed that he had drawn the tale from a book given to him by the Count of Flanders. Now the one great historical tie between Glastonbury and Flanders is to be found in the life of St. Dunstan, and since this saint's history has many curious links with Grail legend, it will be worth while to study it.

His mother's name was Keondrud or Kynedritha. (A name curiously like that of Kundrie, which Wolfram chose for the female who could become a goddess or a Loathly Damsel or a pure maiden.) Dunstan's father was a nobleman at the Court of King Athelstan. The boy, being a younger son without expectations of property, was sent to the famous school at Glastonbury kept by the Irish monks at St. Bridget's chapel of Beckery, a mile or two from the Abbey. As the reader will presently learn some very interesting facts connected with this chapel, it will be convenient to say here that it was dedicated to St. Mary Magdalene, and that in it were preserved the embroidery tools of St. Brigit; hence the attendance of Irish monks; and it was probably originally a shrine of the Celtic goddess Brigit. Dunstan became a clerk in minor orders. His duties would, therefore, have included a knowledge of exorcism. Then his uncle was raised to the Primacy at Canterbury, and the Archbishop introduced the youth to Court. Dunstan had already shown himself to be of outstanding intelligence: a great musician and a student of metallurgy. It was probably this last interest in a science which was always suspect that brought him into disgrace. Is it coincidence that just in the period when Alchemists were at the height of their preoccupation and search for a means to transmute metals (transmutation), the Church in the Lateran Council of 1215 established the doctrine of Transubstantiation? Both dealt with the conviction that one element could be changed into another. As a Catholic I am content to believe what the Church has decreed to be part of the Deposit of Faith, but my sympathies go out to the Alchemists who were struggling to understand chemistry. So Dunstan's study of metallurgy coupled with a possible visit to Wookey Hole led to the accusation that he practised Black Magic. He had to fly for his life from the Court at Kingston to Winchester, where another of his uncles held the episcopate and gave him shelter. He was then persuaded to become a monk, and for many years he lived a life of great austerity at Glastonbury. Athelstan's successor raised him to the Abbacy, but, before Dunstan followed in the footsteps of his uncle and attained the Primacy, he was once again forced to flee for his life. This time the reason was political entanglements. Thus the Abbot of Glastonbury took refuge at the Court of Count Arnulf of Flanders, where for two years he lived quietly. He would no doubt have occupied himself as a scribe, and very probably presented some of his works to his patron. One can see, therefore, how the Flemish royal family might have acquired a book about the Grail. After two years Dunstan was recalled, became Archbishop of Canterbury, and was virtually ruler of England from 959 until his death in A.D. 988. So great was his interest in metallurgy that he was credited after his death with having written a tract on the Philosopher's Stone; and we have seen that this mythical talisman was in fact a memory of the Grail which could turn all things into golden fire. One cannot help wondering whether it was not Dunstan himself who taught the monks to use the symbolism, which they employed in writing his biography, completed only twenty years after his death. For they use this symbolism in the account of Dunstan's birth at Candlemas, as will be seen in the following translation from the Latin.

"While the holy child was yet in his mother's womb, the day of the purification of the holy and perpetual Virgin Mary dawned. And when the folk of the neighbourhood were flocking from every side to the church of Glaston dedicated to the same Virgin, to perform the duty of their devotion on that solemn occasion to Christ, the King of kings, it happened that Herstan, the father of the child, came with his wife Kynedritha, and with lighted candles took part in the sacred solemnities of the Mass. And now the priest had finished the greater part of the day's service, and the recitation had now begun of how his parents brought the child Jesus to the Temple, when suddenly the majesty of the Lord appeared in the church, extinguished the candles of all and shrouded the whole house in darkness and gloom. Then an icy fear ran through the limbs of all, their hair stood erect, their knees knocked together. Thus they stood transfixed, showing their bewilderment by gazing at one another. But in order that it might be clear to all what was intended by the majesty that appeared, forthwith a light sent from heaven shone forth into the church, and kindled the taper which the pregnant woman held in her hand . . . so to this candle all came, and from this candle light was given to all." Another slightly later biography says the people "saw a flame of fire gliding down from heaven, and perceived the candle, which Dunstan's mother was holding, kindled from the flame." Dunstan declared later that he identified his own mother with Mother Church. (The candle of St. Genevieve of Paris was snuffed out by the Devil and relit by an angel, a repetition of the same symbolism.)

Another strange link between him and the Grail legend is shown in the *Concordia*, the great work wherein the monks noted all the reforms and institutions ordered by the Archbishop. Although fire was no longer conjured from the sky, yet the Christians like the Jews required "pure" fire for the altar. It was and still is kindled with iron and flint at the church door. In Dunstan's day according to his *Concordia*, a procession went down to the church door on Maundy Thursday bearing a staff (in Latin a *Hastam* meaning spear) which ended at the top in the shape of a serpent. A flaming candle came out of the serpent's mouth, a flame lit from iron and flint. If we compare this with Malory's account of how after Matins and the first Mass there was seen in the churchyard a stone, of how Arthur pulled Excalibur lightly and fiercely from the stone, and of how then "he tooke the sword between both his hands and offered it up to the altar where the Archbishop was", we shall be delighted to find the sword of Fairy was never lost for long in the mere, but still twinkles in our churches. Arthur had to re-perform the feat of drawing the sword from the stone at succeeding feasts of the Church: namely All Saints (the Druid Samhain when all fires were extinguished until the king had relit his brand) Candlemas; Easter (when the Paschal candle is lit); and Whitsun (commemorating the descent of the fire of the Holy Spirit). The Paschal Candle of Easter is taken out of the water of the font before being lighted and identified with Christ by five marks (wounds) incised in the wax. To go back for a moment to Dunstan's *hastam*: When "The Lord said unto Moses, make thee a fiery serpent, and set it upon a pole," did it have a burning flame at the top? Because when Christ says "And I, if I be lifted up will draw all men unto me," it has always been assumed that he was speaking of being lifted up onto the cross, but actually He continues the declaration by saying "While ye have light, believe in the light." (Numb.XXI. 8 and John XII v. 32-36).

If Dunstan was perhaps responsible for writing the little book which was later found in Flanders, how was it that he or any man of his time had preserved knowledge of the Grail? I think that a crystal, similar to the one treasured at St. Denis, was kept at Glastonbury together with its history. It is fully time that I redeemed my promise to show that such a talisman was preserved in the Abbey, and had been gifted by no less a person than King Arthur. Arthur was probably of Roman blood. Bede refers to him not as a king, but as the

Dux Bellorum of York. He was perhaps the last Roman to hold a nominal appointment from the Eastern Emperor, and it is more likely that he was in command of the remnants of the Roman Field Army, than that he himself was an anointed king. He probably brought this army to the help of the various petty kings, which explains why his battle grounds range from Bath to Loch Lomond. The regular legions had been withdrawn, and the brilliant young soldier gathered the Roman-Britons round him. He realized that the only way to defend the coasts from the Saxon pirates was with light mobile cavalry, for the Saxons arrived horseless from their ships; and the legend of King Arthur's knights is therefore almost certainly true and describes the heavily armoured Roman *equites* of the period, the armour of a Roman legionary being exactly like that on Plate I where the god Horus is dressed as a Roman legionary.

The Orphic had given place to the Mithraic religion, and the cult of Mithras was the great rival of Christianity in the 3rd century. Indeed it threatened at one time to overcome the Church, but by Arthur's day sometime in the fifth to sixth centuries A.D., Christianity, thanks to the Emperor Constantine, was winning. However, as with everything else, Mithraism probably survived in this island longer than on the Continent. As the chapel from which Arthur took the crystal sounds curiously like a Mithraeum, we had better pause for a moment to study the religion of Mithras.

The Iranian demi-god was born as a fully grown youth from a rock situated beneath a sacred fig-tree. Possibly that was why at Frécamp the crystalline ball was enshrined or enveloped in a fig-tree. Mithras rose out of the rock, carrying a torch in one hand and a knife in the other. With the knife he cut the fruit of the tree (like Adam) ate it, and then clothed himself with the leaves. He was allied by a supernatural effluvium to the Invincible Sun, who bade him slay a certain magic bull. Mithras did so, and from the flesh and bones of the bull sprang the seed of all creation. So far it is the same old story of Adam stealing fire, of the institution of human sacrifice (the bull is probably a late substitution for the yearly slaying of the Divine Youth), and the fertilising of the fields with the remains of the sacrifice, as in the case of Osiris. Mithras then held a farewell banquet with his chosen devotees and thereafter ascended into heaven to be re-united with the Invincible Sun. It will be understood why the Early Fathers thought that the Devil had invented the cult for the special purpose of caricaturing the Last Supper and Ascension of Our Lord.

Before the altar of a Mithraeum there lay always an open tomb, wherein the neophyte was buried to simulate the death of sinful nature and rebirth as an Illuminatus. At some time during the rites his eyes were bandaged. I understand the Freemasons carry out a similar pantomimic interment and blindfolding today.

The entry to a Mithraeum, which was generally below ground level so as to resemble the cave in which Mithras had slain the bull, was always guarded by two images of youthful figures: one with an uplifted and one with an inverted torch. They were known as Cautes and Cautopates and represented the seemingly eternal battle between light and darkness, life and death. A so-called perpetual fire was tended on the sacred hearth, and fire and water played a part in the ritual, being represented symbolically on the sculptures by a lion and a cup respectively. The great mystery revealed to the neophyte was to see the sun shining at midnight, probably meaning that it was recognized that the moon was the giant reflector of the sun, which although below the horizon was not dead nor sleeping nor in peril, but was still shining brightly from its nightly position into the mirror of the heavens. In Egypt the moon was referred to as the "painted eye of the sun".* A figure of Mithras slaying the bull was generally portrayed above the altar in the prescribed costume: a red cloak and a crown of sun-rays, with an inscription to say that the demi-god should be revealed crowned with fire.

Such a chapel has been discovered in the vicinity of the

---

* *The Dawn of Civilisation* by Professor Maspero. p. 207 and note 2.

Roman Wall, and from the following story from both the *Prose Perceval* and *Y Seint Greal* it seems likely that a similar one existed at Beckery near Glaston.

Arthur's squire goes to a chapel where the body of a "dead" knight lies before the altar. The Blessed Virgin and Satan are each struggling for the possession of the knight's soul. The squire is tempted to steal the *candlestick* which lights the bier. (There always seems to be a bier lying around the vicinity of the adventures of the Grail, but perhaps the knight is not after all dead but merely undergoing initiation.) The squire's theft is discovered, and as punishment he is mortally wounded in the thigh. At the end of this episode it is to be noted that just as the Nemean priesthood could only be held by a runaway slave, and just as Beowulf's dragon was woken by a serf stealing a golden cup, so the adventure of Arthur begins with the misdeeds of his varlet.

Arthur then sets out for this chapel to ascertain what mystery is contained therein. Here the reader must understand that the king's experiences are cloaked in Christian language. Arthur finds within the chapel a hermit, and this old man begins to say Mass. The king then sees a beautiful lady, called the Blessed Virgin, but who is really the virgin vessel, the Grail. There is a Christian interpolation about the Sacraments at Mass, but we must recall that Mithras also had a Last Supper. But then Arthur witnesses the old mystery. "He looked towards a glass window, that was opposite to the altar, and there he saw a flame coming through the window, a hundred times brighter than the sun when its heat is greatest, descending on the altar." And when Mass was finished, "La flambe qui descendue estoit parmi la verrière s'an ala."

In actual fact Arthur was probably born and died a Christian, but as a hero he was credited by the common folk with the characteristics of a solar hero, hence the greeting of the sun on May morning from Athur's seat in Edinburgh. The people may also have assumed, though wrongly, that a Roman soldier was likely to be a follower of Mithras who was a very popular god among the legionaries. Certainly the

account just given resembles a Mithraeum, but all this, of
course, is only legend. Now however we come to an historical account of the same adventure. A certain monk, known
as John of Glastonbury, who lived in the last half of the 14th
century, wrote the history of his own Abbey. His account of
Arthur's experience tallies with that of *Y Seint Greal* and the
Prose Perceval, except for some additions. After the death of
the squire Arthur rides alone to Beckery, but he is fearful of
entering the place for the door is guarded by two hands
which hold fiery "swords". (This sounds very like Cautes
and Cautopates.) Arthur falls to his knees in prayer and the
swords are then withdrawn, and he enters and hears Mass.
At this point of the story the monk John is so carried away
by his devotion to and interest in the Lady and the
Sacraments, that he forgets to tell us about the flame
descending upon the altar. But what he does tell us is of
even greater importance: "When Mass ended, Our Lady
His glorious Mother, gave the king for a sign of what he had
seen a crystal cross which to this day, by the gift of the king,
is honourably preserved and kept in the treasury of Glaston, and yearly in Lent it is carried on Wednesdays and
Fridays in procession by the monks – those days were
appointed because this miracle took place on a Wednesday,
in fact on Ash Wednesday." John goes on to tell us that
Arthur's faith in Christ and his Mother was firmly
established from that day, and that he thenceforward bore
on his coat of arms the silvery cross together with Our Lady
and the Holy Child. It seems we must conclude that the
crystal cross, which was treasured in the Abbey in the late
14th century contained a jewel which at some time had
been used for bringing down fire-from-heaven. The crystal
probably resembled the one from St. Denis and probably
was engraved with a representation of Christ and placed at
the centre of the cross like a Celtic cross's boss.

No major disasters such as fire or pillage occurred to
trouble the monks between the 14th century and the Dissolution of the Monasteries. There is therefore no reason to
suppose that the crystal cross would have disappeared in
the intervening centuries. Amongst the list of treasures

looted from the Abbey by Henry VIII and recorded in Dugdale's *Monasticon* no mention is made of a cross set with crystals.

The inference to be drawn is that some of the monks, perhaps the office-bearers, had preserved a knowledge of the old mystery. If so the talisman would have been a treasure of great price, for it was the link – the possible bridge of approach – between Jewry and Christendom. In the lost Urim might lie the hope of Israel, the Lame King, and of such a rediscovery by the Jews of their own secret history as would set it on a common road with Christendom to the advantage of both, and end forever its persecution and the desolation of the wasteland. No doubt, therefore, the crystal would have been buried in the Abbey grounds to safeguard it from the rapacious Henry. Curiously enough the last Abbot – Abbot Whiting – although he had signed the Act of Supremacy, was martyred on the Tor because he was accused of having hidden certain treasures from the king.

Perhaps one day Glastonbury will find its Grail, and the Jews their Ark of the Covenant with the Urim. But if both Jews and Christians should find a crystal, then we must not fail – as the neophyte of Grail legend at first failed – to ask what are the secret words, the words of power, of which de Borron wrote:

Relate to him how God did visit thee (meaning St Joseph of Arimathea)
In prison, and the holy vessel took
In his two hands, and to thy care consigned:
Reveal the holy words he spoke to thee
Whose sweet import and precious warranty
Proclaim them meet and proper to be styl'd
The Secrets of the Grail.

Since Christ declared at his trial that he had spoken nothing in secret, we must presume that these words of the Grail are to be found in the Gospel, but that they held a special significance for those who understood the old language of symbolism. I can think of no more perfectly fitting words than these: "Except a man be born of water and the Spirit, he cannot enter into the kingdom of God." From water and light the sacred flame was lit through the Grail, and in the Church the Holy Spirit comes through the water of Baptism. Nicodemus is puzzled and asks, "How can a man be born when he is old? Can he enter the second time into his mother's womb . . . How can these things be?" And Jesus replies: "Art thou a Master of Israel and knowest not these things?" What was the knowledge which Jesus expected a Jewish Rabbi to have, but which Nicodemus lacked? Could that knowledge be the secret of the lost Urim, the hidden Grail?

In our study of the Grail heroes as demi-gods, initiates, and Children of the Sun, do not let us lose sight of the beauty of Malory's human characters. Like Wagner he had intuitive understanding. Therefore he gave us in Lancelot a man whom we can love. "Of all earthly knights," says a nun, "I have the most pity of thee, for I know thou hast not thy peer of any earthly sinful man." We can watch and sympathize with his struggles, and share in his heartfelt sigh: "Now I am sure that I am more sinfuller than ever I was!"

With Galahad we have nothing in common. We suspect that such a man is pure and innocent because he suffered no temptations. Very true, if Galahad *was* a man, but in fact Malory has preserved with perfect intuition of the truth, the purity of the Second Person of the Trinity: a purity incomprehensible and terrifying to human flesh and blood until the moment when He takes possession of it. Galahad, who issues from Elaine (the crystal) is the flame *born in* Lancelot. That is why Lancelot is suffering and struggling. The birth of Galahad is the entry of the Lord into his human temple, the body of any ordinary sinner, and the miracle can only take place at the point where the rays *cross*: that is to say at Calvary. We see Lancelot toiling up the Via Dolorosa until at last his desire for the Queen and his pride of arms are renounced, and on the Cross of Lancelot's crucifixion Galahad is born: A Galahad completely lovable and approachable because he has known suffering and temptation. It is the moment of Re-Dedication of the Temple – "Sing and rejoice, O daughter of Zion; for, lo, I come, and I will dwell in the midst of thee saith the Lord."

14 THE CHOICE

In this chapter I would like to give the reader my personal beliefs on the vexed questions of Evolution and the story of the Fall.

With increased understanding and considerably more study of linguistics which I am not myself qualified to undertake, I think neither question need be vexed.

Let us take first the subject of Original Sin. All the "People of the Book", that is to say Christians, Jews and Muslims, believe that there was an initial act of disobedience to the command of the Almighty, probably due to man's pride, which caused him to be excluded from a paradisical condition in which, it seems, he was in communication with nature, with the animal world, and with the voice within him, which was and is God's usual way of communication with His creatures. But neither Jews nor Muslims believe that this first disobedience of man (let us call him Adam) was a heritable taint transferred forever to his seed. They believe that every man stands or falls by his own individual sin when it comes to the Judgment.

How did a belief that every man was tainted come to be held by the Church? Amongst the Early Fathers, Clement of Alexandria, Chrysostom of Antioch and later Abelard refuted such an idea. Aquinas held that the first sin had not affected man's nature but only his supernatural gifts; in modern parlance, he was divorced from his inner voice, the true Self, while losing also communication with nature and the animal world, for which nowadays he has a growing nostalgia. The doctrine of Original Sin as such, i.e. an

inherited taint, only became the official teaching of the
Church as late as the Council of Trent (1545–1563) which is
very late indeed.

The Church has never asked anyone to believe in the
fabulous "apple" (though artists delight to portray it). In
Genesis, and the Koran the term "fruit" is used: an
ambiguous word, for we can use it in several senses, such as
for instance speaking of the "fruit" of one's labours, or as in
Genesis "the Fruit of Knowledge."

It is easy to conceive of an act of disobedience by Adam,
but almost impossible to imagine what that act consisted of
unless we have certain clues. If we believe, as all the "People
of the Book" do, that God is a loving Father, the "All merciful", we cannot credit that any loving father, even a merely
human one, would forbid any good thing to his children
without a right and proper reason and a desire for their
welfare. The child might not understand the reason, and
therefore obedience would be a proof of love and faith in
the father, rather than an intellectual agreement that the
father had foresight. So we have to consider what the
Almighty's foresight might prohibit, the infringement of
which might damage the child irretrievably.

The answer, I believe, is the control of fire. Just as an
earthly father will say to his offspring, "Don't touch the
matches", so the loving and obedient child will show respect and love and trust by obeying, without understanding
the danger from which the father wishes to protect him; but
if he *does* disobey, the house may burn down and his life will
then depend on the quick appearance of his father to rescue
him.

The "Fruit of the Tree" was the symbol of knowledge,
and knowledge is power: power for good or evil. What
greater power is there than the control of fire? From the
days when primitive man first hardened a wooden spear-
point in the flame, right through the centuries of making
arrows, javelins, swords, stink-pots, gun-powder, rifles, not
to mention metallurgy which depends on fire and gives us
machines, motor cars and all the paraphernalia of oil-rigs
and the present threat of nuclear war, the term fire-power

has become synonymous with aggression.

I am not suggesting that any so-called Prometheus (the name means "before thinking')', a primitive, thoughtless prototype of *homo sapiens*, did not occasionally pick up a burning brand from a forest fire and play with it, in the same way that the rook on Plate VII plays and delights in toying with a burning twig. But there is a great difference between animal or bird "play" and the seizing of power and knowledge by "thinking man" (Epimethius) against the prohibition of his Creator. Not only did he lose easy communication with his inner voice (the Almighty's directions) but he began to regard fire as a god, a very live god. We still in the English tongue speak of "feeding" the fire or we declare "the fire is dead".

Genesis informs us that the "fruit" of the Tree of Knowledge is "good for eating". This could refer to cooking food over a flame, for various foods such as meat are well-nigh uneatable unless cooked. Those scholars who are favoured with a knowledge of archaeology, cuneiform writing, Sanskrit etc. really need for all our sakes to study more closely the various nuances in the languages of the Near and Middle East which can be attached to the word "eat".

Let us take some examples. First from the Bible: you can "eat up" sin, Hosea IV.8; "The zeal of thine house hath eaten me up" John 11.17 and Ps. LXIX; "I did eat thy words", Jeremiah XV.16; Ezekiel "ate the scroll" Ez.XXXI; and you can "taste" death in various passages of the New Testament. In Sumerian you could be the "eater of the price you paid for ransom of a friend".* You can to-day be consumed by jealousy, and you can swallow your pride.

In Genesis we have the earliest conjunction of swords and fires, written long before the invention of shining steel or even bright iron or bronze, for the Cherubim guarding the Tree of Life were armed with a flaming sword. The knapping of flints, particularly in contact with an iron meteorite or pyrite causes sparks, and thus a blade and fire were conjoined in imagination from the first. The *Aggadah*

* *The Epic of Creation* by Professor S.H. Langdon.

says that the Holy One Himself showed Adam, who was terrified in the dark after his ejection from paradise, how to strike two stones together to make fire.

I had the privilege and interesting experience some years ago of making friends with a circus-performer, Stromboli, the Human Volcano, and his wife Silvia, because I wanted to know more about fire-eating. His real name is Mr Danny Lynch, a British seaman who was seconded to running a camp for our Japanese prisoners at the end of the War. From his travels in the Far East he acquired the ability to become both a fire-eater and a fire-walker.

Fire-eating is of course a trick (I am not suggesting that Adam practised it) but a trick that requires phenomenal breath-control, for the flame must never be breathed *in* but only *out*. Breath control in many religions is demanded as a spiritual exercise, known in India as prànàyàma in Yoga. Fire-walking is of much greater importance, and is still practised in the Far East. Stromboli himself has given public performances of this phenomenon and left me a photograph of his doing so. Vedic writings of 800 B.C. give an account of two priests competing to see which of them was the holiest by challenging each other to an exercise of fire-walking.* Stromboli tells me that great care has to be taken to have the necessary length of burning hot coals at exactly the right temperature, and that the naked feet must be brushed carefully at the end of each ordeal to see that no burning cinders are adhering to the flesh. I am personally convinced that the ordeal in Daniel's account (III.19) of how Shadrach, Meshach and Abed-nego went unscathed in and out of the fiery furnace at the insistence of King Nebuchadnezzar is but another instance of competitive fire-walking similar to that undergone by the Vedic priests. The King was counting on his own favourites to win, but they were slain. I do not doubt that the king saw a "fourth man" in form "like the Son of God" walking "in the midst of the fire", for there have been many instances of persons such as explorers, climbers, sailors, near to death by misadventure, becoming

---

* Hasting's *Encyclopedia of Religion and Ethics* under "fire".

conscious of an extra person in their company whose identity they could not pin-point, and only afterwards came to realise was a being not of this world. Medieval painters were fond of the subject of Christ's presence in the fiery furnace, and I see no reason to suppose that the king's vision was false.

If it were once conceded that the act of disobedience (the Fall) was the seizing of power over fire, which is apparently essential to all material progress, then Man was irrevocably set on a course of irreversible progression towards his own destruction. You cannot "uninvent" an invention. It is not so much a taint in the blood as a process, which once begun cannot be stopped. If anyone doubts the power of fire, let him look around – at the bricks of his house, the clothes on his back, the nails that hold his shoe-leather, his supper on the hearth. He could never wish to be without these amenities, but scientific discovery cannot be halted, and much of it leads to warfare and destruction. There is an inevitability about the progression of scientific knowledge, and if it leads to a holocaust the important thing will be, not the death of one person or of many or of millions, for "as in Adam all die" so must we all die. The important thing is in what frame of mind we meet our end.

What do we know about the creation myths of other civilisations apart from the Jewish account in Genesis? The attempts to bring order out of chaos (a monster who generally has to be dissected and scattered) and the plethora of gods, who all have to be allotted female consorts, make such accounts degenerate into absurdity and pantheism. The only creation myth comparable in dignity and simplicity to the Hebrew story was written down by a Phoenician called Sanchoniathon of Beirut possibly as early as the 12th century B.C., and was translated into Greek by Philo of Byblus who lived in the 1st century A.D. According to Sanchoniathon, Heaven and Earth were born of El (Semitic for the Most High God). The Creation began with chaos, darkness, water; and the wind or spirit (as in Genesis) moved or embraced the waters. The sun, moon and planets then came into being, and creatures, male and female,

awoke and began to move on land and sea. Next the wind or
spirit produced Aeon and Protogonos who derived their
nourishment from the fruit of trees. Here I think we have
the Missing Link to please the Evolutionists, for Aeon is
simply the Greek for an age or era or epoch of the universe,
and Protogonos is a mis-spelt *protogenes* a Greek word meaning primitive or of early origin. Why fundamentalists
should think it a belittling of the Almighty to suppose that
He created at other than the speed *they* favour, when we
know that time was measured by men first by the moon,
subsequently by the sun, and for all we know the angels
keep Galactic time, while the Almighty is outside time any-
way, is to me an anachronistic curiosity. St. Augustine is
quite open-minded as to how the days of creation should be
interpreted. Let us speak then of "periods". And Sanchoniathon designates a period for a primitive original species
feeding off trees. When they come "down from the trees",
they beget Genos and Genea, which I deduce is the best that
Philo, a native of Phoenicia, could do with the Greek *Genos*
and the Latin *Gens* to indicate an entirely new species (i.e.
Adam and Eve) a male and female. They in turn begot –
what? Why, Light, fire and flame!

After this first dignified beginning, Sanchoniathon's
account degenerates into the usual Greek and Near Eastern
muddle of gods begetting gods, begetting more gods, until
nymphs, trees and rivers join the pantheistic throng. After
all, Sanchoniathon was a priest in Beirut and therefore subject to pagan ideas. But his beginning is important. He
seems to be postulating a mutation from the primitive half-
animal species of Aeon and Protogonos to *homo sapiens*. And
why not? God is the great Architect of the Universe, the
greatest artist, the superb musician. Do we expect him to
create according to our little notions of speed and time? "A
thousand years in thy sight are but as yesterday". So why
should we presume to criticize the time He took to consider
His final creation? He began to prepare a body for the final
reception of a soul. In Egypt the god Chnum made it of clay
on a potter's wheel (We are back to ceramics again.) In
Babylon the god Ea mixed clay with his divine blood,

anticipating the addition of the divine spark. In Genesis God formed man of the dust, the earth. All of these similes relate to the potter and are in turn related to the ancient liturgy of the Church on Ash Wednesday: "Remember, Man, that thou art dust, and unto dust thou shalt return."

But there is a big difference between the primitive creation of the prototype animal species who fed on the fruit of trees, and presumably lived more or less in the trees, and the new mutation into *homo sapiens*. How was it affected by this incredibly inventive and artistic Creator? How? Why, God not only formed man (the primitive prototype), but then "breathed into his nostrils the breath of life: and man became a living soul"; the potter's vessel, the lamp, has come alight! Gen. II. 7. *

Thus we come back to ceramics and the importance in religious symbolism of Breath, symbol of Life, symbol of the Holy Spirit. Is it not significant that Christ on his first meeting with the apostles after the Resurrection "breathed on them and said unto them: Receive ye the Holy Spirit?" (John XX.22), as though he were lighting the lamps of these dusty vessels, and positively identifying Himself with the Creator. As a man he had given his blood, symbol of earthly life. Now he gives his breath, the breath of spiritual life, without which the "missing link" of the Evolutionists, the primitive prototype, could never have been changed, mutated, created (choose whatever term you prefer) into *homo sapiens*: "and man" says Genesis, "became a living soul". I give in the notes various references to this breath of life. Brahma, the ultimate Almighty but unknowable god of the Hindu Brahmins is also believed to be the source of this breath of life. We find in the cosmology of the Vedas: "There was nothing else save the One, which breathed, breathless, of its own power." †

If the Original Sin was the seizing of fire for knowledge of both good and evil, would this upset Catholics bound to regard the mother of Jesus as immaculately conceived, that

* Exekiel XXXVII 5 & 9 Job XII.10 John XX.22.
† See under 'Indian Philosophy' in Encyclopedia Britannica.

is to say born without the taint of Original Sin that we are supposed to inherit from Adam? There is a rather charming verse in one of the Ethiopic scripts which runs: "No man has carried fire without being burned, and there is none that hath not committed sin except our Lady Mary." As I have said, once set upon the course of scientific discovery there is no going back. It would be *reductio ad absurdum* to suppose that the mother of Jesus did no cooking or that Jesus, the carpenter, did not employ forged tools for his work. But it is perfectly sensible to suppose that neither Our Lady Mary nor Christ ever misused their power or abused their talents. The reason for the prohibition of the "fruit" (fire) of the tree was that man was insufficiently mature to use such power for good only. As Lord Acton has said, "All power tends to corrupt. Absolute power corrupts absolutely." To be born with incorruptible power is but another way of describing the Immaculate Conception.

I have already likened the situation to that of a loving father who forbids his children to touch a box of matches, and trusts in their love of him to prove themselves obedient, although as yet they know nothing of the danger of disobeying. But they do disobey, and they set the house on fire, and will certainly perish in the flames if it were not for the fact that the father Himself (in the person of Christ) races back swiftly to the rescue, enters the burning building (the earth), encounters in his own person the danger, suffers Himself the agony of his injured flesh, and from the well of the stairs shouts to the wretched children, trapped on the floor above and cut off by the flames, "Jump, my children! Jump into my arms. I promise to catch you. But jump now and quickly." So man's scientific progress towards final self destruction is not irreversible, for "The Eternal God is thy refuge and underneath are the everlasting arms." It is not a question of changing our fire-power politically. Politics are far too intricate for amateurish opinions to have any value; but of allowing Him to change us into the mature beings who can exercise power but only for good and never for evil.

We are approaching the subject, so mysterious, of the two

kinds of fire. The fire which Adam seized has caused so
much pain by man's wrong use of it, that it has become
identified finally with pain itself and with Hell, so that we
speak of the fires of Hell and almost in the same breath
we pray:

"Come Holy Ghost our souls inspire
And lighten with celestial fire."

I trust the reader will see nothing irreligious, sceptical or
atheistic in my supposition that the fires which descended
upon the altars of Moses, of Elijah and of Solomon were
induced by focusing sun-rays. We are told the fire came
from heaven, a loose term for the sky, and we know that the
purpose of these altar fires was to roast the sacrificial meat.
In other words ordinary combustion was to take place, and
if the reader feels that lightning is more miraculous than
focusing sun-rays, he is at liberty to choose lightning, but
when all the races of the Mediterranean used the sun, then
the sun appears the most likely choice.

But how about this celestial fire? It is in quite a different
category. No one has ever suggested that the heads of the
apostles were scorched at Pentecost! The Rabbinical
schools themselves believed in a "radiance", called by
them the Shekinah, and it denoted the presence of God
without detracting from His unity; and it was demonstrated
at the Transfiguration of Our Lord and at Pentecost and by
the haloes of certain saints.

There is all the difference in the world (and beyond this
world) between the radiance of the Holy Spirit or Shekinah
and the combustion and conflagration which can destroy.

So now I end with T.S. Eliot's verses from his "Four
Quartets".

The dove descending breaks the air
With flame of incandescent terror
Of which the tongues declare
The one discharge from sin and error,
The only hope, or else despair
    Lies in the choice of pyre or pyre –
    To be redeemed from fire by fire.

Who then devised the torment? Love.
Love is the unfamiliar Name
Behind the hands that wove
The intolerable shirt of flame
Which human power cannot remove.
   We only live, only suspire
    Consumed by either fire or fire.

EPILOGUE

I was introduced to Lady Flavia Anderson's work through the British Museum. Lady Flavia and I were both interested in the two Carolingian engraved crystals in the museum's collection, I from the point of view of an art historian and Lady Flavia in her quest for the Grail.

At a much earlier date than my own work, Lady Flavia had seen the possibilities that crystals were fire bringers, an idea she expounded in 1953, in her book *The Ancient Secret* where she skillfully makes use of cultures, myths and legends in her search for an explanation of the sacred object that is never seen but is revered above all others.

I have been struck throughout her work by how frequently and how closely our paths of research cross and as a means of adding one additional thread to the intricate tapestry of her work I shall briefly outline the pattern of my own work.

My research has been concerned with a group of eight particular crystals, engraved in the ninth century, probably in the workshops of Charles the Bald, which could have been used to generate fire for a liturgical ceremony performed on one or all of the three days preceding Easter Sunday.

The Ceremony of lighting the New Fire is documented *in Consuetudines* from the tenth century, although there are earlier references, as being accomplished with either crystal or flint. The fire was lit outside the darkened church from which in turn a candle was lit to be carried into the church in order to ignite the other candles before the altar and the

Paschal candle. In Lotharingian reform monastic houses
the candle was held in a serpent shaped candlestick. The
association of a serpent and a crystal is also noted by
Flavia Anderson.

These eight crystals have engraved on their undersurface
a motif which also appeared on ivory carvings and manuscripts between 850-1050. It consists basically of a crucifix
with a coiled serpent at its foot which is gazing upwards. In
some cases fire comes from the serpent's mouth, as in the
Coronation Sacramentary of Charles the Bald or it holds in its
mouth a small, straight object like a candle, as in the Gerard
Ivory. In the later example a small boy holds it up by
the tail.

Because of the association of the serpent with the New
Fire and its role in lighting the altar candles, where
symbolically the sacrifice of Calvary is re-enacted at the
consecration of the mass, I have argued that an object
engraved with this motif must also be associated with the
Easter ceremony. Further, it may well be that this ceremony
is linked to the Baptismal ceremony which was the major
event of Easter in medieval times.

There is an interesting mention by Pope Zachary in the
eighth century regarding the use of the crystal. He replies to
an unknown question by St Boniface with the information
that crystals were not used in Rome for lighting the New
Fire. He may have been unfamiliar with the use of a lens but
he does not proscribe it elsewhere. Presumably the Romans
used flint. We know this was the alternative from various
other references to the ceremony. In the twelfth century
Rupert, Abbot of Deutz, leaves the procurement of fire by
the use of flint or crystal as optional depending on the
weather conditions. The crystal which lit the New Fire
seems to have been held in great esteem. St. Ulric,
Bishop of Augsburg, in 924 describes the crystal as a precious stone which, with great reverence, was carried in procession and stored throughout the year.

I was therefore interested to read that this association of
the crystal with Easter was also made by Lady Flavia in her
description of a hanging pyx which held the host to be

viewed by the faithful during Easter. Indeed, I had once wondered if my group of eight crystals were set in the lids of similar pyxes (pyxides) for the *Depositio,* a liturgical drama performed at Easter. Lady Flavia has also argued that the central crystal lens was encircled with a bejewelled setting. Certainly the crystals I am interested in were, and some still are, held in frames. Their upper surfaces are bevelled for this purpose. These settings would have allowed them to be worn like the Urim or reset in a monstrance as was the Freiburg crystal in the fifteenth century.

The engraved crystals were obviously valued as more than just gems as they were reset and treasured and displayed in sacred places. The larger British Museum crystal was from the Abbey Church of St. Denis where, before the revolution, it hung above the altar. The crystal given to the monastery of Conques by Charles the Bald was reset a century later in a sumptuous reliquary to Ste. Foy. Lady Flavia mentions the four large crystal balls which surmount the throne-shaped reliquary. However, in the back of the throne is the beautiful engraved crystal. Another of the group of crystals was reset in the twelfth century in a Mosan triptych and now resides in the Victoria and Albert Museum. The rest of the eight crystals have wandered into collections in Venice, Paris and Esztergom.

Some interesting points emerge when my research is viewed in the light of Lady Flavia's arguments. All the legends of the Grail are from Northern Europe where crystals were particularly revered; but it was from a Near Eastern source that Flavia Anderson drew the idea to light a fire with a globular glass of water and ingeniously created tinder from a tree fungus one cold spring day in Tuscany. She did in fact do a similar demonstration for me with the help of her brother, a scientist, the Earl of Halsbury, F.R.S., by drawing the hot sun's rays through a watch glass of cool water on a summer's day in Kensington.

It is exciting that our individual avenues of research, prompted by an entirely different question, should have arrived at the same answer. I, myself, have profited from Flavia Anderson's impressively complex work and was especially enlightened to see my own, somewhat narrow interest, set within the wider context of her investigation.

In particular Lady Flavia's book has given me valuable material for my continuing work on Carolingian baptismal ceremonies as the unifying solution to some art motifs. Lady Flavia has found her answer in the association of Baptismal water and fire "From water and light the sacred flame was lit through the Grail, and in the Church the Holy Spirit comes through the water of Baptism."

ELIZABETH A. KIRBY,
   Tallahassee, Florida 1986.

Index